SEX-RELATED
COGNITIVE DIFFERENCES

SEX-RELATED
COGNITIVE
DIFFERENCES

An Essay on Theory and Evidence

By

JULIA A. SHERMAN, Ph.D.

Director, Women's Research Institute of Wisconsin, Inc.
Madison, Wisconsin

CHARLES C THOMAS • PUBLISHER
Springfield • Illinois • U.S.A.

Published and Distributed Throughout the World by

CHARLES C THOMAS • PUBLISHER

Bannerstone House

301-327 East Lawrence Avenue, Springfield, Illinois, U.S.A.

© *1978, by* CHARLES C THOMAS • PUBLISHER

ISBN 0-398-03781-7 (cloth)

ISBN 0-398-03782-5 (paper)

Library of Congress Catalog Card Number: 78-880

Printed in the United States of America

OO-2

Library of Congress Cataloging in Publication Data

Sherman, Julia Ann, 1934-
  Sex-related cognitive differences.

  Bibliography: p.
  Includes index.
  1. Sex differences (Psychology)
  2. Cognitive styles. I. Title.
  BF692.2.S5   155.3'3   78-880
  ISBN 0-398-03781-7
  ISBN 0-398-03781-5 pbk.

To my parents
Roy V Sherman
and
Edna Schultz Sherman

PREFACE

Since publication of *On the Psychology of Women: A Survey of Empirical Studies* in 1971, many people have urged me to revise it. The explosion of knowledge in the area of the psychology of women has been so great, however, that a thorough updated review of all the relevant topics and literature would now require an encyclopedia. Even so, the time has come for a cogent reanalysis of one specific topic, sex-related differences in cognitive functioning

This analysis will proceed by first considering some historical and sociological perspectives relative to questions of sex-related cognitive differences. Succeeding chapters will give particular attention to a variety of conceptual and methodological problems and summarize available knowledge on the extent of sex-related cognitive differences. The last section will present and evaluate current biological and psychological theories and hypotheses of sex-related cognitive differences in intelligence. Primary emphasis in the discussion will be on sex-related cognitive differences relevant to women's potential.

Since the impossibility of avoiding bias in social science is recognized, much has been made of the salutory effect of making public one's value viewpoints. This line of reasoning might suggest that one need only acknowledge one's bias and then freely indulge in it. In my own work, I prefer to reject bias as much as possible. That is, I attempt to be aware of my biases for the purpose of *not* falling prey to them, for in its ideal form I conceptualize scientific work as unbiased.

Some persons who have not carefully read my work have assumed, because of the emphasis on sex-typed practice found in my 1967 article, that I have taken an entirely environmental view of the development of sex-related differences in cognition. In fact, that is not true either in that article or since (Sherman,

1971, 1976a, particularly see 1976b). I have never ruled out biological bases as a source of differences between the sexes. In fact, following in the steps of Darwin, I have looked most closely at data contradicting the hypothesis of sex-typed practice presented in the 1967 paper. As I have studied this topic more intensively, and particularly in the course of writing this book, I have found direct biological bases for sex-related cognitive differences increasingly less convincing, though, as we shall see, some contributions from this source cannot be ruled out.

The reader may be interested in some of the ethical questions I struggled with in the course of preparing this book, for example, the advisability of giving examples illustrating conceptual and empirical problems. On the one hand, respect for the courtesies and proprieties of scholarly intercourse weighed against doing so. On the other hand, there was a danger that points would be missed entirely unless examples were given. In the end, I decided that it was better to give examples.

The question of the social risk of the research findings to be reported also required some thought. Social risk refers to negative consequences to a group stemming from research findings. An example might be a finding that a particular group lacked a gene necessary for a high level of intellectual achievement. Such a finding might lead to discriminatory behavior toward that group, their exclusion from training programs, hesitance to hire them for creative, high level intellectual tasks, or a tendency to discount their work. In view of these possibilities, the ethical dilemma presented to the researcher would be whether or not to publish such findings. Or, if publishing the finding, what precautions should be taken in its interpretation and dissemination to the scholarly world and to the public. The terms of this controversy have centered about freedom of inquiry versus social consciousness and responsibility. Some have cried academic freedom and others have cried freedom is academic indeed. The main focus of this issue has been the controversy regarding differences between blacks and whites in intelligence (Jensen, 1969; Herrnstein, 1971), but the issue has arisen in regard to other matters, notably the question of whether XYY persons were being stigmatized as violent (Culliton, 1974, 1975).

Very little concern has been focused on questions of social risk to the XX group. Pierre van den Berghe (1973) complained that a feminist group tried to stop him from teaching a sociology course on a systematic analysis of age and sex in social structures. Van den Berghe successfully fended off this effort and subsequently published the lectures in book form. Though sexism has never generated the power and concern of racism, the issue has sometimes been joined. As one who has suffered negative consequences from proponents of both sides of this controversy, I have, nonetheless, concluded that the best course is not to censor or exclude any theories or data, but to attempt to present the material in as socially responsible a way as possible. It is my belief that the future of the sexes is better based on reality than ideology and that scientific method constitutes one of the most successful procedures yet devised for ascertaining reality. On the other hand, it is important to avoid the Naturalistic Fallacy, which concludes that what is, should be. Human plasticity is such that reality, to a large degree, can be what we wish to make it.

One note about the form of this book. In order to increase the precision of expression, the neuter pronouns "tey," "ter," and "tem" have been used when the sex of a person is not known, or when "person" is used in a generic sense. They are the singular equivalents of they, their, and them. For example: The scientist pursues "ter" work; "tey" reads avidly and strives to overcome obstacles that beset "tem." This usage, while doubtless repugnant to linguistic traditionalists, is strongly recommended for scientific use. It is surprisingly unobtrusive in speech.

Parts of the manuscript have been developed from material of an earlier project supported by the National Institute of Education. Any opinions, findings, and conclusions, or recommendations expressed in this publication are those of the author and do not necessarily reflect the views of the National Institute of Education.

My thanks to Jeanne Gomoll for her faithful assistance in

library research and preparation of the manuscript and to Stanley Payne for his critical reading of the text.

Madison, Wisconsin   Julia A. Sherman

CONTENTS

SEX-RELATED
COGNITIVE DIFFERENCES

Chapter One

SOME HISTORICAL PERSPECTIVES: SOCIOLOGY OF KNOWLEDGE BY HINDSIGHT

THERE is probably no more controversial topic in the study of the psychology of women than sex-related differences in cognition. Radical feminists insist there are no psychological sex differences (Millett, 1970), and many feminists object to any discussion of the topic at all. Certainly negative opinions about women's intellectual capacities have always played a role in polemics, justifying the inferior status of women (Goldberg, 1973; Tiger, 1969). For the practical person, however, charged with the responsibility of forming governmental or educational policy, questions of sex-related differences in cognition require answers which are as factual and carefully considered as our present state of knowledge permits. For the curious as well, questions of sex-related differences in cognition, their nature, extent, development, and origin, pose a challenge worthy of response. But can this question be pursued objectively?

Gunnar Myrdal (1972) asks, "How scientific are the social scientists?" He doubts that it is possible for social scientists ever to be disinterested. Jessie Bernard (1972) surveyed the literature on sex differences and came to these conclusions: "(1) Research on sex differences achieved few if any of its ostensible objectives; (2) it has had the effect of rationalizing the inferior status of women by explaining it in terms of their demonstrable inferiority (an inferiority which they have themselves accepted); (3) it has been guilty of a male bias in the selection of variables, in the methods used, and in the interpretation of its results, all reflecting the values of a male world in which the cult of macho prevails; and (4) it has had the effect of preserving sex stereotyping."

3

One way of gaining greater insight into the role of bias and its possible function in contemporary society is to examine the heritage of our ideas about women's intellect. In this chapter we will consider some historical views of women's intellectual capacity and early theories of the nature and extent of sex-related differences in intelligence. These views will provide perspective and counterpoint to contemporary opinions. In some cases these viewpoints now seem laughable; in some cases they seem bigoted; but in other cases the quality of analysis, like a fine antique, is in no way inferior to that of contemporary thought.

SOME HISTORICAL VIEWS OF WOMEN'S INTELLECT

Summarizing the attitude toward women's intellect in the Middle Ages, O'Failain and Martines wrote, "Aristotle was still much quoted to the effect that 'the female state is. . . as it were a deformity.' Generally speaking, the arguments against women were a rehash of the old misogynist themes: woman is cursed by the sin of Eve, crooked because made from a rib, bestial by nature, concupiscent but crafty. Education would refine, and hence heighten, her natural depravity. Husbands must defend themselves by keeping wives on a tight rein" (1973, p. 182).

Shields (1975) attributed the first systematic work on individual differences in intelligence to Juan Huarte, a Spaniard writing in 1575. He attributed sex-related differences in intelligence to the humoral qualities that characterized each sex. Humors had been part of Western thought since ancient Greece. The male humors were heat and dryness while the female humors were moisture and coolness. Since dryness of spirit was necessary for intelligence, males possessed greater wit. Maintaining dryness and heat was the function of the testicles. Huarte (1959) observed that the effect of castration was the same "as if he had received some notable dammage in his very braine" (p. 279). This theory of sex-related differences in intelligence was widely accepted through the seventeenth century.

One can discern a much more modern attitude toward

women and women's intellect in the letter of a prominent sixteenth century French nobleman to his daughters. In this letter one sees the now familiar theme that women may be educated but should not use their education. One also encounters the opinion that sanctions against intellectual competence are strongest in the "middling ranks" of society. As far as I can tell, this observation is still valid in the contemporary United States.

> My daughters, your brother has brought you my summary of Logic in French, "Logic for girls," . . . I am letting you have it on condition that you make use of it only for yourselves and not against your companions or superiors, as it is dangerous for women to use such things against their husbands. . . . I have nearly always found that such preparation (a superior education) turned out to be useless for women of middling rank like yourselves, for . . . a disproportionate elevation of the mind is very apt to breed pride. I have seen two bad effects issue from this: (1) contempt for housekeeping, for poverty, and for a husband less clever than oneself, and (2) discord. And so I conclude that I would be most reluctant to encourage girls to pursue book learning unless they were princesses, obliged by their rank to assume the responsibilities, knowledge, competence, administration, and authority of men (O'Failain and Martines, 1973, p. 186).

In the eighteenth century we find the French philosopher Rousseau, writing in *Emile,* "women's entire education should be planned in relation to men. To please men, to be useful to them, to win their love and respect, to raise them as children, care for them as adults, counsel and console them, make their lives sweet and pleasant" (O'Failain and Martines, 1973, p. 247). This view has its modern counterpart in Lynn White, a highly respected historian of science and former president of Mills College, a school devoted to the education of women. White wrote a book entitled *Educating Our Daughters* (1950). In this book, drawing upon his understanding of the psychological literature, he averred that women are not so analytical as men and that education for women should suit them to become the charming companions of men, learning for example the art of mixing a very dry martini. However, not all male views of women's intellect have been unfavorable. Witness the strong advocate for women's rights found in the nineteenth century intellectual John Stuart Mill (1955).

EARLY SCIENTIFIC VIEWS

By the 1870s, when psychology as a science had its beginning, the ideas of Charles Darwin were very influential. His theory of evolution is well-known, though aspects of it have been misunderstood. Darwin's theory of natural selection did not mean, as commonly thought, that the most fit individual survives, but that those who most successfully *reproduce* themselves survive. Also, considering the uses of his work, it is ironic that Darwin thought that the source of variation among persons was not genetic but *primarily environmental* (Teitelbaum, 1976). Mendel's work on genetics was not well-known at that time and was not known to Darwin. Working from an environmentalist view, Darwin's contemporaries developed the idea that evolution dictated an increasing sexual differentiation, with each sex perfecting the characteristics most suited to its role and function. The male traits so generated included courage, intelligence, and resourcefulness and the female traits included a passive maternalism (Fee, 1976).

Scientific views became especially influenced by *Darwinism*, i.e., the particular interpretations of Darwin's theory applied to the social sciences by Herbert Spencer and others. Spencer had been an early supporter of the feminist movement but revised this position in an 1873 article, "Psychology of the Sexes." He stated that since intellectual attributes were not necessary to rear children, these characteristics had not been developed in women in the course of evolution. Spencer added that although "under special discipline" female intellect could equal or surpass that of men, this should not be permitted as it would draw energy away from the maternal functions. He saw women as a case of arrested evolutionary development, a type that fell short in "those two faculties, intellectual and emotional, which are the latest products of human evolution — the power of abstract reasoning and that most abstract of the emotions, the sentiment of justice" (Spencer, 1873). (See Sherman, 1971, for a discussion of sex-related differences in moral judgment.) The idea that females differ less from children than do males was supported by the fact that in some ways females mature more rapidly than males. The male was seen as more highly differentiated, more specialized, requiring more time for development, more highly evolved (Burt and Moore, 1912). Aspects of this view reappear in the thinking of Marañon (1932). The differential maturation rate of the two sexes also figures in contemporary theories of sex-related differences in cognition.

Lombroso, the nineteenth century Italian criminologist, was a famous and well-respected scholar in his day. Most of his work involved innumerable physical measurements and their correlation with mental disorders. Lombroso believed that greater differentiation between the sexes was a sign of a more highly evolved "race." Among what he called more primitive peoples, notably among blacks, the sexes were thought to be less differentiated (Lombroso and Ferrero, 1958). Remnants of this viewpoint may still be found in contemporary discussions comparing the intelligence of black females and black males (Reid, 1975).

Women were said to have "many traits in common with children; that their moral sense is deficient; that they are revengeful, jealous, inclined to vengeance of a refined cruelty.... In ordinary cases these defects are neutralised by piety, maternity, want of passion, sexual coldness, by weakness and an undeveloped intelligence" (Lombroso and Ferrero, 1958, p. 151). Lombroso also explains for us how women have acquired their beautiful appearance through the process of sexual selection: "Man not only refused to *marry* a deformed female, but ate her, while on the other hand preserving for his enjoyment the handsome woman" (Lombroso and Ferrero, 1958, p. 109).

Views in nineteenth century Germany were even less favorable to women. The German physiologist Paul Mobius argued that the mental incapacity of females was necessary for the survival of the race. However, this incapacity also meant that "If woman was not physically and mentally weak, if she was not as a rule rendered harmless by circumstances, she would be extremely dangerous" (Mobius, 1901, p. 630). The opinions of

Weininger (1906), an intellectual companion of Freud, were even more virulent.

The Female Brain

The size and nature of the female brain were often examined for clues that might account for differences between the sexes in cognitive functioning. In the early nineteenth century, the famous phrenologist Franz Joseph Gall claimed that just by looking he could tell the difference between a female and male brain of any species. In addition to gross anatomical differences, he claimed that the cerebral fiber of the female brain was softer, slender and long rather than thick. Phrenology is a discredited school of thought, but the neuroanatomical argument continued, centering about two main views: that the quality of intellect was related to the absolute or relative size of the brain, and that differences between the sexes could be accounted for by differences in the development of various brain centers (Shields, 1975).

The simple idea that since males have bigger brains, males are smarter gave way to the question of whether the male brain is larger than the female brain proportionate to the size of the body. This necessitated many more measures and considerable controversy. By 1908, however, Havelock Ellis concluded that the argument that males were smarter than females because their brains are bigger could be dismissed. It had been learned that brain size in the normal ranges is uncorrelated with intelligence.

The question of whether the sexes differ in intelligence because parts of the brain develop differently is still very much an aspect of contemporary thinking (see Chapter Six). For some time in the nineteenth century, it was thought that the *frontal* lobes were the repository of the highest mental capacities. During this period, several researchers reported that the frontal lobes of men were in every way more extensive than those of women. At the turn of the century, the *parietal* lobes came to be regarded as the seat of the intellect and, in due course, some generality of opinion developed that parietal predominance characterizes males (Shields, 1975).

In their article "The Mental Differences Between the Sexes," Cyril Burt and Robert Moore (1912) speculated that in males the *cortex* might be more highly organized, while in females the *thalamus* might be more organized. Thus the mental life of males would be cortical, that of females thalamic. The overall tone of the Burt and Moore article, however, was rather different in that they stressed the similarities between the sexes. They concluded their lengthy article with this statement, "We incline . . . to that group of writers who . . . agree that in the practical issue 'the question of the future development of the intellectual life of woman is one of social necessities and ideals, rather than of inborn psychological characteristics of sex' (p. 34)." Their quotation was from Helen Thompson's *Mental Traits of Sex* (1903); we will discuss her work later in this chapter.

Shields (1975) concluded that the theory of Geddes and Thomson (1890) was the "most positive evaluation of the female sex offered by nineteenth century science" (p. 746). Geddes and Thomson saw the two sexes as opposites but complementary and hence valued and necessary in their relationship to each other. "Man thinks more, woman feels more. He discovers more, but remembers less; she is more receptive, and less forgetful" (Geddes and Thomson, 1890, p. 271). The basis for this theory was that males are primarily "catabolic," females "anabolic." From this difference in metabolism, from the comparison of the egg and the sperm, Geddes and Thomson derived the principles by which they explained all other physical, intellectual, and emotional sex-related differences. One further corollary of this view was that woman is conservative; man is progressive (Burt and Moore, 1912). This line of thought was consistent with the notion that the female represents the basic human form while males are more likely to vary from the basic form, for good or for ill (Shields, 1975).

The Variability Hypothesis

The variability hypothesis finds its roots in Darwinism and

in the theory of Geddes and Thomson. Its contemporary version states that males are more variable than females and therefore there are more male geniuses and mental defectives. However, while this is the general import of the hypothesis, there has been a paucity of definition and explicit formulation of the hypothesis from the very beginning, and the logical derivation of this hypothesis from evolutionary theory is tenuous. The idea was that if evolution proceeded in part by sexual selection, the males with the most attractive and/or successful characteristics would have their characteristics continued in their more numerous offspring. For natural selection to occur there must be variety. Since in this theory the emphasis was on the female selecting the male, it was thought that there might be more variety among males.

Such an idea, weakly related to theory, and not the strongest part of the theory at that, was bolstered by the common observation that male animals often show a more spectacular appearance than female animals. So the theory that explained the peacock's tail was haphazardly transferred to the human condition and physical appearance applied to the mental condition. The upshot of this not very logical series of thoughts was that by the 1890s the variability hypothesis was commonly accepted as an explanation for why there were more male than female geniuses: "That men should have greater cerebral variability and therefore more originality, while women have greater stability and therefore more 'common sense,' are facts both consistent with the general theory of sex and verifiable in common experience" (Geddes and Thomas, 1890, p. 271).

Havelock Ellis discussed the variability hypothesis in his book *Man and Woman* (1894). It was he who supported the hypothesis with the observation that not only were there more male geniuses, but there were more male mental defectives. Ellis found great social significance in the hypothesis of greater male variability in its importance to human civilization through the production of men of genius. However, he thought that the female's tendency toward the average did not mean inferiority of talent, but simply limited her to "the sphere of concrete practical life" (Ellis, 1934, p. 436).

The pioneer statistician Karl Pearson (1897) took issue with Ellis on a variety of conceptual and empirical grounds. For example, he objected to contrasting the sexes on the basis of abnormalities. Pearson redefined the problem and using anthropometric data, not involving the secondary sexual characteristics, he showed that, if anything, females are more variable than males. He concluded that the variability hypothesis was quite unproven (Shields, 1975).

Late Nineteenth and Early
Twentieth Century American Views

European ideas were very influential in the United States and opinions about women mirrored European thinking, though never reaching the more extreme negative positions held especially by German scholars. There was a strongly held sentiment that women's role did not include development of the intellect (Shields, 1975). These opinions ranged from those of a woman (Hannah More, 1800), to those of psychologists and physicians (Smith-Rosenberg and Rosenberg, 1973). G. Stanley Hall (1918) worried that coeducation might upset the normal development of female menstruation and suggested "stepping a little aside to let Lord Nature do his magnificent work of efflorescence." Dr. Edward Clarke (1873) of Harvard thought women's health and reproductive capacities would be injured by allowing them to study. Pulling energy to the brain would drain the reproductive organs of energy and cause their malfunction. Dr. Clarke presented histories of coed-collapse in his book *Sex in Education*. The dramatic and dire tone of the book was calculated to deter women from pursuing scholarship.

Controversy continued regarding the actual intellectual merits of the female sex. In an article entitled "The Psychology of Women" published in *Popular Science Monthly* in 1875, Professor G. T. W. Patrick of the University of Iowa reviewed the existing scientific literature on sex-related differences and found the sexes equal in many ways; males superior in some ways, e.g., analytical capacity; and females superior in other ways, e.g., memory (Fee, 1976).

In 1903, Helen Thompson at the University of Chicago published the most thorough study of cognitive sex-related differences yet attempted. Twenty-five men and twenty-five women participated in nearly twenty hours of individual testing. Very little difference was found between the sexes. Thompson attributed the small differences which were found to social influences rather than to biological causes.

As we have already seen, Cyril Burt and Robert Moore endorsed Thompson's conclusions, as did W. I. Thomas (1908) and Edward Thorndike (Fee, 1976). In an essay on sex in education, Thorndike (1906) rejected the view that the observable sex differences were inherent. After studying thousands of girls and boys he concluded that "the differences in sheer intellectual capacity are too small to be of any great practical importance to educational theory or practice" (p. 214). In the same essay, however, Thorndike accepted the variability hypothesis, estimating that the intellectual capacity of males is five to ten percent greater than that of females (Fee, 1976). Here Thorndike was in the company of Cattell (1903) and Cora Castle (1913) both of whom were impressed with the apparently greater number of male geniuses.

Leta Stetter Hollingworth, first a student and then a colleague of Thorndike at Teachers College of Columbia University, took up the issue of the variability hypothesis once more, presenting conceptual and empirical arguments against it (Shields, 1975). She concluded (1913, 1914) that the true potential of woman could only be known when she received social acceptance of her right to choose career, maternity, or both. The variability hypothesis figures in contemporary discussions and we will return to it in Chapter Four.

COMMON TWENTIETH CENTURY AMERICAN OPINION

As we move from the past to the present, it may be helpful to be aware of common contemporary opinion regarding women's intellect. There is evidence that both men and women believe that intelligence is more characteristic of men than of women; this is particularly true regarding skill in math-science areas

(Broverman et al., 1972; Rosenkrantz et al., 1968). These beliefs may be very persistent. In the 1940s, Fernberger studied the evidence on sex-related differences in cognitive functioning. He became convinced that there was no evidence to support the view that males are superior to females in intellectual functioning. Fernberger (1948) assessed the attitudes of college students in his classes and found that they believed males possessed superior ability. After a semester, during which Fernberger presented evidence to the contrary, he reassessed his students' attitudes. They were unchanged. Common views of superior male ability express themselves in various behaviors. For example, under many circumstances academic credentials, and intellectual and creative work, will be evaluated less favorably if they are thought to be those of women rather than of men (Frieze et al., 1978).

Contemporary Political Perspectives

In a democratic society espousing equal opportunity, the ideology demands that many, if not most, high status positions be *achieved* — awarded on the basis of merit. In theory, everyone of adequate "ability" is allowed to compete for these positions. "Ability" is thought to be basically inherited but strongly influenced by educational experiences. For this reason, part of equal opportunity is thought to be equal access to education. The equalizing function of the educational system is in direct opposition to another major function of the educational system, selection — the separating of those of more "ability" from those of less "ability." The selection function works by teaching those of less "ability" that they are intellectually less able and should not aspire to unsuitable positions. This learning is part of the system maintenance. What would happen if many persons thought they *should* have positions for which they were judged inadequate? Obviously, serious strains would develop.

In a situation of limited high status positions, but presumably open opportunity and education, it is advantageous for the maintenance of the system to reduce the number of possible competitors. This is done by the selection process and other procedures that convince large numbers of persons that they are unfit for high status positions. When obvious, gross barriers to high status positions cannot be used for ideological reasons, more subtle, sophisticated, and complex means may achieve the same ends. These could include the widespread conviction, even accepted by women themselves, that they are unfit for high status positions. Such means might include a negative assessment of female intellectual ability vis a vis males. Because the belief in women's intellectual inferiority so obviously supports the status quo, one is justified in being skeptical of these theories. Of course, evidence that theories serve to justify the status quo does not mean, ipso facto, that such theories are untrue. The truth or falsity of the theories must be independently established.

Chapter Two

CONCEPTUAL, METHODOLOGICAL, AND DESIGN PROBLEMS

WE dealt briefly with some perspectives on cognitive sex-related differences from the sociology of knowledge, some historical views of women's intellect, and some early scientific attempts to cope with the topic. In this chapter we will consider a variety of interrelated definitional, conceptual, and methodological problems regarding cognitive sex-related differences. A parallel account of these issues with particular attention to British writers can be found in Lloyd (1976).

DEFINITIONS AND TERMS

While people usually understand what is meant by the female sex and the male sex, there are some points of possible confusion. As used here, the human, female sex refers *only* to XX persons; male sex refers *only* to XY persons. XX and XY persons with sexual, physical abnormalities, including those with an abnormal influence of sex differentiating hormones during their pre- or postnatal development, will be considered as female or male respectively but will be considered apart from the others.

The major problem of misclassification in discussions of the sexes occurs when XO persons are described. These persons, to be discussed in more detail in Chapter Four, have only one sex chromosome, not two as is normal. XO persons have the external appearance of females in childhood, though during adolescence they fail to develop the usual secondary sex characteristics (unless given exogenous hormones). They do not have the chromosomes, hormones, or internal organs of the female sex, nor of the male sex for that matter. XO persons are considered female for *social* purposes, since they externally

15

look more like females than males. This practice, however, can cause confusion. Consider this statement: "In girls with Turner's syndrome, an XO condition, there is a profound defect in spatial perception" (Hamburg, 1974, p. 389). To the only casually informed, such wording lends itself to the interpretation that some *girls* have a profound defect in spatial perception. Bock and Kolakowski (1973) stated, "spatial proficiency in Turner's syndrome . . . has been observed to be typically female." Since persons with Turner's syndrome often perform at a mentally defective level on spatial tasks and have been described as suffering from "space-form blindness," the Bock and Kolakowski statement could be readily misinterpreted to mean that such performances are typically female. Such misinterpretations can occasionally be found.

The term "sex-related differences" is used in preference to "sex differences" or "gender differences." "Sex differences" denote differences that are attributable to biological sex. The term "sex differences" has been used simply to mean any differences demonstrated between the groups, *without* the assumption that they can be attributed to biological sex (Maccoby and Jacklin, 1974). However, usage of the term in this manner facilitates misinterpretation. If the differences are not attributable to biological sex, why call them "sex" differences? "Gender differences," on the other hand, denotes differences which can be attributed to social causes, since gender is a term of social role. "Sex-related differences" seems the most clear, easily understood, and neutral term to describe differences observed between male and female groups without implying either biological or social causation.

"Cognition" refers to intellectual processes as opposed to motivational and emotional processes. We will not deal with all possible aspects of cognitive differences but will concentrate on the most important areas: verbal, spatial, and mathematical. Other terms which may need clarification will be defined in the context of the discussion.

CONCEPTUAL PROBLEMS

Confounded Treatment Effects

The problem of confounded treatment effects is endemic to research regarding the differences between the sexes. Scientific conclusions about a variable require the control or randomization of all other factors relevant to the variable under investigation. For example, if you wish to know whether Seed A or Seed B yields the greater amount of corn, the two seeds might be planted on randomly assigned plots of ground and thereafter given the same treatment in terms of watering, fertilization, pest control, and time of harvesting. In this way the merits of Seed A and Seed B can be ascertained independently of the other factors. However, these conditions are not met in the comparative study of the two sexes. Research involving human males and females necessarily fails to control or randomize relevant factors. Therefore, the data reviewed will only allow us to make informed assessments.

Null Hypothesis

A set of fundamental conceptual problems is associated with the null hypothesis. The null hypothesis states that there is no difference between two conditions or, in this case, two groups, i.e., the difference is zero. It has been pointed out that, in practice, data based on large numbers of subjects will show statistically significant differences almost any way they are divided: male, female; North, South; rural, urban (Bakan, 1970). These statistically demonstrated differences often have little or no meaning and present us with a statistical paradox. On the one hand, an intuitive approach suggests that the more subjects one has the better the data. On the other hand, very large numbers of subjects increase the power of the statistical test to such a degree that almost any comparison would be statistically significant. In evaluating sex differences research, it is necessary to understand this statistical paradox. (See Morrison and Henkel, 1970, for discussion.)

The null hypothesis method of scientific investigation presents an additional problem. Let us say that we have decided to reject the null hypothesis if the t or F value should be large enough that, assuming all underlying assumptions have been adequately met, there will be only five chances in one hundred that the hypothesis is true even though we rejected it. Hence we are running a 5 percent risk of a Type I error (risk of rejecting a true hypothesis). What happens, however, if we do *not* reject the hypothesis? Does that mean the hypothesis is true? For example, would that indicate that there are no differences between the sexes?

In many facets of experimental work, failure to demonstrate an effect means an inadequate procedure. This line of reasoning is not necessarily appropriate when applied to comparison of the sexes. However, it is sometimes implicitly assumed that "failure" to demonstrate a sex-related difference means inadequate procedure. In any case, a finding of no difference is not interpreted to mean there is no sex-related difference but that the results are inconclusive. If, when we do not reject the null hypothesis, we do not accept the null hypothesis then in essence, we are taking *no* risk of a Type II error (risk of accepting a false hypothesis). Ordinarily in research design one seeks to balance the risks of the Type I and Type II errors. The risk of accepting a false hypothesis that there are no cognitive differences between the sexes does not appear serious. Indeed, in terms of negative social consequences, the risk of a Type I error would appear to be far more serious. The philosophical underpinnings of the null hypothesis approach clearly have detrimental effects in the "sex differences" area.

It is widely acknowledged that studies with negative results are much less likely to be published. Moreover, in the case of findings of no sex-related differences, these results tend to be selectively ignored in favor of findings supporting the concept of sex differences. For example, the study of Corah (1965) did not find clear sex-related differences in favor of males in the performance of various spatial perception tasks. This was not reported in the abstract nor was it reported in the Oetzel bibliography in Maccoby (1966). Instead, this study was frequently cited in support of the X-linked hypothesis of male inheritance of superior spatial perception. Ironically the X-linked hypothesis was supposed to explain why males were superior to females in space perception, yet the Corah study itself did not clearly demonstrate such superiority.

Naturalistic Fallacy and Evolutionary Determinism

Some writers have assumed that what is, must be, and what was, should and shall be. This reasoning is rampant in the study of sex-related differences. Some authors suppose that finding a partial biological basis for a sex-related difference means that this difference is immutable and/or desirable. Neither assumption is necessarily true. Explanations of the possible role of sex-related differences in natural selection have likewise been presented in a deterministic framework assuming more rigidity for biological factors than can reasonably be supported. Archer (1976) has soundly criticized the speculations of Hutt (1972), Tiger (1970), and Gray and Buffery (1971) on these grounds.

Extrapolations from Animal Data

While animal data may provide useful hypotheses for evaluation with humans, no conclusions can be made about humans solely on the basis of animal data. Indeed, inferences cannot be drawn from one animal species to another. There is so much behavior variation between nonhuman primate species that even generalization from one group to another is impossible (Lancaster, 1976). Extrapolations from rats, guinea pigs, chicks, and peacocks to humans are even more suspect. A writer's failure to state clearly that tey is relying on animal not human data can lead nonprofessional persons to erroneous conclusions. Hutt (1972), for example, noted that testosterone increased attention and her account implied that the studies were carried out on men (actually the subjects were male chicks). By the time the finding was reported in a popular book (Stassino-poulos, 1973), the subjects were arbitrarily described not merely as men but were fancifully endowed "with large chests and biceps" (Lloyd, 1976).

Duality and Bipolarity

There are strong tendencies in our culture to think in terms of dualities and bipolarity. This leads to a bias in which characteristics tend to be rather arbitrarily divided into two groups. The unexamined expectation is that males will have one group of characteristics while females will have the *opposite* characteristics: strong, weak; active, passive; analytical, global; rational, emotional. It is what can be described as the Yin-Yang fallacy. It is the fallacy of false dichotomous grouping stemming from an unrecognized adherence to Yin-Yang thinking, belief in the Female and Male principles. This fallacy exhibited in the theory of Broverman et al. (1968) is discussed in more detail in Chapter Five. Cognitive traits were quite arbitrarily divided into those that were described as simple and repetitive and those described as complex and requiring restructuring. Females were thought to do better on the simple, repetitive tasks and males were thought to be better on the complex, restructuring tasks. A dualistic, bipolar theory induces a certain specious comfort in the reader who is often not sufficiently critical to challenge the surface validity of the concepts involved. (See Fairweather, 1976, for cogent comment on this problem.)

Faulty Cross-Sex Inferences

Female subjects are not so often studied as male subjects (Carlson and Carlson, 1961; Carlson, 1971; Schwabacher, 1972). The assumption is made that what applies to males, applies to females or that whatever applies to males, the *opposite* applies to females. In fact, neither assumption is likely to be true. Typically the sexes are more alike than different, but complex differences exist in timing, triggering, and meaning. Often the sex of the subjects is not reported (Miller, 1971) or the data are not analysed by sex (Bakan, 1969). Maccoby and Jacklin (1974) pointed out an example of researchers making faulty inferences about *between* sex differences from *within* sex data. For example: Bell reported that activity level was high in newborn boys who had suffered birth complications, compared with those who had not. He hypothesized that since boys more often suffer birth complications, this might explain a higher activity level among neonatal boys. Later this was reported by others as an instance in which boys had been found to have a higher activity level than girls, though Bell had not studied girls. In the first printing of their book, Maccoby and Jacklin (1974) fell into a similar error in discussing the "bent twig" hypothesis (Sherman, 1967, 1971). This hypothesis, based on the law of primacy, suggested that since females are apparently verbally accelerated compared to males, they come to rely on verbal approaches to problem solving more than males do, i.e., they develop a preference for a verbal approach to problem solving. In addition to misrepresenting the hypothesis, Maccoby and Jacklin suggested that the way to test the "bent twig" hypothesis is to see whether boys who speak late have better spatial skills than boys who speak early. On the surface this appears to follow logically but, in fact, it does not. The converse of a true statement cannot be assumed to be true. An assertion that verbal precocity in girls more than boys leads to establishing a preference for the verbal approach in females, does not logically permit the inferences they made. Shifts were made from girls to boys, from between sex differences to within sex differences, from the verbal area to the spatial area, and from preference for a verbal approach to skill in spatial performance. However, some light could be shed on the validity of the bent twig hypothesis by determining if a verbal approach preference and lower spatial skill can be observed in girls and boys who talked early, compared to girls and boys who talked later, controlling for relevant factors such as possible brain injury and socioeconomic background. A more detailed discussion of the bent twig hypothesis will be found in a later chapter.

Inferences from Cross-cultural Data

It has been assumed that findings of differences between the sexes common to all cultures indicate a biological basis for the differences observed. It is also assumed that differences that fail to replicate across cultures have no biological basis. Neither assumption is completely accurate. If a difference between the sexes is found in one culture but not in another, it suggests that the difference does not stem from *incorrigible* biological sources, assuming that the two sexes have been similarly sampled in the two cultures. Such an inference is not the same as saying that there is *no* biological basis for the difference, though that may be true. On the other hand, there may be some biological factor that manifests itself under some conditions but not others. Though in one sense it seems to be a reasonable inference that differences that are found in all cultures have a biological basis, in another sense, the meaning of this may be more complex than at first assumed. Modern technology has produced many changes, including changes in what is essentially the biological role of women, i.e., newly available methods of relatively safe childbirth, artificial feeding, abortion, and birth control have altered women's lives. Some differences between the sexes may be the indirect result of ubiquitous differences in sex roles which were based on biological differences that are no longer effective factors. Hence, differences that have appeared ubiquitous may no longer seem so in the future.

Pitfalls of Age-related Inferences

Sometimes it is thought that any difference between the sexes at birth must surely be biologically based. This is a sound inference, if the many factors which affect neonatal behavior have been properly controlled, evaluated, and interpreted for the two sexes. This is no easy task (Fairweather, 1976). A biological influence may be involved, but not necessarily in the manner one supposes. As mentioned, more males have difficult deliveries which can lead to greater activity. However, this greater activity could be incorrectly attributed to greater testosterone levels in males, and these data could be used to support a very different line of reasoning, e.g., testosterone results in greater activity and hence as a result of hormonal differences males are active and females are passive.

The common assumption that differences between the sexes that occur later in childhood can be attributed to socialization is also not clearly true. Many biological developmental events occur after early childhood and one cannot assume that later changes are independent of these. Nor can one assume that changes occurring at puberty can be attributed to biological changes of puberty. They may instead be attributable to changes in sex role behaviors which are cued to biological changes. The timing of differences is important to causal attribution, but it is not a simple and infallible guide to correct attribution.

Statistical versus Practical Significance

Besides the *statistical* significance of a finding, one may be concerned with its *practical* significance. Many apparently demonstrated sex-related differences are so small that they are of essentially no practical importance. For theoretical reasons, however, even a small difference, if it appears to be a valid one, may be of interest. The pitfall of seriously considering small but highly significant sex-related differences is illustrated in the failure of Wechsler's Masculinity-Femininity index. Impressed by the consistency of findings of sex-related differences in specific subtests of the Wechsler Intelligence tests, Wechsler attempted to use scores on these subtests as an indicator of masculinity/femininity. The predictive power of such small differences has been totally inadequate and it has not proven possible to validate the index (Matarazzo, 1972).

PROBLEMS OF MEASUREMENT AND DESIGN

Bias in Measures

What constitutes a cognitive difference between the sexes? The overwhelming majority of reports of cognitive sex-related differences refer to differences in test scores. Usually the report is of a difference between a mean score of a male group compared to a mean score of a female group. Studies of the effect of bias in the content and wording of tests on sex-related differences on test performance have shown negative effects for the female group (Donlon, 1971; Donlon et al., 1976; Ekstrom et al., 1976; Tittle et al., 1974). There is evidence that female subjects scored better when tested by females than when tested by males, though the sex of the examiner did not affect male performance (Pedersen et al., 1968). When global ratings or judgments are made, even greater distortion can be expected in measurement. There are several studies that have experimentally demonstrated that work labeled that of a woman is likely to be judged of poorer quality than if it is thought to have been done by a man (Goldberg, 1968; Pheterson et al., 1971; Rosen and Jerdee, 1974).

Another interesting aspect of measures of sex-related differences lies in the possibility of test constructors unwittingly selecting test items which maximize differences between the sexes. In test development, a common method is to select items having the largest variance. Selecting such items hopefully means that the test will discriminate better among persons. If the pool of subjects used to develop the test consists of both males and females (the usual practice) and if items with the highest variance are selected, the possibility exists that items maximizing sex-related differences will be selected.

Some have argued that if one's goal is to maximize individual differences, then it makes no difference if the individual differences are maximized about the sex variable or about some other variable. There are problems, however, with this argument. First of all, the test developer may mistake artifact for reality. Having unwittingly created a test maximizing sex-related differences, tey may say "Aha! We have strong sex-related differences!" People may be more impressed with the finding than they would be if they realized that the test development procedure facilitated the appearance of sex-related differences. The situation becomes very serious if the items do not validly relate to criteria. What if they have to do with aspects of wording of content irrelevant to the basic purpose of the test? There is no way of knowing the extent of this problem in the psychological literature because it would be deeply embedded in the production of the measures themselves.

Artifacts of Measurement: Rod and Frame Test

Some further examples of the possible role of artifactual, uncontrolled factors can be illustrated by the Rod and Frame Test. This test has often, but not always, shown a superior male performance (Sherman, 1974). From such results it was ultimately incorrectly concluded that males are more "analytical" than females. The chain of faulty inference and weak empirical findings that resulted in this conclusion has been explained more fully elsewhere (Sherman, 1967). The test itself and spatial perception are discussed at greater length in the next chapter. Here let us simply examine aspects of the measure with an eye toward sources of effects that could confound sex-related differences.

First of all, the test must be conducted in nearly total darkness. That factor alone could produce sex-related differences in performance. Female subjects being tested by a male experimenter might well be more uneasy than male subjects. Such situations have been known to elicit unwanted sexual advances. The apparent greater ease of female conditionability as found in eyelid conditioning studies was ultimately attributed to greater female anxiety, an anxiety that may well have been situational, given the subject's nearly prone position in an isolated, dark room. The "same" conditions may not be the same for males and females. This example is only meant to be illustrative and though it has doubtlessly confounded some results with some subjects, it could not account for all the variance of differences between the sexes on the Rod and Frame Test (e.g., with the portable version).

The conditions of the Rod and Frame Test also require that the experimenter move the rod in small increments at the subject's direction until the subject is satisfied that the rod is vertical. Subjects who are not assertive in character (dependent persons) or subjects not used to assertive behavior as part of their role, might be less likely to "bother" the experimenter

enough to get the rod adjusted just right. The assertive behavior required as part of the experimental design could result
in sex-related differences on this basis rather than because of
differences in spatial skill. Relationships were sometimes found
between Rod and Frame Test scores and dependency (Witkin et
al., 1954, 1962) though they were not considered artifactual, but
further evidence of an overarching cognitive style.

An important source of confounding effects is the sex-role
appropriateness for females of good performance on a spatial
task. Spatial tasks are sex-typed male (Stein and Smithells,
1969) and it has been demonstrated that the sex-related difference in Rod and Frame performance disappeared when the rod
was a human figure and the task was described as one of empathy, a female appropriate task (Naditch, 1976). Sex-role effects on cognitive performance will be discussed in more detail
in Chapter Seven.

Achievement versus Ability Tests

An overall measurement conceptual problem in cognitive
studies is the confusion about ability or aptitude versus
achievement. Questions related to such terms as "aptitude,"
"ability," and "achievement" have been discussed at length
(Green, 1974). These terms have been variously defined; "aptitude" has even been defined to include motivational and attitudinal factors (Carroll, 1974), but it will not be so used in this
review. The terms "aptitude" and "ability" carry connotations
of being inherited while the term "achievement" does not, it is
specifically defined as being learned. Problems have arisen with
(a) the use of achievement tests of such generality as to be very
similar to ability tests; and (b) misuse of tests and terms in ways
increasing social risk to certain groups, e.g., using ability tests
as the only pre-post measures of intervention programs, finding
sex-related differences on achievement tests between groups un-
equal in mathematics background and from this implying the
sexes are different in mathematics ability.

It is widely acknowledged that experiential factors strongly
affect performance even on ability and aptitude tests. Thus,

even with these tests, one cannot assume that group differences reflect genetic differences. This fact, acknowledged in the abstract, is forgotten in concrete interpretation of results. Moreover, there is one major exception to the general assumption that experience affects performance even on ability tests; spatial perception has been widely believed to be relatively uninfluenced by training (Bock and Kolakowski, 1973). Evidence to the contrary and the effects of practice and training on space perception will be discussed in more detail in a later chapter.

Because of their implications, the terms "aptitude" and "ability" will be seldom used. Terms of potentially lower social risk will be preferred, e.g., "skill," "performance," "disposition" (Humphreys, 1974). These terms are to be considered neutral in that no assumption is made that they imply inheritance or lack of it.

Selection Factors

If one wishes to make any inferences comparing the sexes, one must have a rather clear idea of how one's sample of males and females has been selected and if the two sexes are equitably represented in the sample. One must also decide what equitable means. Should complete or at least random samples of an *entire* population be compared? If more males are brain-injured at birth (Taylor, 1974), is it equitable to include brain-injured persons? If "abnormal" males are excluded, how does this affect the comparison? Could it be that since females are more viable, there are more compensated brain-injured females in the seemingly "normal" population?

In a certain sense, any live male population is more select than the female population. One hundred and twenty males are conceived for every one hundred females, and there are one hundred and six male live births for every one hundred females. Males die off at faster rates than females at every decade of life (Childs, 1965). In middle age there are about equal numbers of the two sexes, while there are many more females than males in old age. If the more intelligent samples of the genotype are more likely to survive, every comparison of a male and female group involves the comparison of a more select male group with a less select female group.

Questions of selection have more commonly concerned whether or not comparison of the sexes in high school populations is equitable since more males than females drop out of school. This kind of differential drop-out would mean that a more select group of boys would be compared to the overall group of girls. Another common observation is that many colleges have had different admission standards for males and females. Typically, females have had to have better records than males in order to be admitted. Comparison of the sexes at such colleges would mean that a more select group of females has been compared to a less select group of males. The point has generally been made that comparison of the sexes in college populations is biased since there may generally be a tendency for only the most intelligent of the females to continue with college education while males of even fairly average intelligence might continue. Such a bias is possible but not universally the case in college settings. Even very intelligent females do not necessarily continue in a college education. This is particularly true if they are from a lower socioeconomic class (Alexander and Eckland, 1974).

Neglect of Important Control Factors

Sex-role divergence is sufficiently pervasive that the sexes have different experiences from very early ages, with the divergence increasing at least until young adulthood. These sex-role divergences mean that separation of the effects of genetic sex and the effects of sex role is extremely difficult, if not impossible, to accomplish. There are, however, variations in the degree to which obvious relevant differences are controlled. For example, one would hardly think it worthy of note to report that people who have studied four years of mathematics do better on math problems than people who have studied two years of mathematics. However, much was made of the fact that male and female groups, years of study of mathematics uncontrolled, greatly differed in mathematics performance (Mullis, 1975). The researchers certainly realized that the difference in performance cannot be attributed to the sex of the subjects per se; however, people reading newspaper reports of the research could hardly be expected to interpret the results correctly. Such research, if properly interpreted for the professional and lay reader is, of course, useful for it is helpful to know that females are performing far below males in mathematics. It is important, however, that such findings not be used to infer differences between the sexes attributable to sex per se. Many of the studies of mathematics performance cited by Maccoby and Jacklin (1974) failed to control previous mathematics education. These studies contributed to the conclusion of Maccoby and Jacklin that males are superior to females in mathematics "ability."

A more subtle form of failure to control relevant variables lies in the failure to control course of study in investigations of spatial perception. Performance on spatial tasks is improved by participation in certain courses, e.g., drafting (Blade and Watson, 1955; Johnson, 1976; Zimmerman and Parlee, 1973). Failure to control for course of study can increase the amount of apparent difference between the sexes.

Maturation Rate

A controversial question is the extent to which differences between the sexes in physical maturation are paralleled by differences in cognitive development. In skeletal development, for example, females at age five are a year ahead of males and two years ahead at age thirteen. Girls also stop growing earlier. On the average, girls reach 98 percent of their final height by sixteen and a half, boys at seventeen and three-fourths (Tanner, 1962). However, simple generalizations that females mature more quickly than males are misleading since females do not mature more quickly on all indices. For example, males are ahead in sexual behavior and in attaining fertility (Siecus, 1970). People often mistakenly assume that menstruation completes female sexual maturation, when it is only a midpoint in the process of maturation. More closely related to the intellectual area are findings related to brain lateralization. While lateralization of verbal function to the left hemisphere has been thought to occur earlier in girls than in boys, Witelson (1976) found that lateralization of spatial function to the right hemisphere occurred earlier in boys than in girls.

Investigators, however, have long debated the general question of whether accelerated female physical development is paralleled mentally. Anastasi (1949) thought not. Maccoby (1963) pointed out that faster physical growth may be correlated with faster maturation of certain motor and perceptual abilities that underlie intellectual performance, though performance of these tasks does not necessarily imply anything about ultimate levels of intellectual achievement.

In general, Maccoby (Maccoby and Jacklin, 1974) has not been impressed with the idea that female precocity in some aspects of physical development is paralleled by mental development. She has based her opinion largely on Nancy Bayley's (1956) data from the Berkeley Growth Study Sample. These data showed boys and girls progressing at the same rate intellectually though at different rates for growth in stature. Bayley described intelligence as accelerating most rapidly up to five or six years with another spurt between nine and eleven. Height, on the other hand, increased rapidly in the first two years with adolescent spurts between ten and twelve for girls and eleven and fifteen for boys. While there was a positive relationship between height and intelligence, mental and physical rates of growth in the individual child were not concomitant. Tanner (1961) concluded that compared to other children the same age, physically advanced children show a small but consistent superiority in mental age. Ljung (1965) found a general agreement between mental growth pattern and physical growth pattern at adolescence, using group data. Mental acceleration of girls preceded that of boys.

Maccoby's contention appears to be that because Bayley did not find a correlation between mental and physical development, then one is justified in inferring that differences between the sexes in physical development are also not paralleled by differences in mental development. However, one cannot make inferences about group comparisons from individual longitudinal data. For example, within individuals the physical growth spurt might not correlate with the mental growth spurt. Nonetheless, *groups* could differ, with both the physical and mental growth spurts coming earlier in females.

Garai and Scheinfeld (1968) decided that girls *are* mentally accelerated compared to boys and that comparing boys and girls of the same chronological age is inappropriate. Therefore, any comparison of the sexes of the same age which did not show female advantage was interpreted as an instance of *male* mental advantage. This procedure is arbitrary and introduces confusion in the literature.

At present, no easy resolution for the question of whether or not the sexes differ in cognitive maturation is available. On the one hand it is unwise to ignore this possibility. While differences between the sexes cannot be great, it may be that there are some differences in the best timing of exposure to various educational experiences. It is also possible that comparing the sexes of the same chronological age is a procedure biased against males as Garai and Scheinfeld (1968) contend. This danger would appear to be greatest in the preschool years. While there is no strong evidence for their contention, we will pay particular attention to data on sex-related differences at older ages (sixteen plus) in order to avoid making inferences that some might regard as biased in favor of females.

Cyclic Phenomena

Englander-Golden et al. (1976) hypothesized that some apparent performance differences between the sexes might be artifactual in the sense that after adolescence, the possibility exists that an unstressed male group could be compared with a female group containing variable numbers of women under menstrual stress. They hypothesized that some women react to stress stemming from menstruation phenomena with decrements in performance on complex tasks. They formulated their hypothesis focusing particularly on the performance of complex spatial tasks, since a difference between the sexes in the performance of such tasks has been thought to emerge at adolescence. They did not predict any main effects of phase of the menstrual cycle on intellectual performance since there is very little evidence of such effects (Sherman, 1971; Sommer, 1972).

Englander-Golden et al. (1976) demonstrated that women who are repressors, as measured by Byrne's (1961) Repression-Sensitization scale, showed a performance decrement during the menstrual phase of the cycle but not during the premenstrual or mid-cycle phase (days seven to thirteen). Performance decrements were found on both a complex spatial task and a complex verbal task (Space Relations test and Verbal Reasoning test of the Differential Aptitude Test, Bennett et al., 1952). They did not find such effects for a simple repetitive task (Digit Symbol subtest from the Wechsler Adult Intelligence Scale, Wechsler, 1955). These results raise the possibility that some or all of the performance differences between the sexes in postpubertal groups can be attributed to the presence among the females of greater numbers of persons coping poorly with stress related to menstruation. Replication of these findings and careful comparison of the sexes with larger samples, controlling for menstrual cycle phase, will be needed to shed further light on this possibility.

STATISTICAL CONSIDERATIONS

Faulty Inferences

Considering the sophisticated techniques available for statistical analysis, or perhaps because of them, there is a large amount of faulty inference in the area of sex-related difference. For example, in some instances the correlation for one sex is significantly different from zero but the correlation for the other is not. These facts are then interpreted as if there were a significant sex-related difference between the correlations. In fact, the difference between the sexes is not tested or is not significant. There are many instances in which correlations significant for one sex but not for the other are interpreted in this way. Sometimes such spurious findings are the beginning of a speculative analysis of why such supposed differences should occur.

The same sort of faulty inferential procedure can occur with analysis of variance. Sometimes a significant effect is found for one sex but not for the other leading to a faulty inference of a sex-related difference. Such an inference properly requires a significant interaction effect. A recent example of this error is the study of Hannay and Malone (1976b). They concluded that there is less complete lateralization of linguistic function in females in comparison to males. This inference was made without any direct statistical comparison of the two sexes.

In another instance, a sex-related difference was inferred by comparison of an overall correlation with the correlation of a female group. McGlone and Kertesz (1973) found that the correlation between Block Design and an Aphasia battery for seventy-two patients was .12, while the correlation for the twenty-two females with left-hemisphere lesions was .63. They interpreted this finding to indicate that following injury to the left hemisphere the degree of language impairment is to some extent predictive of visual-spatial disability in women but not in men. The proper statistical test however, would have been to compare the correlation for males, .23, with the correlation for females, .63. This comparison is not significantly different. The conclusion of McGlone and Kertesz may ultimately be shown to be correct but, contrary to their report, their current data do not provide statistical support for their conclusion.

Another kind of error, pointed out by Maccoby and Jacklin (1974), occurs when different patterns of findings within each sex are mistaken for a sex difference. For example, Sears et al. (1965) found that for preschool girls verbal aggression was more frequent than physical aggression, but for boys physical aggression was more common than verbal aggression. Though correctly presented in the original report, the results were later interpreted as showing that girls were higher than boys in verbal aggression. In fact, boys showed both more physical and verbal aggression than girls.

More Appropriate Statistics

The discussions of meaningful versus statistical significance of the difference between the means of the two sexes indicate the need for more appropriate statistical indices. A statistic recommended very early was a simple measure of overlap, e.g., the percentage of males exceeding the median for females (Burt and Moore, 1912). This measure permits comparison from study to study and across characteristics. Maccoby and Jacklin (1974) used the standard score of the difference between means to accomplish a similar purpose.

Tresemer (1975) provides an excellent discussion of the problem with several alternative recommendations. The measures discussed are free from the effects of sample size and difficulties of the null hypothesis logic. They are based on how much more accurately one can classify an individual on the characteristic in question by knowing that individual's sex. There are a variety of these measures which can be presented more or less equivalently. (See Friedman, 1968, for a useful table of equivalence.) They include R^2, eta squared, phi squared, and various overlap statistics, though omega squared may be the most useful (Hays, 1973). These measures provide an opportunity to make a more intelligent evaluation of the size of the effect of differences between the sexes. Unfortunately most studies do not use these statistics and sufficient data for calculating them are often not reported.

An Illustration

Recent data (Fennema and Sherman, 1977) may be used to illustrate some points about statistical reporting of sex-related differences. An analysis of variance of mathematics test scores (Test of Academic Progress, Scannell, 1972) was performed for over 1,000 9th to 11th grade students. Mathematics background was controlled. There was a highly significant difference between the sexes in favor of males, $F(1,\infty) = 27.47$, $p < .001$. That looks like a very impressive difference. Let us examine, however, the *extent* of the difference. Using omega squared as our measure of association, we find that sex accounted for *two percent* of the variance of the math achievement scores. This is a trivial difference and not at all impressive.

Further perspective on the data is provided when one notes that there is a statistically significant school by sex interaction. In two schools there was a significant difference between the sexes and in two schools there was not. When one addresses the question of the conditions eliciting differences between the sexes, one moves to another, more fruitful level of discussion than when one deals solely with the question of what "sex differences" there are. We will return to data from this study as our discussion proceeds.

CONCLUSION

These problems of concept, methodology, design, and statistics have proven formidable indeed. Unfortunately, they have been very commonly ignored. One can only strongly agree with the Oxford professor Hugh Fairweather (1976, p. 267) in his assessment that "the majority of the studies . . . are both ill-thought and ill-performed. Whilst in other circumstances this may be regarded as the occupational hazard of scientific enterprise, here such complacency is compounded by the social loadings placed upon these kinds of results."

It is disconcerting indeed to see, by contrast, the methodological care lavished on rats. Dawson (1972), for example, warned that space perception measures, mazes in this case, should not be mistaken for a general intelligence measure as this would seriously confuse the literature on the topic. This insight so carefully applied to rodent intelligence is even more aptly applied to the case of human female intelligence (Sherman, 1967).

It may be that some improvement in the quality of how material is reviewed and what is published in journals and books could be accomplished by adoption of research guidelines by funding agencies and journal editors. These guidelines would then need to be widely available and distributed.

From this introduction, the reader may correctly anticipate that our task in discerning valid findings in the area of sex-related cognitive differences will be a difficult one. In practice, one finds that studies comparing the sexes sometimes find significant differences between them and sometimes do not. However, the fundamental question is not asked. "Why are significant results found in one study and not in another?" The fact that this question is rarely addressed in a serious fashion is a sign of how little we understand sex-related differences in cognition.

Chapter Three

SEX-RELATED COGNITIVE DIFFERENCES: EMPIRICAL FINDINGS

INTRODUCTION

OUR discussion of this topic will be handicapped by lack of information. No existing work on sex-related differences has come close to incorporating properly the conceptual and statistical approaches discussed earlier. In many instances this can only be done when one has access to the raw data. Almost invariably, however, it will involve calculation of new statistics measuring the extent of difference between the sexes. Such a task is beyond the scope of this book. Our task is further complicated by the fact that the most recent major review of the material, Maccoby and Jacklin (1974), is a work seriously marred by conceptual, interpretive, and empirical errors. (For further detail see reviews by Block, 1976a, 1976b, and Sherman, 1975.) Our main topics of interest are sex-related differences in general intelligence, verbal, spatial, mathematical, and problem solving skills. These topics do not exhaust the possibilities but appear to be the most important. Our purpose is not an exhaustive review but a reexamination of the evidence for its reliability, validity, and meaning.

GENERAL INTELLIGENCE

David Wechsler, one of the nation's foremost authorities on intelligence, has concluded, "It may be possible to demonstrate a measurable superiority of women over men so far as general intelligence is concerned" (Wechsler, 1944, p. 107). But alas, this apparent female advantage was shortlived; the 1955 revision of the Wechsler Intelligence Scale removed the female advantage (Matarazzo, 1972). Are we to suppose that females were more intelligent than males before 1955 and now males are as intelligent or more intelligent than females? Of course not. Intelligence has been inferred from a test with specific items on it and how a particular group scores depends on the content of that pool of items.

Curiously enough, the only recent opinion favoring the view of superior female intelligence comes from Arthur Jensen, noted for his defense of important genetic sources of variation in intelligence (1971). Most writers in recent years have described the sexes as equal in general intelligence; the focus of controversy has switched from the question of general intelligence to questions of differences in specific dispositions, especially spatial and mathematical dispositions, and to some extent the verbal disposition.

VERBAL DISPOSITION

Verbal skill is probably the single most important aspect of intelligence and in this area females are usually conceded to have well-developed powers. Females are generally thought to be verbally precocious compared to males. Males eventually catch up but females are thought to retain a slight edge in all areas of verbal functioning. These generalizations characteristic of Tyler (1965), Maccoby (1966), and Guilford (1967) have been challenged and questioned but still appear valid, though the demonstrated differences are so small as to be trivial. In our discussion, we will pay special attention to the foci of change and controversy.

Examination of Evidence

Verbal Reasoning

Garai and Scheinfeld (1968) thought that males were *superior* to females in verbal reasoning and comprehension, including vocabulary. Their review, however, did not include all relevant studies. Moreover, as discussed, they used a highly questionable procedure to handle the possible impact of differential rates of maturation for the two sexes. In the years before maturity, they counted all equal performances of the sexes as instances of male superiority. One would have preferred comparisons of mature groups of similar background and training. This procedure would avoid the necessity of drawing conclusions based on the speculative assumption that equality really means male superiority. This arbitrary procedure has introduced an unnecessary element of confusion to the literature with scholars citing the same study to opposite ends. For example, Garai and Scheinfeld cited Bennett et al. (1959) as evidence that boys are better in verbal reasoning. (The Verbal Reasoning subtest of the Differential Aptitude Test involves analogies.) This same study was cited in the Oetzel (1966) as showing *no difference* between the sexes. Let us attempt to resolve this question by looking at data from older subjects.

The Maccoby and Jacklin (1974) discussion of cognition builds on a previous work (Maccoby, 1966). In order to gain a complete picture of the views of these authors, one must study both works. In the 1966 book, Maccoby did not address the specific question of whether males are superior to females in verbal reasoning, including vocabulary. The classified summary of research by Oetzel (1966), however, catalogued results of relevant studies. The 1974 review covers nonoverlapping material. If one avoids the maturity controversy by examining the results of the reported studies using subjects age sixteen or older, one has a somewhat better basis for an objective opinion. These studies are tallied in Table I. Examination of Table I makes clear that males are *not* superior to females in verbal reasoning including vocabulary. Garai and Scheinfeld are incorrect even when applying a test favorable to their viewpoint (i.e., use of older subjects).

Maccoby and Jacklin (1974) described the usual female advantage in the verbal area as about .25 SD. They were at pains to point out that the female verbal advantage includes "higher-level skills, such as comprehension of complex written text, quick understanding of logical relations expressed in verbal terms, and in some instances verbal creativity" (p. 84). These

TABLE I

VERBAL REASONING: SUBJECTS > AGE 16

Variable	Number of Results	Female Superior	Male Superior	No Difference
Oetzel (1966)				
Vocabulary	4	2	0	2
Verbal Problem Solving	1	1	0	0
General Verbal Skill	4	1	0	3
Abstract Reasoning	4	1	1	2
Maccoby and Jacklin (1974)				
Tested Verbal Abilities	25	8	1	16
Droege (1967)	2	2	0	0
Total	40	15	2	23

data indicate that the slight verbal advantage that females retain in adulthood applies not only to word fluency (e.g., name as many words as you can think of beginning with *B*), but to verbal skill in general.

Female Verbal Precocity

The issue of female verbal precocity is interesting in its own right and also as part of an explanation for further development of cognitive differences. Sherman (1967, 1971) has hypothesized that the early female verbal advantage bends the twig toward female preference for verbal approaches to problem solution. This bent is then increased by the verbal emphasis of the educational system and by aspects of sex roles that do not encourage girls' development of visual-spatial skills. Maccoby, however, is no longer so sure that girls are verbally precocious compared with boys. Let us examine Maccoby's position first in 1966 and again in 1974, and then look at evaluations of Harris (1977) and McGuinness (1976).

> Through the preschool years and in the early school years, girls exceed boys in most aspects of verbal performance. They say their first word sooner, articulate more clearly and at an earlier age, use longer sentences, and are more fluent. By the beginning of school, however, there are no longer any con-

sistent differences in vocabulary. Girls learn to read sooner, and there are more boys than girls who require special training in remedial reading programs; but by approximately the age of ten, a number of studies show that boys have caught up in their reading skills. Throughout the school years, girls do better on tests of grammar, spelling, and word fluency (Maccoby, 1966, p. 26).

Eight years later, Maccoby and Jacklin were more cautious in their conclusion. They stated that the "presumed advantage of girls in the first two years of life is tenuous" (p. 77). They went on to explain:

We suggest that there are distinct phases in the development of verbal skills in the two sexes through the growth cycle. One occurs very early — before the age of 3. We emphasize that the studies documenting sex differences at this age are very old. More recent studies tend not to show superiority for girls in spontaneous vocalization or in picture vocabulary after the understanding of speech has begun. Whether a sex difference would still be found with large samples on age of beginning to speak, age of first combining words into sentences, or mean length of utterance, we do not know. If girls do have an early advantage with respect to these aspects of language development, it is short-lived. At about 3 the boys catch up, and in most population groups the two sexes perform very similarly until adolescence. When there are differences, they favor girls; these exceptions tend to occur in populations of underprivileged children, where girls maintain an advantage to a later age. It is about age 10 or 11 that girls begin to come into their own in verbal performance. From this age through the high school and college years we find them out-scoring boys at a variety of verbal skills (Maccoby and Jacklin, 1974, pp. 84-85).

Their final word on this topic concludes, "It is probably true that girls' verbal abilities mature somewhat more rapidly in early life, although there are a number of recent studies in which no sex difference has been found" (Maccoby and Jacklin, 1974, p. 351).

First let us discuss these quotations with regard to the question of girls' verbal precocity. Basically Maccoby and Jacklin seem to be saying that results of studies from 1966 to 1974 are not easily compared with results of earlier studies. Examination of the bibliographic summaries in the two books shows that earlier studies used larger and less select samples and different sorts of measures. The 1974 review does not include the categories of Age of First Speech, Articulation, Verbosity and Verbal Fluency, Length of Statement, Grammar, etc. Moreover, how large the difference appears to be probably depends a great deal on the extent to which boys with speech and reading problems are or are not included in the sample. Differences in criteria of who is in a "normal" sample could be a factor in the differing evaluation of the precocity question over time. Boys greatly outnumber girls in speech and reading problems (Bentzen, 1963; Garai and Scheinfeld, 1968).

Before moving on to more recent evaluations of the precocity question, two internal contradictions in the 1974 material should be pointed out. The first concerns ambiguity regarding when Maccoby and Jacklin think female verbal superiority begins. In one instance they say "adolescence" and in another, "age 10 or 11." These can refer to rather different times and, if taken seriously, have some different implications. The second internal contradiction involves a contrast between what appears in the tables and what is stated in the text. Their statement that female verbal advantage (after age three and before age ten?) persists longer among underprivileged children is not supported by their own tabled data. While their inference may be supportable, it is not clear from their presentation. They made a similar error in their discussion of general intelligence (Block, 1976b).

Harris (1977) evaluated sex-related differences in the growth and use of language utilizing several categories of comparison, e.g., rate of acquisition of phonemes, age of first words, vocabulary size and complexity in early childhood, articulation, loquacity. Phonemes are the basic speech sounds out of which mature language is built. Harris concluded that, although differences are small, girls make a variety of these sounds earlier than boys. Harris agreed with the Maccoby (1966) assessment that girls speak their first word earlier than boys. In regard to vocabulary size and complexity, Harris pointed out that findings of female precocity span a seventy-year period of research. Since some sex-related differences have proven labile over time, it is important to note that studies subsequent to those included in the Maccoby and Jacklin (1974) review continue to support this generalization. Katherine Nelson (1973) found that girls acquired an average of fifty words by eighteen months, boys by twenty-two months. Nearly all the boys were slower than the slowest girl. Girls' speech has also been found to be more complex in twenty-four to fifty-month-old children. Harris' conclusion regarding articulation and loquacity likewise supports the earlier opinions of female precocity. McGuinness (1976) also concluded that females are precocious in language. She emphasized the fact that, altogether, these data indicate more effective verbal communication for very young girls compared to boys. This point is important to the bent twig hypothesis since it supports the possibility that more girls than boys might establish verbal communication as a preferred mode of interacting with the environment.

Conclusions

One can conclude from this resurvey that girls probably have a headstart in verbal skill and certainly girls and women more than hold their own in all aspects of the verbal area including verbal reasoning and vocabulary, as well as verbal fluency. Garai and Scheinfeld's conclusion of male superiority in verbal reasoning and vocabulary was incorrect, though the extent of female verbal superiority is very small. Maccoby and Jacklin (1974) indicated that the typical difference in favor of females was .25 SD. A better idea of how very small the differences are can be gained from examining the results for the vocabulary subtest from the 1955 standardization of the Wechsler Adult Intelligence Scale (Matarazzo, 1972). These data are based on 850 females and 850 males, ages sixteen to sixty-four. While females scored significantly higher than males, the amount of the variance accounted for by sex (omega squared) did not even reach 1 percent. There are also signs that sex-related differences in verbal skill are culture bound, a facet of the data that will be discussed in more detail in a later chapter.

SPATIAL DISPOSITION

Introduction

Unlike the verbal disposition, the spatial disposition, its meaning, importance, and development, is much less understood, for spatial skill has been less studied. It has already been mentioned that females are less often studied than males and this is also the case in the area of space perception. Many more studies have utilized male than female subjects. For this reason, we know even less about spatial perception in females than in males. However, while females are generally conceded to have well-developed verbal skill, such is not the case in the spatial area. Thus space perception is a more problematic area with possible important social implications in terms of current controversies regarding women's potential. For these reasons the spatial disposition will be discussed in more detail.

Definitions

WHAT IS SPACE PERCEPTION? Let us look first at a general definition of spatial cognition, "the knowledge and internal or cognitive representation of the structure, entities, and relations in space; in other words the internalized reflection and construction of space in thought" (Hart and Moore, 1973). Spatial skill is described as the "practical facility in manipulating and utilizing these mental representations of the structure of, and relations in, space." Space perception could refer to audio-spatial perception, tactual-spatial perception, or visual-spatial perception (perception of ears, skin, or eyes). Visual-spatial perception has been by far the most commonly studied. There was an attempt to make a general statement about perceptual types across modalities (Witkin et al., 1954, 1962). Males and females were thought to differ in regard to this dimension. This generalization has proven to be faulty in a number of respects (Sherman, 1967), and the cross-modal inference has too little supporting data to warrant its acceptance (Maccoby and Jacklin, 1974; Sherman, 1967). Since nearly all theory and data concern only visual-spatial perception, we will not discuss the other modalities further.

VISUAL-SPATIAL PERCEPTION. Spatial skills were orginally regarded as especially important to success in fields such as engineering, mechanical arts, and aviation, but in recent years their relevance to other fields such as architecture and mathematics has been noted (Bennett et al., 1966; Fruchter, 1954; Sherman, 1967; Smith, 1964). Because of its importance, the relevance of space perception to mathematics performance will be discussed in more detail in the next section.

There is general agreement that there is more than one space factor and that the factors are highly related. There is not, however, agreement on how many spatial factors there are, their names, and how they differ from each other. As a result it is extremely easy to become confused. For example, the Space Relations test of the Differential Aptitude Tests (Bennett et al., 1966) measures spatial visualization and *not* spatial relations, which is the name given to another factor. Some scholarly consensus, however, emerged from a 1957 synthesis (Michael et al., 1957). One factor, Spatial Relations and Orientation, is considered to involve comprehending the arrangement within a visual stimulus pattern with the subject's body as a frame of reference, e.g., tests such as Flags or Cards. In contrast, the Visualization factor requires mental manipulation of an object or parts of the configuration, such as with the Space Relations test (Bennett et al., 1966). A third factor appears to involve right-left discrimination.

Yet another factor has been called Gestalt Flexibility in the space perception literature (Thurstone, 1944) and elsewhere called other names, e.g., field dependence versus independence (Witkin et al., 1954) or global versus analytical cognitive style (Witkin et al., 1962). This skill involves retaining a configuration so as to be able to pick it out in spite of perceptual distractions of an organized nature (Coates, 1974). It has also been called visual disembedding and field articulation. The latter term will be used in this review. It has been measured by a laboratory test, the Rod and Frame Test also briefly discussed in Chapter Two. In this test subjects are seated in a completely darkened room. Several feet away is a forty-inch-square luminous frame, bisected by a rod. The subject must adjust the rod to true vertical against the distracting and misleading influence of the tilted surrounding frame. Other common measures of Field articulation are the Embedded Figures Tests, which involve searching out hidden figures.

RELEVANCE OF THE SPATIAL DISPOSITION TO MATHEMATICS. The relationship of verbal disposition to mathematics is well-accepted; however, the relationship of spatial disposition to mathematics has not been so obvious to scholars. This is curious because, from another vantage point, mathematics itself can be viewed as the symbolization of spatial relationships. Since mathematics involves such diverse activities as computation, mathematical problem solving, integration, and topology, it is obvious that the quality and type of cognitive skills involved differ with the task. Spatial skill is important to integration and topology, for example, but not to computation. Spatial visualization is related to mathematics performance and it has been hypothesized that sex-related differences in space perception might partly account for sex discrepancies in mathematics performance (Sherman, 1967).

In a large scale investigation of this question, for both sexes vocabulary *and* spatial visualization were found to be moderately correlated (typically, .40 to .50) with mathematics achievement in grades six to twelve (Fennema and Sherman, 1977, 1978). The correlations between spatial visualization and math achievement were consistent from subsample to subsample of the overall sample of nearly 3,000 students, building further confidence in the reliability and validity of the results. (For further evidence of the relationship between spatial visualization and mathematics see also references in Sherman, 1967, and data in Bennett et al., 1966.)

The main source of the opinion that spatial visualization is not related to mathematics achievement appears to be Very (1967), who in turn seems to have based his opinion on Murray (1949). Murray's data were based only on males and showed a definite influence of spatial visualization on geometry grades, but less on Murray's geometry test which was, by his own description, verbal in character. Murray's point had been that one cannot assume geometry to be based *primarily* on spatial skill. In this, of course, he is correct. Memorizing definitions and theorems is not a spatial task.

Hyde et al. (1975) found that sex-related differences in mathematical problem solving can be accounted for by sex-related differences in spatial disposition. Furthermore, tests of spatial ability, "field independence" (field articulation), and mental arithmetic emerged together as a single factor. Overall, the evidence is very clear that spatial visualization is substantially related to many forms of mathematics achievement.

Examination of Evidence

Sex-Related Differences in Visual-Spatial Perception

It has been generally thought that males are superior to females in visual-spatial perception. This opinion is found in Fruchter (1954), Anastasi, (1958), Smith (1964), Tyler (1965), Maccoby (1966), and Maccoby and Jacklin (1974), though the latter authors found reason to question and delimit some previous conclusions. Werdelin (1961) thought that any sex-related differences were limited to the visualization factor, which involves more difficult tasks than the spatial relations-orientation factor. Yen (1975a), however, concluded that spatial orientation tasks more often showed significant heritability than visualization tasks. Hence, she expected the sexes to differ most on orientation tasks, but found them different on both the orientation and visualization tests. What Yen has considered an orientation test, however, others have considered a visualization test (Vandenberg, 1977). Spatial tests differ greatly in difficulty and those most likely to show differences tend to be the most difficult, whether they are considered tests of visualization or tests of orientation. Some differences between the sexes have also been reported in right-left discrimination.

FIELD ARTICULATION. By far the greatest amount of research and attention has focused on sex-related differences in field articulation. Field-dependence-independence and later global versus analytical cognitive approach were presented as crucial dimensions of human development upon which the two sexes differed (Witkin et al., 1954; Witkin et al., 1962). Females were supposed to be field dependent and males were supposed to be field independent. These terms fit into stereotypes about females being otherwise dependent and males being independent. The terms are not logical descriptions of the measure since the score on the Rod and Frame Test, one of the most common measures, is not based on the extent to which one's errors *depend* on the field. The score is simply based on deviation from the vertical, whether or not the error is in the direction of the surrounding field. Not only are the terms inaccurate but feminists have considered them prejorative to women.

The terms global cognitive approach versus analytical cognitive approach are even greater sources of difficulty. Women were supposed to take a global approach and men an analytical approach. These terms also feed into stereotypic thinking and are inaccurate. The term "analytical" implies a generality not justified by the evidence (Sherman, 1967). While Witkin hoped that the dimension would extend to include the verbal area, this did not prove to be the case (Witkin et al., 1962). All the measures of analytical approach are spatial measures (Sherman, 1967, 1974; Wolf, 1971). Whatever difference there may be between the sexes on these tasks appears to lie in the spatial nature of the tasks and not in their "analytical" nature. Unfortunately Witkin's work has been occasionally cited erroneously as "scientific proof" that women are not as analytical as men. Sherman's 1967 critique was accepted by Fairweather (1976) and by Maccoby and Jacklin (1974).

Some writers have wished to emphasize the positive values of the "global" approach. However, one must remember that scores on these tasks represent accurate or inaccurate performance. In the final analysis, it is difficult to justify the virtue of inaccuracy compared to accuracy. It seems likely that knowing "up from down" will always be considered a virtue. (This is not to say that Witkin's extreme analytic cognitive type represents an ultimate virtue with no drawbacks.)

A further difficulty with the Witkin work was the implication that individual variation in field articulation, e.g., spatial performance, was uniquely innate, uninfluenced by practice or training. This view was a logical outgrowth of the Gestalt heritage of this line of research. The implication was, however, that any difference between the sexes would likewise be inherent. This was never explicitly stated and in some instances cultural causations have been emphasized (Witkin, 1967). There had been general evidence of spatial learning (Gibson, 1953), but Witkin's (1948) didactic training methods had failed to produce much learning. Since then, however, both Kato (1965) and Sherman (1974) have demonstrated practice effects with the Rod and Frame Test and Goldstein and Chance (1965) have done the same with the Embedded Figures Test. Brinkmann (1966), Blade and Watson (1955), and Johnson (1976) have demonstrated spatial learning, even from participation in a drafting course. We will return to this topic again in later chapters.

PREVIOUS REVIEWS. As mentioned earlier, for many years there has been a firm opinion that males are superior to females in space perception. Fairweather is highly critical of past reviewers for the strength of their conclusions compared to the paucity of their evidence, for example, the frequently quoted reference work for studies in spatial ability by MacFarlane Smith (1964). Says Fairweather (1976, pp. 248-249) of Smith's work:

> Five references to studies concerning sex differences are made, none of these concerning children under the age of 14 years. The first two (pp. 122-123) report boys' superiority in geometry at high school. The third (p. 209) reveals that 14-year-old boys outscore girls on drawing tests if proportionality is the measure, but that this sex difference is reversed if accuracy is measured. The fourth (p. 235) reports that a spa-

tial factor correlates with gregariousness in men but not
women. The fifth (p. 255) actually does not consider men and
women as separate groups though here MacFarlane Smith
manages to report "a marked sex difference" in favor of
males; whilst simultaneously failing to quote his own study
(1948) of Scottish schoolchildren 12 to 14 years, which did
find an overall difference in favor of boys. Nine tests included
some essentially similar to those now called Block Design,
and embedded figures, and others concerning the matching
and classifying of sizes and shapes of objects. Elsewhere may
be found the following remarks: ". . . the well-known fact
that girls are inferior to boys in visualizing ability" (p. 123);
". . . it is well known that tests with high spatial loading
show a marked sex difference in favor of boys" (p. 210); and
". . . men doing better than women as nearly always occurs
with spatial tests" (p. 255). To none of these statements is
there attached even a single reference, stuff indeed to make a
myth.

In 1966, Maccoby concluded, "While very young boys and
girls do not differ on spatial tasks such as form boards and
block design, by the early school years boys consistently do
better on spatial tasks, and this difference continues through
the high school and college years" (Maccoby, 1966, p. 26). In
1974, the conclusion was that "visual-spatial tasks that involve
disembedding and those that do not have a similar developmental course. The male advantage emerges in early adolescence and is maintained in adulthood for both kinds of tasks"
(Maccoby and Jacklin, 1974, p. 94). The age at which Maccoby
placed the differentiation of the two sexes has risen from "early
school years" to "early adolescence." Maccoby and Jacklin also
noted that not all the field articulation studies showed sex-
related differences even among adults, a fact brought out by
Parlee (1974). These changes in the literature evaluation signal
the labile nature of the results.

EXTENT OF DIFFERENCE. Relying on two large scale studies
(Droege, 1967; Flanagan et al., 1961), Maccoby and Jacklin
concluded that "boys' superiority on this factor (space) increases through high school, and that the boys' scores exceed
the girls' by at least .40 standard score units, on the average, by

the end of this time." This can be regarded as a maximal estimate of difference since: (a) The end of the high school years
marks a sufficient degree of maturity that we can be sure that
any sex-related differences are not masked by possible differences between the sexes in maturation rate (Garai and Scheinfeld, 1968). (b) Differences between the sexes in spatial training
have not been controlled and doubtless favor males. It is also of
interest to look at a measure of relationships — omega squared.
Schonberger (1976) reported the omega squared for the results
of the spatial test used in the 12th grade Project Talent Study
(Flanagan et al., 1964). Sex accounted for only 5 percent of the
variance. This difference is very small.

It is also instructive to look at the extent of the differences
between the sexes in the 1955 standardization sample for the
Block Design subtest of the Wechsler Adult Intelligence Scale
(Matarazzo, 1972). The Block Design subtest is a highly respected test of spatial visualization. It has also been used as a
measure of field articulation. Since the sample consists of 1700
persons sixteen to sixty-four they are mature enough so that
comparisons could not be considered biased against males.
Males scored significantly higher. A measure of the extent of
difference, omega squared, calculated from these data showed
that sex does not even account for 1 percent of the variance.

RECENT DATA. Such small differences or even nonexistent
differences are consistent with my own observations (Fennema
and Sherman, 1967, 1978; Sherman, 1974). Sherman (1974)
found no significant differences between small samples of college males and females on the Rod and Frame Test, Embedded
Figures Test (Witkin et al., 1971), and Draw-A-Person Test, all
spatial measures of field articulation. A significant difference
was found for spatial visualization (Bennet et al., 1959). The
absence of a sex-related difference on field articulation tasks
even in an American population is not very unusual (Maccoby
and Jacklin, 1974; Parlee, 1974; Witkin, 1949); however, many
people have believed that such differences are nearly always
demonstrated. Findings of no difference tend to be greeted with
skepticism. (I was asked if the female students in my study had
been feminists.) After reflecting on these results for some time

and after the appearance of further findings relating course of
study and spatial skill (Fennema and Sherman, 1977; Johnson,
1976; Zimmerman and Parlee, 1973), it has occurred to me that
the lack of difference might be attributed to the large percentage of the female subjects who were nursing students. Since
nursing is a stereotypic female occupation, this may seem implausible; however, nursing students at the University of Wisconsin, Madison must take difficult science courses. Thus, this
sample may have been less biased in favor of males than many
other reported college samples in which males have taken many
more math/science/technical courses than the females.

The results from the very large samples of the Wisconsin
Study showed no sex-related differences at all for spatial visualization (Bennett et al., 1973) in grades six to eight (Fennema
and Sherman, 1978). The Wisconsin Study high school sample
consisted of mathematics students in a four year sequence of
math courses beginning with algebra and ending with calculus
or advanced algebra (Fennema and Sherman, 1977). (See the
Appendix for further discussion of sampling.) To facilitate
discussion of the age at which sex-related differences might
occur, data were analysed by grade. Among 9th grade and 12th
grade students, there were no significant differences in spatial
visualization. A sample, representative of all 9th grade students
at School 4, also showed no significant differences in spatial
visualization (Sherman and Fennema, 1978). Significant differences were found in grades ten and eleven, i.e., not before about
age sixteen.

Let us first make some observations from these data and then
look at the data sliced in a different way. As will be recalled,
Maccoby and Jacklin (1974) set "early adolescence" as the time
for the appearance of a sex-related difference in space perception. The large representative samples of Wisconsin students,
however, did not show any significant difference before about
age sixteen. This is later than suggested by Maccoby and
Jacklin (1974). It may well be that as (and if) curricula become
more similar for the two sexes, fewer and fewer performance
differences will be discernible. For example, in grades six to
eight, both female and male students in the Wisconsin study

had been required to take industrial arts, a course including drafting as well as a variety of manual skills. The lack of a sex-related difference between the 12th grade math students, a very select group, serves to illustrate once more that even among older students, sex-related differences are not always found.

Using the Maccoby and Jacklin (1974) preferred measure of difference, the standard score of the difference between means, the value for the 10th grade was .25 and .37 for the 11th grade. The measure of the extent of the relationship, omega squared, was .01 and .03; sex accounted for 1 percent of the variance of spatial visualization scores in 10th grade (age sixteen) and 3 percent in the 11th grade (age seventeen). Again, the amount of the variance accounted for is very small.

Another very interesting aspect of the high school data is that the differences between the sexes varied from school to school, being significant at two schools and not at two other schools. In this case, no difference was apparent at the schools of families of upper-middle-class socioeconomic status while the difference appeared at the schools of families of middle, lower-middle and lower-class socioeconomic status. When the number of courses taken judged to have important spatial content, e.g., drafting, was controlled, even these small differences between the sexes became nonsignificant. Omega squared for sex for the two schools with significant differences were .02 and .03, accounting for a very small amount of the variance.

Conclusions

Although a significant difference between the sexes on spatial tasks has often, but by no means always, been demonstrated, even with minimal control of variables related to sex role, the size of the difference between the sexes is very small. It is my judgment that the extent of the differences between the sexes in spatial performance is much smaller than believed by psychologists and by the public, certainly much smaller than one would expect on the basis of most of the material written on the topic.

MATHEMATICS AND PROBLEM SOLVING

Introduction: Nature of Mathematics

Mathematics includes a great variety of intellectual activities of varying complexity, involving diverse cognitive skills. Computation, mathematical problem solving, and topology are each very different skills. Even the same material can be taught and/or tested in very different ways. For example, geometry could be taught and/or tested by emphasizing the memorization of definitions and theorems, or by emphasizing visualization of spatial relations. The psychological processes of these activities are very different and are thought to involve different parts of the brain. The common stereotype is that women do not generally possess the same ability as men in mathematics. The stereotype is a broad one which extends from the simple addition and subtraction of keeping a checkbook to the more advanced and arcane skills of mathematics, though women are commonly believed to be even more incapable of dealing with advanced mathematics. Considerable focus has been placed on possible sex-related differences in what has been variously called "word problems," "quantitative reasoning," "arithmetical reasoning," and "mathematical problem solving." The term "mathematical problem solving" will be used here and defined as finding the solution to a stated problem involving mathematical ideas when one does not possess a standard solution.

Review of Evidence

Sex-Related Differences in Mathematics

From our discussion of the nature of mathematics, it is apparent that the best approach to the question necessitates dealing with at least some aspects of mathematical performance separately. The question of genius and greater variability in male mathematics performance will be discussed in the next chapter. Let us look first at the conclusions from Maccoby

(1966) and Maccoby and Jacklin (1974) and then examine sex-related differences in specific aspects of mathematics with some particular attention to recent data.

MACCOBY, 1966 COMPARED TO MACCOBY AND JACKLIN, 1974. In 1966 Maccoby presented her main conclusion about mathematics as follows:

> Girls learn to count at an earlier age. Through the school years, there are no consistent sex differences in skill at arithmetical computation. During grade-school years, some studies show boys beginning to forge ahead on tests of "arithmetical reasoning," although a number of studies reveal no sex differences on this dimension at this time. Fairly consistently, however, boys excel at arithmetical reasoning in high school, and the differences are substantially in favor of men among college students and adults (Maccoby, 1966, p. 26).

In 1974, Maccoby and Jacklin considered mathematical "ability" one of the "sex differences" fairly well established. They summarized their findings as follows:

> The sexes are similar in their early acquisition of quantitative concepts, and their mastery of arithmetic during the grade-school years. Beginning at about age 12-13, boys' mathematical skills increase faster than girls'. The greater rate of improvement appears to be not entirely a function of the number of math courses taken, although the question has not been extensively studied. The magnitude of the sex differences varies greatly from one population to another, and is probably not so great as the difference in spatial ability (Maccoby and Jacklin, 1974, p. 352).

There are numerous problems with these latest conclusions. One's confidence is not encouraged by an examination of Tables 3.5 and 3.6 upon which they were based. These tables contain numerous errors, inconsistencies, and irregularities: (a) Table 3.5, headed "Quantitative Ability," contains a study of "physics achievement" and two studies of the Digit Symbol subtest of the WAIS. Neither of these can be considered measures of quantitative ability. (b) The results of Droege (1967) are tabulated and discussed in three different ways. While Table 3.5

showed boys significantly *superior* in three of four comparisons of high school age subjects, with no significant differences for the fourth comparison, the text stated, "Droege (1967), also using thousands of cases, finds no significant difference in high school" (Maccoby and Jacklin, 1974, p. 85). In Table 3.6, for the Droege (1967) study, *girls* are listed as scoring significantly higher than boys in three of four comparisons, with boys doing slightly better than girls at age seventeen. (Apparently this is the correct version.) (c) Consulting the Droege (1967) article itself, one finds further problems. The students tested would more accurately have been described as ages fifteen to eighteen, not ages fourteen to seventeen. (d) Statistics of sex-related differences were not reported in the Droege article and the sex-related difference in Numerical Aptitude was not discussed because the differences were so small. (The significant difference in favor of girls in Table 3.6 must have come from new calculations by Maccoby and Jacklin.) (e) The sex-related differences in mean gain in mathematical skill from grades nine to twelve, ten to twelve, eleven to twelve were statistically tested and reported. Males increased *statistically* more than females in mathematics skill (math coursework not controlled). The differences were so small that Droege ignored them. In the abstract of the study he stated "the average increases in aptitude scores attributable to practice and maturation were about the same for boys and girls" (Droege, 1967, p. 407). However, this study appears to be the source for the Maccoby and Jacklin conclusion that after age thirteen, "boys' mathematical skills increase faster than girls" (p. 352). Contrary to the Maccoby and Jacklin presentation, the Droege study basically showed very little difference between the sexes in mathematics performance. Differences favoring females in several instances were so small as to be considered inconsequential by the author.

A further problem with the Maccoby and Jacklin (1974) conclusion involves the puzzling discrepancy between their recognition of the need to control mathematics background and their conclusion. While they pointed out that the effect of males taking more, and more advanced, mathematics, science, and technical courses has not been adequately studied, they nonetheless made a firm conclusion about "sex differences" in mathematical "ability."

Some of the studies they tabulated made an attempt to control for mathematics background. Hilton and Berglünd (1974), for example, equated the sexes for years of mathematics study, within *one year*. However, a one year difference in mathematics study can be an important difference and sufficient to account for the small group differences observed. Likewise in the Project Talent study (Flanagan et al., 1961), Maccoby and Jacklin reported that the sexes were matched on *number* of math courses. This also provides insufficient control of previous mathematical background since males tend to take more advanced courses. Let us now consider sex-related differences in specific types of mathematics with some particular attention to recent data and to questions of the extent and meaning of the differences.

COUNTING AND COMPUTATION. Maccoby (1966) separated studies having to do with mathematics into three sections — counting, computation, and mathematical reasoning, the equivalent of mathematical problem solving (Oetzel, 1966). These studies showed girls to be ahead of boys in counting during the preschool years. Counting is essentially a verbal activity and this finding is consistent with the many studies of female verbal precocity.

The studies of computation usually showed no differences between the sexes; when there were differences, they favored girls. The summary of studies did not include any past the high school years (Oetzel, 1966). Essentially no differences in computation, except an occasional one in favor of girls, was found in the Wisconsin Study for grades six to eight (Fennema and Sherman, 1978).

The National Assessment of Academic Progress used large, representative samples of the population of the United States. The results showed the sexes performing equally, or girls better, on exercises dealing with numbers and numeration at ages nine and thirteen. At age seventeen and during adulthood, however, males were superior (Mullis, 1975).With age, the sexes are exposed to greater differences in curriculum and to increasingly different experiences and expectations related to sex role.

OTHER MATHEMATICAL SKILLS. Very often studies do not include sufficient detail to explain exactly what sort of mathematics was tested. In other instances distinctions are somewhat misleading. The problem of inferences made about "ability," with its connotations of inherency, has already been mentioned. However, "achievement" tests are sometimes thought of as more ephemeral than they are. Most standardized "achievement" tests are of a generalizability approaching that of "ability" tests. For example, the mathematics "achievement" tested in the Wisconsin Study involved performance on standardized tests of sufficient generality to be considered "ability" or "aptitude" tests nearly as much as tests commonly labeled as "ability" or "aptitude" tests.

In this section we will discuss some recent data on mathematics performance. Many of the measures used were standardized "achievement" tests though results from some "ability" tests will also be reported. We will consider results for a variety of noncomputational mathematics performance including mathematical problem solving. The question of analytical "ability" and problem solving will be discussed in a later section.

Unlike the case with computation, the National Assessment of Educational Progress found that girls scored below boys at ages nine, thirteen, seventeen, and at adult level in measurement, geometry, variables and relationships, probability and statistics, and consumer math. At ages nine and thirteen differences were small but they became larger. The author stated that "the advantage displayed by males particularly at the older ages, can only be described as overwhelming" (Mullis, 1975, p. 7). Presentation of data was not complete enough to permit calculation of the extent of the differences.

Girls encountered especially great difficulty in word problems. Mullis found this puzzling since females often computed and read better than males. Many word problems had a "male" content, e.g., finding the difference between a rocket target and the actual landing point, but no assessment of the possible role of bias in the items is available. One assumes, however, that the large discrepancy in performance could not be fully accounted for simply on the basis of test bias. This study leads one to expect that groups of the adult sexes unmatched for math background will greatly differ in mathematics performance (assuming that the differences actually were as large as described).

This finding is in contrast to a follow-up study of Project Talent (Flanagan et al., 1964). Among about 1,800 9-11th grade students, males scored only about half an item better than females on the noncomputational math. *Less* difference was found between the sexes in 1975 than in 1960 (Flanagan, 1976).

The National Longitudinal Study of Mathematical Abilities collected data in 1967, with controls for previous math background. Their results regarding sex-related differences were not presented in much detail. They did conclude, "Differences favoring girls were for variables at the comprehension level (the lowest cognitive level tested) and the differences favoring the boys were for variables at the application and analysis level" (Wilson, 1972, p. 95). It is difficult to figure out the extent and significance of the differences from their reports. (For further comment, see Fennema, 1974, 1977.)

The massive international study of Husén (1967) found statistically significant differences between the sexes in mathematics performance in some countries but not in others. There were large differences in math performance *between* countries; *within* countries boys tended to score higher than girls. Lower-scoring girls of one country, however, scored higher than the higher-scoring boys of another country. These results suggest a cultural, not biologic, cause for sex-related differences in mathematics performance.

The Wisconsin Study gathered data in 1975 to 1976 from about 3,000 students, grades six to twelve. The noncomputational measures of math performance used in grades six to eight (Fennema and Sherman, 1978) were the Mathematics Concepts subtest of the Science Research Associates Assessment Survey (Naslund et al., 1971) and the Romberg-Wearne Problem Solving Test (Wearne, 1976). In grades nine to twelve, the Test of Academic Progress (Scannell, 1972) was used (Fennema and Sherman, 1977). This test has overlapping items to cover progressively more difficult mathematics from 9th grade level to 12th grade level mathematics. Of the tests given in grades six to eight, it is most similar to the Math Concepts test. In order to test an hypothesis about mathematical problem solving, the Mental Arithmetic Problems test (Stafford, 1965a) was given to a representative sample of 9th grade students at one school. This is considered very much an "ability" test. For this 9th grade sample, it correlated .72 with the Test of Academic Progress, the "achievement test" (Sherman and Fennema, 1978). As already indicated, the standardized achievement tests were of a generality characteristic of "aptitude" tests. (See the Appendix for a discussion of sampling and procedural issues in the Wisconsin Study.)

At ages twelve to fourteen in grades six to eight (n = 1,330), there were no overall significant differences in mathematics performance between the sexes in the area by grade by sex analyses of variance. Schonberger (1976) also found no differences in math problem solving in a Maine sample of 7th grade subjects. To facilitate comparison with the high school data and because of some significant variations in sex-related differences from area to area, data were also analysed separately by area. Small differences in favor of males were found in one area, traceable to one school. These differences were in problem solving.

At the high school level, no difference was found between the sexes in mathematical problem solving in the 9th grade (age fifteen) sample (*n* = 313). Small differences in favor of males, ages fifteen to eighteen, were found in math achievement at two schools but not at two other schools (*n* = 1,233). The difference between the sexes did not increase with age and/or difficulty of the material.

It is important to remember that the samples used in the Wisconsin Studies were controlled for previous math background. With this important variable controlled, the extent of the differences between the sexes was very small, even when statistically demonstrated. For example, in the attendance area where there were differences in two aspects of problem solving in grades six to eight, these differences measured by omega squared were .01 and .02. That is, sex of subject accounted for 1 and 2 percent of the variance depending on the specific problem solving measure. At the high school level, omega squared for School 1 was .02 and .06 for School 4. (No significant differences had been found at Schools 2 and 3.) These variations in differences between the sexes by school will be discussed in greater detail in Chapter Seven. In the instances of greatest difference, however, sex accounted for only 6 percent of the variance. Even among these older subjects, when the sexes were matched for math background, very little difference was demonstrated between them.

Data are not easily available to calculate omega squared for the studies Maccoby and Jacklin (1974) tabulated. However, they reported another measure of extent of difference, a standard score of difference between means. The *highest* standard scores for the difference between means in favor of males (not controlling math background) were .36 and .64 for ages fourteen and seventeen respectively for the Project Talent data (Flanagan et al., 1961) and .47 for eighteen-year-olds from the American College Testing program 1966 norms (Monday et al., 1966-67). In other words, the *largest* differences were much less than one standard deviation. These findings suggest that when even only grossly obvious variables are controlled, the differences between the sexes in mathematics performance are small. Again, the Wechsler data are instructive. Males, ages sixteen to sixty-four, scored significantly higher than females on the Arithmetic subtest in the standardization sample of the Wechsler Adult Intelligence Scale (Matarazzo, 1972). The Arithmetic subtest consists of word problems. Omega squared calculated from these data showed that sex accounted for only 3 percent of the variance.

CONCLUSIONS. There is consensual agreement that there are no sex-related differences in mathematics performance before the ages of twelve to thirteen. If differences are found before ages twelve to thirteen, they are likely to favor girls. Differences in favor of girls are most likely to be observed during the preschool years on tasks such as counting. During the grade-school years girls sometimes score better than boys in computation.

Maccoby and Jacklin's (1974) summary of research and Mullis (1975) emphasize the difference between the sexes after ages twelve to thirteen, especially differences in mathematical problem solving, i.e., word problems. When previous mathematics background was controlled, as in the Wisconsin Study, differences in mathematics performance between the sexes, including performance in mathematical problem solving, was found to be nonexistent or minimal (Fennema and Sherman, 1977, 1978; Sherman and Fennema, 1978). Of major interest are the factors that affect the variation in differences between the sexes. Data related to this question will be discussed in Chapter Seven.

Analytical Skill and Problem Solving

Since so much attention has been focused on questions of sex-related differences in analytical skill and problem solving, it is perhaps unwise to leave the topic of sex-related cognitive differences without addressing this question more directly.

Some aspects of this problem we have already dealt with in our discussion of space perception. Field articulation skills have at times been described as analytical cognitive approach and even as analytical ability, though they are spatial measures (Sherman, 1967). Certainly they do not qualify as general measures of analytical skill. To some extent it seems fair to say that the field articulation tasks involve visual-spatial analysis; however, it is doubtful that they differ greatly from the more difficult tests of spatial orientation and visualization in the amount of analysis required. A general case for superior analytic skill in males cannot be made solely on the basis of the field articulation data.

"Analytical style" has been used to describe a type of performance on Sigel's sorting task. A descriptive-analytic behavior would sort objects on the basis of some characteristic of a part of the object, ignoring the whole. For example, dog and chair would be grouped together because they both have four legs.

Only one of six studies reviewed found males more "analytical;" Maccoby and Jacklin (1974) concluded that an inference that males are more analytical is unwarranted.

We have also discussed problem solving in connection with mathematical problem solving. As already indicated, the extent of differences between the sexes appears to depend strongly on the extent to which relevant background factors are controlled. For example, a representative sample of students as old as fifteen did not show a significant sex-related difference in mathematical problem solving (Sherman and Fennema, 1978). In the Wisconsin Study, high school seniors of similar math backgrounds, age eighteen, also showed no sex-related difference in mathematics achievement, the test being one of "mathematical problem solving" in the sense of being a very difficult mathematics test. The test, however, is not recognized as a test of mathematical problem solving.

There are, however, other kinds of problem solving that do not involve translation of the problem to mathematical ideas. These kinds of problems are also varied in the possible approaches, knowledge, and skills involved. They include Luchins' water jar problems (1942). This type of problem is thought to involve "breaking set" and "restructuring." The subject is given a set of problems that can be solved by one particular method, but later problems can be solved more easily by another method. The point of interest is how quickly the subject "breaks set" and shifts to the easier method. It has been thought that females do less well on this type of task and that the difference between the sexes lies in "breaking set," "inhibiting an obvious response," and/or "restructuring." Most of the relevant studies of problem solving were done in the 1940s and early 1950s. In view of the fact that the number and size of sex-related differences appear to be decreasing, it might be that well-designed studies with contemporary subjects would no longer show differences between the sexes.

In any case, dealing with the results of these earlier studies, Maccoby and Jacklin (1974) pointed out that Nakumura (1958) found sex-related differences were the same for college-age subjects on tests involving restructuring and tests not involving restructuring. This hypothesis (that restructuring is the crux of sex-related differences) has been popular partly because of the Broverman et al. (1968) theory that males are superior to females on complex tasks that require inhibition of an immediate response. Maccoby and Jacklin (1974) showed, however, that anagram tasks, which require restructuring, most typically show female, *not* male, superiority. These authors further noted that if there are differences on the inhibition-impulsive dimension in a general sense, it would be extremely difficult to show that they favor males being less impulsive. If any differences are ultimately shown to characterize the cognition of the sexes, it is doubtful that "breaking set" will describe them.

ANALYTICAL SKILL AND PROBLEM SOLVING: CONCLUSIONS. Many aspects of generalizations that girls and women are not as analytical as boys and men are not supported by the evidence available. The mental processes involved in analytical performance and problem solving are poorly understood and analytical thinking and problem solving are rarely explicitly included in curricula. These remain tasks upon which people are tested, not trained. One suspects, however, that the development of these skills does not occur independently of training, example, and practice. Evidence from the 1940s and 1950s favors males in performance of some kinds of problem solving tasks. Further well-designed studies with contemporary subjects might shed more light on this question.

SEX-RELATED COGNITIVE DIFFERENCES: CONCLUSIONS

Assessment of the comparative cognitive skills of the sexes has proven to be a perilous enterprise. There are numerous conceptual and methodological problems in obtaining an accurate and scientific assessment. The size of the differences between the sexes is greatly dependent upon the similarity of the background factors. Given the inadequacies of data generated from a strongly sex-role divergent culture, one can only observe the sex-related differences under various conditions and come to more or less reasoned conclusions as to their meaning.

The long-standing conclusion that girls are verbally precocious compared to boys is still the prevailing opinion. This topic is discussed further in connection with the bent twig hypothesis. Generally speaking, with the exception of the greater number of boys with language deficits, the sexes are very similar in verbal performance, though Maccoby and Jacklin give females the edge in all areas of verbal function after the age of eleven. In any case, the differences are very small; they estimate a quarter of a standard deviation. Female curricular concentration in languages and humanities is doubtlessly relevant to the differences between the sexes observed in older samples.

In the area of space perception, it is possible to demonstrate larger differences between the sexes, in this case in favor of males. The difference between the sexes, however, is still very small, accounting at most for 4 percent of the variance. The difference does not occur in the grade-school years. In fact, at the preschool level, girls are sometimes found to be superior to boys on the spatial tasks of field articulation (Coates, 1974). There now seems to be general agreement that no difference between the sexes in favor of males is observable until adolescence. The Wisconsin Study found no difference between the sexes until age sixteen. The extent of the difference is not so great as people imagine; however, it is probably possible to demonstrate large differences between certain groups strongly divergent in sex role, such as housewives versus male engineers.

A similar situation may well exist with mathematics. The popular view of male superiority in mathematics is supported by comparison of random samples of adult males and females unmatched for relevant background (Mullis, 1975). Most of the studies of mathematics performance have not matched the sexes for mathematical background. Indeed, the more frequent reports of divergence of the sexes in cognitive performance at adolescence is probably at least partly related to the failure to control for diverging curricular and extracurricular experiences.

There is general agreement that there is no difference between the sexes in favor of males in mathematics performance below the age of ten. (There are in fact, some reports of female superiority on such tasks as counting and computation.) Maccoby and Jacklin (1974) marked the point of divergence of the sexes at some place past ages twelve to thirteen. The Wisconsin Study found no differences in mathematics achievement between the sexes until age fifteen; even then, no difference was found in mathematical problem solving. Differences that have been reported (except possibly for Mullis, 1975) are very small. The sexes overlap tremendously and sex has accounted for, at most, a few percent of the variance.

Grasping the limited extent of the cognitive differences between the sexes, one is struck by their inconsequential nature at least in terms of any kind of evidence that would warrant advising boys and girls to pursue difference courses or careers on the basis of sex differentials in ability. Such counseling would be clearly contraindicated by the available evidence. On the other hand, the large extent of the differences that can develop in cognitive skills between the sexes is a matter for concern. Has it been our intent to divide the population into the pinks and the blues and to develop one set of cognitive skills in the pinks and another set in the blues? If this is not our intent, the educational and social practices that have occurred "naturally" will need reexamination.

From a theoretical point of view, even very small differences between the sexes can be of interest. The sizes of the differences between the sexes when some of the most obvious variables are controlled are very small. In some instances, e.g., verbal skill, it may be that the differences are smaller than they would "naturally" be if it were not for the strong cultural emphasis on verbal education. In other instances, e.g., math and spatial skill, our culture probably serves to emphasize sex-related differences. However, even without total control of relevant sex-role variables, i.e., even when likely environmental sources of variance are left uncontrolled, the amount of variance attributable to sex is typically *at most* 5 percent. Hence any biological factors contributing to these differences are relegated to a very small role. It is not even easy to imagine plausible factors. The effects are certainly too small for there to be common X-linked factors and/or gross differences between the effects of male and female hormones. Theories of these kinds exist however and one suspects that many investigators have simply not appreciated the small extent of the differences between the sexes.

Given these facts, theories which attempt to acount for cognitive performance differences between male and female groups on the basis of biological variables associated with sex suffer acute embarrassment. There are instances in which their theories explaining sex-related differences have actually been published with some of their own data showing no significant differences between the sexes (Petersen, 1976; Stafford, 1972; Waber, 1976).

Chapter Four

THEORIES: THE VARIABILITY
AND X-LINKED HYPOTHESES

INTRODUCTION

IN spite of the fact that differences between the sexes in cognition have been small, there has been no lack of theories to account for them. Such is the fascination of the topic, notes Matarazzo (1972), that hundreds of small sample studies were published about IQ sex-related differences even though the IQ tests had deliberately been developed in a way so as to eliminate any difference between the sexes in Full Scale IQ. The interest in sex-related differences is thus a hardy one, and, in addition to the question of differences themselves, some scientists have hoped that the biological and cultural bases of cognitive development itself might be illuminated. Some writers, e.g., Hutt (1972) and Bardwick (1971), have assumed that the biological bases of human female behavior have been neglected. In fact, though topics related to the psychology of women have been neglected, research and theory directed toward biological bases of sex-related cognitive differences appear to have been less neglected than other topics and are far more studied and developed than theories and hypotheses utilizing cultural and/or environmental variables. The wealth of material in the next chapters attests to the activity in this area.

In this chapter we will examine some prominent and current biologically based theories of sex-related cognitive differences, including those of greater male variability and the X-linked hypotheses. Subsequent chapters will deal with metabolic and hormonal explanations and explanations based on hypothesized sex differences in brain laterality. Finally, Chapter Seven will deal with social and cultural factors in the development of cognitive sex-related differences.

68

In an essay as complex as the present volume, it does not seem appropriate to present introductory biological material. Interested readers, however, will find the work of Hamburg and Lunde (1966) a helpful introduction to sex hormones. Levitan and Montagu (1971) provide a useful introduction to genetics while Federman (1968) describes genetic and endocrine abnormalities of sexual development. The volume edited by Cancro (1971) contains clearly written papers on the nature-nurture debate and intelligence, though the focus was on race-related differences, not sex-related differences.

GREATER MALE VARIABILITY

Conceptual Analysis

As one analyses the variability hypothesis three questions arise: (a) Is this a biological, *explanatory* hypothesis? (b) What sampling procedures provide appropriate evidence to test the variability hypothesis? (c) What measures are appropriate to test it in terms of the question of whether or not the tests measure innate or learned qualities? While social factors will be discussed in a later chapter, some discussion of these factors is necessary here as well. Let us examine each of these questions in turn.

Biological Basis

As discussed in Chapter One, the variability hypothesis has been loosely derived from Darwin's theory of sexual selection. Its claim to being a biologically based explanation rests on the expectation that since females choose their male mates, one could well expect special diversity among males to facilitate the hypothesized sexual selection and evolutionary processes. This idea was propounded initially as a possible explanation for the greater diversity in the appearance of male animals. While, of course, certain species (e.g., birds) show greater diversity in male than female appearance, this phenomenon can be accounted for by other interpretations. Moreover, as previously mentioned in Chapter One, the generalization that males are more variable than females in physical characteristics was not supported. Borrowing on the prestige of evolutionary theory, however, the idea has persisted that perhaps for some vague biological reason, males are more variable in intelligence than females.

At first glance, the theory of Ounsted and Taylor (1972) could provide biological underpinning for the idea. They proposed that the Y chromosome is responsible for slowed maturation. They see the effect of earlier maturation as not merely the fact that it is earlier, but suggest that for males at each stage of development, more genetic information can be transcribed into phenotypic characteristics. The fuller transcription of genetic material can be for good or ill but would lead to greater male variability. Curiously enough, Pearson's old findings that males are *not* more physically variable than females are inconsistent with the theory. Thus it seems unlikely that this theory is valid. Though there is no biological evidence or theoretical necessity that males need to be more variable than females, the emptiness of the variability concept when applied to human intelligence often passes unnoticed. Hutt (1972, p. 24), for example, refers to it as the "law of greater variability" as though greater variability was a well-established fact with explanatory power. If males are more variable than females in intelligence or in specific aspects of intelligence, this becomes a datum requiring explanation, and the importance of this datum should be separated from the excess meanings it has acquired through its historic association with evolutionary theory. Moreover, note that a finding of greater male variability would be a datum to be explained, *not* an hypothesis which can account for sex-related differences in cognition. This datum in itself is merely descriptive and devoid of explanatory power.

Sampling Questions

The sampling issue has two aspects: (a) Should you include only normal persons in the comparison or should you include everyone in a given population? (b) What sorts of biases that affect the sexes differently might be present in the sampling procedures?

Long ago, Karl Pearson pointed out that if what was being studied was the extent of normal variation in the two sexes, then only normal persons should be included in the sample. If one is seriously evaluating the *variation* idea within the evolutionary context, use of only normal subjects is appropriate. However, much of the evidence cited in discussing this idea, from Havelock Ellis to the present, dwells on the percentage of mental defectives and geniuses among the two sexes. Pearson considered such data inappropriate. The fact that Pearson's critique has continued to be ignored indicates once more that the emphasis in modern discussions does not lie with the variation hypothesis in the evolutionary context. In fact, "variation" has been translated into "variability" and standard deviations of test scores have been examined for evidence of difference. Typically further examination is then made as to whether any given difference represents an excess of male geniuses or an excess of male mental defectives.

To evaluate *variability* in the population, one must study nearly everyone in a given population to get an unbiased sample, otherwise the data is virtually worthless for assessing the question. Just picking students from ordinary classrooms would not sample mental defectives and possibly not geniuses either. The sexes may differ in how likely they are to be institutionalized. Some have thought women are more likely to be institutionalized though men are more likely to be jailed. Unless nearly *all* the population is studied biasing factors are free to operate. Studies of genius or precocity which allow for self-selection or selection by others is a procedure biased against females. Some writers have been very cognizant of this problem, but others have not, as we shall see. One must also bear in mind that since more males than females are conceived, and since more males than females die in every decade of life, male groups are truly by nature more select than female groups.

Measuring Innate Ability

While it is not possible to discuss fully the question of measuring innate ability, let us at least acknowledge the existence of the problem. Much of the discussion in recent years of the variability hypothesis has not even considered this question. For example, Maccoby and Jacklin (1974) did not discuss whether the data they examined had to do with ability or achievement measures, preferring to ignore any differences between them. Granted that the differences may be ambiguous, nonetheless there are differences between measures in the extent to which they are sensitive to recent learning experiences. To simply compare male and female standard deviations on various tests without regard to questions of selection and/or type of test used is a totally inadequate evaluation of the variability question. In the mathematics area, for example, Fox (1976) reported that precocious boys, much more than girls, spent a considerable amount of time outside of school studying mathematics. Would it be surprising then that more males than females attain high scores? Discussions which purport to evaluate the variability hypothesis must consider these questions.

Discussions of genius often assume that great innate talent suddenly blooms, without recognizing the relevant socio-cultural factors. Socio-cultural factors are clearly involved in the development and in the social recognition of genius status. They begin with the valued expectation of a male child, his infusion with aspirations, his nurture, his status, and the opportunities that then seem to unfold "naturally" for him as a young adult. These factors include the very judgment of the worth and importance of cultural creativity and intellectual achievements. Even the attribution of discoveries is affected by socio-cultural expectations. Are we really to believe that it was Ikhnaton with his grotesquely deformed body, a victim of inbreeding, who thought of the concept of one god, or was it his "wife," the beautiful Queen Nefertiti?

Variability in the Twentieth Century

Much of the focus in this century has been on the question of genius and why there seem to be so few women of genius

(Terman et al., 1925). It gradually became clear that not only have women of genius seemed scarce, but that there have also seemed to be more mentally retarded and defective males than females. Attempts have been made to ascertain if this is true and to explain these phenomena, but it is likely that no single explanation will prove satisfactory. The factors that account for the excess of male mental defectives are probably different from those that account for the excess of male geniuses. For example, biology may explain the former while social factors may explain the latter.

Some of the best data and most thorough consideration of this question are old. Extensive surveys with very little selection bias were conducted in Scotland in 1932 and 1947 (Scottish Council, 1933, 1949). These surveys used objective tests, largely verbal, to survey eleven-year-old children. Slightly larger standard deviations were found for males (15.92 versus 15.02 in the 1932 survey and 16.68 versus 15.44 in the 1947 survey). Because of the very large samples, these differences were statistically significant. Upon further analysis, such sex-related difference was found to result largely from an excess of males with very low scores. Moreover, more males had physical handicaps which could have adversely affected performance (Anastasi, 1972).

One might get consensus that there are more male mental defectives (Freier-Maia et al., 1974), though, that had previously been questioned (Nance and Engles, 1972). Some of these excess male mental defectives may be attributable to the fact that males do not have the protection of a second X chromosome. This explanation has been given for the fact that males are more subject than females to a great many maladies (Childs, 1965). The finding of more frequent male mental deficiency, but not greater male superior performance, is consistent with the fact that positive effects are usually genetically dominant and hence if found on an X chromosome would be equally expressed in males and females, whereas negative effects tend to be recessive and hence if found on an X chromosome would be expressed more in males than in females.

Stanley et al. (1974) attempted to locate mathematically and scientifically gifted children by staging well-advertised contests during which the children took various tests measuring their skill in these areas. They located many more precocious boys than girls and their top winners have been male. These authors have been intrigued by this sex-related difference but have not come to any definite conclusion as to its cause. Astin (1974) explored these data, noting many differences between the male and female children in their attitudes and opportunities. For example, boys were given more books and equipment related to math and science; many of the gifted girls' parents did not even plan to send them to college. Curiously the test scores of 8th grade girls were *lower* than those of 7th grade girls. Ordinarily one would expect progressive intellectual development with age and grade. These data provided some definite clues about socio-cultural factors affecting this sex-discrepancy in math-science precocity, but they are not strong evidence.

The very troublesome research problem of bias in sampling was present in the Stanley et al. (1974) procedure as in the Terman et al. (1925) study, a fact both research teams have been well aware of. That is, more boys than girls may present themselves or be presented by others as precocious. For this reason, data which is based on less than an entire population is virtually worthless. Maccoby and Jacklin (1974) discussed this issue, recognized the problem of selection bias, but then examined results of *selected* samples, comparing the sexes in variability. They cited the Stanley et al. (1974) study as evidence that there is indeed an excess of males at the upper end of the distribution of mathematics performance. In regard to verbal skills they concluded that the evidence was not clear, while their files contained too few relevant studies of spatial skill to make any evaluation. Because of possible selection bias and because of their disregard for what was being measured such comparisons are unjustified and inappropriate as evidence bearing on the variability idea. Such uncritical presentation of data merely perpetuates the mystification of the variability hypothesis.

Conclusions Regarding Variability

The variability hypothesis is lacking in explanatory power.

The idea has been poorly defined from the beginning and has persisted with an aura of excess meaning and mystification, borrowing on the prestige of the theory of evolution. The best available data suggest that males may be more variable in performance on intelligence tests than females. This increased variability, however, can be traced to the increased number of males with various physical, sensory, and mental defects. There is no evidence of greater variation in normal males nor is there evidence of a greater number of unusually gifted males. The apparent excess of gifted males appears attributable to measurement problems and to socio-cultural factors rather than to any greater number of innately gifted male children.

X-LINKED INHERITANCE OF ABILITIES

Introduction

The idea of X-linked inheritance of cognitive skills was first proposed in its modern form by O'Connor (1943). Basically the X-linked hypothesis is that high potential is carried as a recessive characteristic on the X chromosome. The term "X-linked" is preferred to "sex-linked" because of its greater precision (Levitan and Montagu, 1971). If the X-linked hypothesis were true, it would mean that many more males than females would evidence high potential. In fact, the proportion of females showing high skill should be the square of the proportion of males showing high skill. This is because if the characteristic is recessive and carried on the X chromosome, males would need to inherit only one X with the gene on it to evidence the characteristic while females would need to inherit two Xs with the gene on it in order to manifest the characteristic. The probability of inheriting two such Xs is the square of the probability of inheriting one. X-linked inheritance has been proposed for mathematical problem solving (Stafford, 1972) and spatial visualization (Stafford, 1961). Stafford (1972) thinks that each ability is carried as a separate recessive gene on the X chromosome (Stafford, 1965b).

At a superficial level it seems that if true, this hypothesis would go a long way toward accounting for the scarcity of women in math and science and in high level positions in general. However, even if true, this hypothesis would still not account fully for the scarcity of women since by the estimate of these researchers, one third of the high ability persons would be female, and, of course, women are not found in anything like those proportions in math, science, or in high level positions in general. The X-linked hypotheses have gained considerable acceptance (Deaux, 1976; Maccoby and Jacklin, 1974; Wittig, 1976) and have now found their way into introductory psychology textbooks as *facts* (e.g., Hyde and Rosenberg, 1976). For these reasons it is important to evaluate the hypotheses carefully.

Tests of the X-linked Hypotheses

There are various possible ways to test the X-linked hypotheses: (a) comparing monozygotic male and female twins, (b) observing the variations in intra-familial correlations, (c) examining score distributions for their conformity to theoretically predicted distributions. The rationale of these approaches will be briefly explained, and then pertinent evidence for the X-linked inheritance of mathematical problem solving and spatial visualization will be examined.

The Lyon (1961) hypothesis, which is widely accepted by geneticists, holds that a few weeks after conception, one of the female X chromosomes is randomly inactivated in each female somatic cell. (This inactivated X chromosome is believed to form the Barr body which serves as a basis for a test of chromosomal sexuality.) Assuming the Lyon hypothesis is correct, and assuming X-linked cognitive characteristics, one would expect greater variability in intelligence among female than among male identical twins. Such findings have been reported but their statistical reliability has not been established (Maccoby and Jacklin, 1974). Consequently this method of testing the X-linked hypothesis will not be discussed further.

Given certain assumptions, such as no significant bias introduced by assortative mating, it can be predicted that X-linked genes will contribute to the observed variance in continuous characteristics in the following manner: (a) Father-son correlations should be approximately zero because males do not receive an X chromosome from their fathers. (b) Father-daughter correlations and mother-daughter correlations will be greater than zero because females receive one X chromosome from each parent. (c) Father-daughter correlations will be higher than mother-daughter correlations because females always receive their father's only X chromosome but may receive either of their mother's X chromosomes. (d) Mother-son correlations should be equal to father-daughter correlations because in both cases, half of the X chromosomal inheritance of the female member of the pair is identical to the X chromosomal inheritance of the male member of the pair. Thus the predictions are (mother-son ≈ father-daughter) > (mother-daughter) > (father-son=0).

Another test of the hypotheses lies in the fact that they predict a bimodal distribution of scores. The score distributions should show specific, predictable sex-related differences. The proportion of females showing evidence of high skill should be the square of the proportion of males showing high skill. If the characteristic is recessive and carried on the X chromosome, males would need to inherit only one X with the gene on it to evidence the characteristic while females would need to inherit two Xs with the gene on it in order to manifest the characteristic. The probability of inheriting two such Xs is the square of the probability of inheriting one.

X-linked Inheritance of Mathematical Problem Solving

Stafford (1963) studied the intrafamilial correlations on the Mental Arithmetic test of 104 fathers and mothers and their teenage sons or daughters. These data have been presented at various professional meetings and also in a later paper (Stafford, 1972). The correlation pattern did not follow that predicted though it was described as best fitting the X-linked hypothesis; no statistical tests of differences between correlations were run. The father-daughter correlation of .21 should have been about the same as the mother-son correlation of .62, which it clearly was not. Both should have been higher than the mother-daughter correlation of .25 which they clearly were not. As predicted, however, the father-son correlation was lower, .08, and close to zero. (Consistent with the assumption of nonassortative mating, the father-mother correlation was .07.) Averaging these correlations with some reported by other investigators in the 1920s and 1930s, the correlations fell somewhat more in line with what was predicted, but still not to a convincing degree and still not buttressed with statistical tests (Stafford, 1972). Williams's (1975) finding of a significant correlation of .31 between fifty-five fathers and sons on the Wechsler Arithmetic subtest is not consistent with the X-linked hypothesis since according to the latter, the correlation should be zero. (Correlation between parents was nonsignificant indicating no violation of the assumption of nonassortative mating.)

Stafford (1972) reported score distributions of the Mental Arithmetic Problems test. On the basis of the distribution of averaged monozygotic twin scores, he estimated the location of the antimode. Then male and female subjects (300 pairs of twins of various sorts), ages twelve to eighteen, were sorted as to whether their scores fell above or below the antimode. On the basis of this analysis, Stafford estimated the gene frequency as .43. The proportion of females above the antimode was .33. However, the hypothesis predicts that this value should equal $.43^2$ or .18 which was not the case.

Using the male proportion above the antimode as the estimate of gene frequency, .43, Stafford tested the observed score distributions of 181 dizygous twin pairs (fraternal twins of the same sex) on the Mental Arithmetic Problems test against the predicted distribution. The fit for males was adequate; however, the fit for dizygous (DZ) female twins deviated significantly ($p<.001$) and the fit for heterozygous (HZ) twins (fraternal twins of different sexes) also deviated significantly ($p<.05$). The fit of these results was described as "not too bad for HZ twins, but somewhat off for DZ girls" (Stafford, 1972, p. 197). In fact, these deviations are clearly significant and these data provide no support for the X-linked hypothesis. Yet Stafford at the end of the article says, "In conclusion, it appears that in general there is an underlying hereditary component for a proficiency in quantitative reasoning which fits the sex-linked recessive model fairly well" (Stafford, 1972, p. 198).

Sherman and Fennema (1978) examined the Mental Arithmetic Problems score distributions of 161 male and 152 female 9th grade students for their fit to X-linked predictions. The proportions of males and females in the upper range of the mathematical problem score resolutions were grossly out of line. The female proportion (.49) was not close to the square of the male proportion ($.53^2 = .28$). While a bimodal score distribution was not rejected for either sex, the means of the two curves were similar and single normal curves were not rejected as fits of the data. This sample did not show a significant difference between the sexes in mathematical problem solving, a finding also inconsistent with the X-linked hypothesis.

There is no acceptable, scientific evidence of X-linked inheritance of mathematical problem solving.

X-Linked Inheritance of Spatial Visualization

Stafford (1961) published part of the results of his dissertation (Stafford, 1963) in which he studied intrafamilial correlations on a variety of cognitive tests. The one which best fit the X-linked hypothesis was Identical Blocks, a measure of spatial visualization. For this test, the ordering of the size of the correlations conformed to theoretical predictions, that is (mother-son$\approx$father-daughter)$>$(mother-daughter$>$father-son=0). Stafford, however, did not statistically establish that the correlations were significantly different from each other. Moreover, he found the magnitude of the correlations consistent with an estimated gene frequency of .20 while Bock and Kolakowski (1973) found the correlations consistent with a gene frequency of .50. This discrepancy has not lent credence to the findings.

After Stafford's report, Corah's (1965) finding of a higher mother-son than father-son correlation for the Embedded Figures Test was sometimes cited in support of the X-linked hypothesis. However, the difference between these two correlations was also not statistically tested and the rest of the correlations did not conform to the X-linked predictions. Corah himself did not conduct the study with the X-linked hypothesis in mind.

Bock (1967) found the distribution of spatial ability in a sample of forty-five families inconsistent with the X-linked hypothesis. The results of Hartlage (1970) conformed rather well with the X-linked predictions. Bock and Kolakowski (1973) took these results, those of Stafford (1961), and averaged them with some results of their own in order to demonstrate statistically significant differences between the correlations, providing support for the X-linked hypothesis. Bock and Kolakowski (1973) also reported that the spatial visualization scaled score distribution for over 700 11th grade students was better fit by two normal curves than by a single normal curve. That is, bimodal score distributions were found for each sex as predicted by the X-linked hypothesis.

Yen (1975a) studied sibling correlations and within-sex score distributions for four paper-and-pencil spatial tests in a population of 2,508 white high school students. Part of the results supported the X-linked hypothesis but most did not. It is also of interest to note that Yen (1975b) did not find any difference in handedness between those of presumably high or low genotype for space perception. This would imply no relationship between the hypothesis of X-linked inheritance and Levy's laterality hypothesis, both presented as explanations of sex-related differences in space perception. However, neither hypothesis appears to have empirical support (see also section on Levy).

The report of Stafford (1966) that the scores of the Space Relations test of the Differential Aptitude Tests were bimodal as predicted was not accompanied by sufficient data and/or statistical tests to permit evaluation. Guttman (1974) is sometimes cited in support of the X-linked hypothesis of the inheritance of spatial skill but provides neither strong nor appropriate support for the hypothesis (see Chapter Nine).

Since 1975, however, several negative results have been obtained. Williams (1975) did not find the predicted correlations for the Block Design test in a sample of fifty-five Canadian families. A large scale study in Hawaii of Americans of European ancestry (739 families) and Americans of Japanese ancestry (244 families) found that neither the scores of five different spatial tests nor the score of the spatial factor produced correlations consistent with the X-linked hypothesis (DeFries et al., 1976). Bouchard and McGee (1977) found that the familial correlations among members of 200 families did not order themselves as predicted by the theory that human spatial visualization is under the control of an X-linked recessive gene. Likewise results from a Korean sample have failed to support the hypothesis (Park et al., 1977). Sherman and Fennema (1978) did not find the predicted bimodality of scaled score distributions of the Space Relations test of the Differential Aptitude Test in a population of over 300 9th grade students, nor did the sexes significantly differ in their scores. It should be noted that instances of no sex-related differences in spatial visualization are also not consistent with X-linked hypotheses.

Sex-Limitation

Sometimes a gene is only expressed in one sex or the other because of hormonal influences. Baldness is an example. Suggestions have been made that space perception may be a sex-limited cognitive characteristic. Curiously enough, this hypothesis originated because data from Turner's syndrome cases embarrassed the theory of the X-linked recessive inheritance of spatial visualization. Rather than decide that the X-linked theory must be incorrect, this additional hypothesis was offered (Garron, 1970; Bock and Kolakowski, 1973). Bock and Kolakowski based their argument on data from persons with chromosomal and/or hormonal abnormalities. They assumed that some minimal level of testosterone is necessary for expression of the X-linked gene for good spatial visualization. Let us look now at the data from persons with chromosomal and/or hormonal abnormalities.

Typically persons with Turner's syndrome have only forty-five rather than forty-six chromosomes. (A few are mosaics with atypical characteristics.) For sex chromosomes they have only one X chromosome and neither a Y nor a second X as is normal. The external genitalia of these persons are female, but they have no functional gonads of any sort and lack normal internal sexual organs. Of course they also do not have gonadal female hormones nor for that matter proper sex hormones of either sex. Various abnormalities are associated with the syndrome, e.g., short stature, webbed neck (Ferguson-Smith, 1965). These persons are often wrongly considered female because of their early external appearance, but they are neither male nor female. They usually live their lives as females in a social sense.

If the X-linked hypothesis were true, one would expect that, as for males, the percentage of Turner's patients expressing the superior gene should be greater than for XX persons, since the recessive gene supposedly would have a full chance to express itself. Instead these patients showed a spatial deficit. Shaffer (1962) reported a degree of what he called space-form blindness in these patients, though below normal spatial performance does not appear in every patient. These findings have generally been extended and confirmed (Buckley, 1971; Money and Granoff, 1965). Garron (1970) resolved this contradiction by adding the hypothesis that the gene had not been able to express itself in the absence of proper sex hormones. Bock (1973; Bock and Kolakowski, 1973) accepted this hypothesis and suggested that a minimum androgen level, specifically testosterone, is required for normal spatial ability.

The data that Bock relied upon for resolution of this question was mainly that of Masica et al. (1969). These authors studied the intellectual functioning of XY males whose bodies are unresponsive to androgens. As a result they are born looking like females and are often reared as females. As adults their sex hormone level for estrogen is between that of normal males and females (Federman, 1968). They are less responsive to androgens than normal females. For example, they have very sparse pubic hair. The Wechsler Verbal IQ, 112, of a sample of fifteen of these persons was higher than the Performance IQ, 102. The Performance Scale measures mostly spatial function. From this it has been inferred that the X-linked gene for superior spatial visualization can only be expressed when accompanied by an adequate level of testosterone. It was then further inferred that spatial visualization is not only X-linked, but testosterone-limited (Bock and Kolakowski, 1973). There are many problems with this line of inference: (a) The Performance IQ was very much in the normal range. Who is to say that the Verbal IQ is not higher than it "should" be rather than that the Performance IQ is lower? (b) What would comparison with an appropriate control group show? (c) The performance of three persons with the same syndrome reported in the same article who were reared as males and not as females was quite different: Verbal IQ 117, Performance IQ 119. If the gene expression is dependent on testosterone, why is Performance IQ even in the normal range let alone above normal, PIQ 119? Normal brain development probably does depend on at least a minimum level of sex hormones, but there is no evidence they need to be androgens nor specifically testosterone.

In general, while there is no question that mental retardation is often associated with sex chromosome anomalies, considerable doubt exists that there is a "space-form blindness." The terms "spatial deficit" or "nonverbal deficit" (Garron and Vander Stoep, 1969) are more descriptive terms. Some reference has even been made to "numerical" deficit, but the evidence for this is negligible. For purposes of comparison, results of studies of intellectual functioning in several groups of sex chromosome/hormone anomalous persons are charted in Table II. It would be of considerable interest to have been able to include results of naturally occurring XX persons who phenotypically look like males (Polani, 1972); however, no relevant studies were found. In at least one case, however, such a person has superior intelligence and works successfully as an engineer (Meissner, 1975).

As can be seen, all three groups with more or less than forty-six chromosomes have an associated mental deficiency. The group with the lowest Performance IQ, which is a fairly good measure of spatial function, is not the XO Turner's syndrome group, but one of the XXY groups. The variation in Performance IQ cannot be accounted for by the assumptions made by

Sex-Related Cognitive Differences

Bock (1973) or by Peterson (1976) about androgen effects. Summarizing the comparison of the Performance IQs one can say (though without benefit of statistical test) that more or less than forty-six chromosomes has an adverse effect on Performance IQ (spatial function) and among those without forty-six chromosomes, more androgens did not improve Performance IQ.

TABLE II

WECHSLER VERBAL AND PERFORMANCE IQS OF PERSONS
WITH SEX CHROMOSOME/HORMONE ANOMALIES

Study	N	Geno-type	Sex of Rearing	Effective Adult Hormones	VIQ	PIQ
Money and Granoff (1965)	45	XO	F	Low estrogen, androgen	106	86
Masica et al. (1969)	15	XY	F	Low estrogen	112	102
Masica et al. (1969)	3	XY	M	Low estrogen	117	119
Money (1964)	23	XXY	M	Fairly low estrogen, androgens	105	88
McKerracher (1971)	12	XXY	M	Fairly low estrogen, androgens	66	76
McKerracher (1971)	20	XYY	M	Androgen, normal?	79	88

These comparisons demonstrate the difficulties of dealing with discrepancy measures. Various factors affect verbal and spatial function. High verbal performance tends to be sex-typed female, but at a broader level, acquisition of a certain level of verbal skill is culturally more emphasized, trained, and important to overall achievement and status in society than is acquisition of spatial skill. The importance of verbal skill is so great that even in instances when the entire left hemisphere is removed in infancy, adequate verbal skill develops in the right hemisphere though probably at the expense of spatial skill (Kinsbourne and Smith, 1974). Perhaps because of the cultural ascendency of verbal skills, brain injury is more sensitively detected by deficits in spatial function.

It is also well-known that delinquent, impulsive persons have poorly developed verbal skill in comparison to their performance skill (McKerracher, 1971; Wechsler, 1958). The interpretation given to this observation is that they have not been willing to benefit from their cultural opportunity to learn. Some of the variation in verbal skill then may be based on noncognitive aspects of willingness to cooperate, attend, persist, self-correct, and hence to learn. These cooperative characteristics, which are very much present in XO persons, are frequently absent in XYY persons though the suspected propensity of the latter for outright violence proved to be exaggerated.

The data from persons anomalous in chromosomal or hormonal sex lack systematic investigation. However, although XO persons have lower spatial than verbal performance, attribution of this pattern of performance to lack of testosterone is unwarranted. The data do not support the notion that a minimum amount of testosterone and/or androgens is necessary for adequate or good spatial function. Neither do the data support the idea that the more testosterone, the better the spatial performance. In fact, data from Broverman et al. (1968) indicate the contrary for males. Peterson (1977) found more androgenized females superior in spatial performance to less androgenized females. However, since androgen effect was inferred from bodily indices, one certainly cannot rule out the possibility that the causal factor was not androgen but some correlated factor, e.g., participation in vigorous outdoor activities and other activities sex-typed male. Obviously if these data are reliable, one also faces the paradox that more androgen effect in males is associated with poorer spatial performance while more androgen effect in females is associated with better spatial performance. Hormonal hypotheses will be discussed in more detail in the next chapter.

Lehrke Hypothesis

Lehrke (1972, 1974) has hypothesized that major intellectual traits, specifically verbal ability, are carried on the X chromosome. Lehrke based his hypothesis on the observations that (a) Stafford (1961) found evidence of X-linkage for space perceptions, (b) males are more variable than females in intelligence, and (c) pedigrees of some forms of mental deficiency, especially involving verbal deficit, seemed to fit an X-linked pattern.

Wittig (1976) has pointed out that there is no evidence for X-linked inheritance of general ability (Erlenmeyer-Kimling and Jarvik, 1963). Stafford's hypothesis about recessive, X-linked inheritance of spatial visualization has been disconfirmed. Moreover, Lehrke's hypothesis specified X-linked *verbal* inheritance. He apparently was unaware of the fact that in Stafford's (1963) dissertation research on which the 1961 publication was based, the author concluded that there was no evidence of X-linkage in verbal ability. This in no way obviates Lehrke's (1974) presentation of pedigree data which seem to indicate an X-linked verbal deficit. That is to say, because verbal ability in the usual or superior groups is not inherited in an X-linked manner does not rule out the possibility that one can inherit some form of mental deficiency in that way. It is possible that males are more variable than females because of the presence of more males with mental and physical defects as already discussed. It may be that Lehrke has found another X-linked, recessive deficit which, of course, would affect males more than females. His observations are not relevant, however, to the question of sex differences in normal persons.

Conclusions: X-linked Hypotheses

The X-linked recessive hypotheses of the inheritance of mathematical problem solving and spatial ability are disconfirmed. The widespread acceptance which the hypotheses found was premature, as pointed out by Sherman (1975), and the subsequent accumulation of negative findings have thoroughly borne out that assessment. The evidence cited as favoring the hypothesis that spatial visualization is a sex-limited characteristic is selective, insubstantial, and does not support the hypothesis.

OVERALL CHAPTER CONCLUSIONS

The poor quality of much of the evidence adduced to support these theories should be evident to anyone who has closely examined the evidence presented. The need for greater rigor and higher scientific standards is self-evident.

Chapter Five

METABOLIC AND
HORMONAL EXPLANATIONS

INTRODUCTION

THIS chapter will consider metabolic and hormonal explanations relevant to sex-related cognitive differences. We will first consider the gout hypothesis and then the hormonal theory of Broverman et al. (1968). Lastly we will look at effects of testosterone on attention and hypotheses and data regarding prenatal hormonal effects on intelligence.

GOUT HYPOTHESIS

The textbook of Hyde and Rosenberg (1976) presents a new explanation for sex-related differences in cognition. The presence of gout in men of genius has been noted historically. Gout is a metabolic disease characterized by elevated levels of uric acid in the blood (BSUA) and its deposit as a salt in various parts of the body, notably in the joints or as kidney stones. These deposits can be a source of extreme pain and interfere with function. About the only consolation gout sufferers have is that they suffer from the "disease of genius."

Since some studies have found lower levels of serum urate in women, Hyde and Rosenberg speculate, "We may be seeing here a biological source of the paucity of professional achievement among women. . . . While feminists may not welcome this view, it does suggest the possibility that women in the future may be able to take a pill that will give them the motivation to complete medical school (by raising BSUA levels!)" (p. 137). Nearly every aspect of this quotation can be questioned. One of the few studies which compared male and female achievement, with some attempt to control relevant variables, did *not* find a difference in achievement (Simon et al., 1967). It is extremely doubtful that Hyde and Rosenberg could empirically support the idea that few women graduate from medical school because they lack the motivation. Moreover, there is an ambiguity in the hypothesis. On the one hand, one is led to infer that a high level of blood serum uric acid is related to intelligence, i.e., genius; on the other hand, the implication seems to be that it is related to motivation. Lastly it should be noted that serum urate level is affected by physical activity which has been an uncontrolled variable in most studies.

There are several propositions relevant to this hypothesis: (a) blood serum uric acid level is related to intelligence; (b) serum uric acid level is related to achievement; (c) these relations are causal; (d) blood serum uric acid levels are lower in females; and (e) serum uric acid relates to intelligence/achievement in the same way in women as it does with men. Each of these propositions will now be examined. (Blood serum uric acid, BSUA, and serum urate will be used with the same meaning.)

Hypothesis Evaluation

Serum Uric Acid and Intelligence

In fact there is no indication of an important relationship between serum urate level and intelligence (Mueller et al., 1970). Serum urate level correlated positively and significantly with the Otis, a group intelligence test, in a group of 817 army recruits (Stetten and Hearon, 1969), but the correlation of .08 is too small to be of practical importance. Likewise a correlation of .10 was found between the Otis and serum uric acid among high school boys, but no relationship was found between serum urate levels and scores on the Medical College Aptitude Test for medical students (Dunn et al., 1963). It seems that if there are fewer female geniuses it is not likely that it is because their intelligence suffers from lack of uric acid.

Serum Uric Acid and Achievement

There appear to be at least some grounds for supposing there is a relationship between achievement and serum urate. Dunn et al. found serum urate levels of 4.77 for over 500 craftsmen compared to levels above 5.30 for 76 Ph.D. scientists, 96 medical students, and over 300 executives (given in order of rising urate level). The executives had the top urate level of 5.73. It is not clear that it is *achievement*, however, that would differentiate the Ph.D. scientists and the executives. Other findings are that high school boys with high serum urate levels participated in more extracurricular activities, received more science awards, and were rated higher by teachers on industry, leadership, and responsibility.

Using age-sex corrected serum urate values, Dodge and Mikkelsen (cited in Mueller et al., 1970) found high levels of uric acid among men in professional and executive jobs and low levels among farmers and those in unskilled jobs. Wives of these men did not show the same differences. Executives enrolled in a development program showed serum uric acid levels higher than men in general or than unselected executives from a small community. This seems to suggest that the more *ambitious* the executive, the higher the urate level. The emphasis seems to fall most correctly on ambition, not intelligence, genius, or achievement.

Brooks and Mueller (1966) found a correlation of .66 between ratings of achievement-oriented behavior and serum uric acid levels in fifty-one professors, but other investigators have not replicated such dramatic relationships (Mueller et al., 1970).

There is some evidence then of a relationship between uric acid level and what may perhaps best be described as ambition.

Serum Urate Causes Ambition

Certainly this is absurd if baldly stated since it is well-known that the biochemical, hormonal substrata of human behavior act in a more indirect, facilitative fashion. However, maximal brain organization and functioning have proven to be a topic of great interest and theories have been advanced as to the best brains and their evolutionary significance (Levy, 1974; Orowan, 1955). Orowan has suggested that uric acid may be an endogenous cortical stimulant. As we have seen, there does appear to be some indication of a relationship between ambition and serum urate, but what is the direction of that relationship?

It is also known that "stress" increases serum urate levels. Very few studies offer any clues to disentangling the causal chain of relationships. Hyde and Rosenberg (1976) state, "The study of Kasl et al. suggests that it is uric acid that influences achievement, since their uric acid measures were taken *before* achievements were realized, and that college attendance (and presumably achievement-related stress) had no influence on changes in serum urate" (p. 136). Actually the evidence presented by Kasl et al. (1966) was not so clear cut. They reported serum urate levels of high school males who, in 1955, had either completed college ($n = 28$), attempted college ($n = 18$), or who had never gone to college ($n = 16$). While there was no difference in the high school grades of the latter two groups, there was a significant difference in serum urate level among the groups and between the latter two groups. This, if replicated, suggests that (a) serum urate level predicts achievement effort when grades are controlled and (b) the relationships found between serum urate and ambition may not be attributable to the immediate stress of the achievement effort. However these data still do not allow us to infer that high uric acid causes achievement. The authors stated that there was no relationship between the amount of change in uric acid level from 1961 to 1965 and pursuing education past high school, but they did not present the data or the results of statistical tests. Furthermore, we have no way of knowing that the ambitious attitudes that led these boys to attempt college were not also present during high school. That is we have no real basis for concluding that the serum urate level caused ambitious behavior. The authors, in fact, made no such inference.

Hence, while there is some reason to believe that high uric acid level is related to ambition, it is not at all clear that high uric acid level causes ambition. When these events are eventually untangled, it may very well be that certain *specific* kinds of attitudes cause rises in serum urates (Graham and Stevenson, 1963).

Serum Urate levels Lower in Women

After age ten, most population studies show that the sexes diverge in amount of serum uric acid (Mikkelsen et al., 1965; Mueller et al., 1970). Differences between the sexes at all age levels from age ten to sixty were found to be significantly different. The period of greatest increase in serum urate level was adolescence for males, while females showed much less rise then but a gradual increase at menopause. These findings, plus the fact that blood uric acid was significantly lower in a sample of pregnant women, have suggested that sex hormones influence serum urate levels, i.e., specifically that estrogens and possibly progesterone have a urate-depressing ability.

Serum Urate Causes Ambition in Women

As the alert reader may have noted, none of the biosocial studies discussed involved women. As already indicated, there is no evidence that serum urate causes ambition; moreover, the merest demonstration of a relationship between achievement and serum urate levels has not been established in women. Dunn et al. (1963) did *not* find a significant association between number of extracurricular activities and uric acid levels in high school girls (Mueller et al., 1970). Gordon et al. (1967) found a significant correlation between serum urate levels and college achievement during the clinical years of a nursing student but no relationship during the earlier, academic years. In short, it is not at all clear that ambition and serum urate level are related in women. There is very little cogent evidence on this point. It should also be remembered that there is no reason to believe that ambition or achievement motivation in women cannot or does not equally develop even if their estrogens acted as a urate suppressant. Perhaps the estrogens themselves or some other biochemicals serve equally well to stimulate the female brain *without* so great a risk of developing gout.

Conclusion regarding Gout Hypothesis

Obviously there is no way this hypothesis could account for

sex-related cognitive differences. It is extremely doubtful that it is even cogent.

HORMONAL EFFECTS ON SEX-RELATED DIFFERENCES IN COGNITION

This section will concentrate on the best known theory of a hormonal basis for cognitive sex-related differences, that of Broverman et al. (1968). The theory will be briefly described and then the validity of its assumptions, conceptualization, and empirical base will be examined. The influence of testosterone on attention and the question of prenatal hormone influences on intelligence will also be examined.

Evaluation of Broverman et al. Theory

It has been hypothesized that (a) there is a negative relationship between performance of simple, repetitive tasks and those complex tasks requiring inhibition of immediate responses to obvious stimuli in favor of responses to less obvious stimuli (cognitive restructuring); (b) females are better than males on simple, overlearned tasks while males are better than females on more complex, restructuring tasks; (c) this negative relationship between performance on cognitive tasks is an expression of the underlying antagonism of the adrenergic (activating) and cholinergic (inhibiting) systems; and (d) estrogens are stronger activators than androgens. This theory has been criticized on numerous grounds (Singer and Montgomery, 1969; Parlee, 1972), and a reply was made to the first criticism (Broverman et al., 1969). After examining each of the propositions of the theory in turn, the data bearing on the theory will be examined.

Negative Relationships between Simple and Complex Cognitive Tasks

Cognitive skills are generally regarded and found to be positively related. The question of a negative relationship between simple, overlearned tasks and complex tasks requiring restructuring is a complicated one involved with factor analytic theory and procedures. The idea emerged from the factor analytic work of Burt (1940) and has played an important role in Broverman's research (1964; Broverman and Klaiber, 1969; see Smith, 1964, for some additional discussion). The primary factor found in these factor analyses was interpreted as "g" or general intelligence and can be understood as a factor based on *between* subjects variance. The secondary factors can be considered as reflecting *within* subjects variance. These secondary factors before rotation were negatively related. Most factor analyses are rotated before the results are presented. The rotation is done to eliminate the negative values. Statisticians differ in their opinion as to which form, rotated or nonrotated, presents the truest reflection of the data. For unrotated results, there is evidence of a bipolar factor characterized at one end by simple, overlearned tasks and at the other end by complex tasks requiring restructuring. What this means in simple terms is that the individual who performs well on simple, overlearned, repetitive tasks is supposed to perform poorly on complex tasks requiring restructuring. These complex, restructuring tasks are not of *all* types but appear to be especially, and possibly only, spatial tasks.

A point of unclarity lies in the possible confusion of dynamic and status predictions. That is, while it is intuitively appealing to imagine performance of simple, repetitive tasks being facilitated by a high level of activation, and impulsivity impairing the greater reflection that might facilitate performance on a perceptual-restructuring task, this does not necessarily translate to a permanent characteristic of people, nor to a characterization of cognitive differences between the sexes. People are not blind respondents, but learn and are taught appropriate strategies for dealing with different tasks. A higher level of activation, even if demonstrated, does not necessarily lead to impulsive, unreflective behavior. The Broverman et al. (1968) theory does not entirely make sense in this regard.

Females Better on Simple, Males on Complex Tasks

The authors have lumped together a variety of tasks on

which females perform better, e.g., color naming, word fluency, digit symbol, and even verbal function, including reading, and called them simple, overlearned tasks. The tasks males were thought to do better on, notably spatial tasks, were put together and called complex tasks requiring restructuring. This division is arbitrary and inconsistent with any other researcher's view (Parlee, 1972). To consider reading a simple, overlearned task is extremely inaccurate. Moreover, the authors' characterization of restructuring as the chief difference between the tests differentiating the sexes has been shown to be incorrect. Maccoby and Jacklin (1974) pointed out that females generally do better than males on anagrams, which is a restructuring task.

Let us look at the extent of differences between the sexes on tasks relevant to this theory. As will be recalled from Chapter Three, differences between the sexes in cognition appear to account for a very small percentage of the variance. Matarazzo (1972) discussed the sex-related differences found in the 1955 Wechsler standardization. Using the critical ratio values presented for 1,700 males and females, aged sixteen to sixty-four, it is possible to calculate some pertinent omega squares to measure the extent of differences. Omega squared for the sex-related difference on the Digit Symbol subtest of the Wechsler Adult Intelligence Scale was .03, females scoring significantly higher; for the Block Design subtest, males scoring significantly higher, omega squared was 0. The Digit Symbol subtest was among those classified as a simple, repetitive task by Broverman et al. (1968), while the Block Design subtest was classified as a complex, restructuring spatial task. The difference between the sexes that the Broverman et al. theory attempts to explain accounts for a tiny percent of the variance.

Some idea of the cross-species evidence Broverman et al. adduced in support of their theory may be gained from the following quotation. "Human females exceed human males on simple perceptual-motor tasks. The same sex difference in analogous behaviors, that is, spontaneous motor activity is true in rats" (Broverman et al. 1968, p. 37). Though this characterization was not intended to be derogatory toward women (Broverman, 1977), it illustrates how easy it is for even well-intentioned and sensitized researchers (Broverman et al.,

1972) to make statements that jar minority group members.

Adrenergic and Cholinergic Antagonism

According to Singer and Montgomery (1969), Broverman et al. (1968) have oversimplified and inaccurately stated physiological facts—equating sympathetic and parasympathetic with adrenergic and cholinergic systems, setting up false and inaccurate antagonisms between the systems, drawing inferences from the peripheral nervous system and applying them to the central nervous system, and selectively presenting evidence of cholinergic action. (See Broverman et al., 1969, for their reply.)

Broverman et al. (1968) indicated that the best evidence of hormonal effects was the fact that the concentration of choline acetylase, an enzyme involved in regulating the amount of acetylcholine available as a transmitter substance, rises in the hypothalamus of castrated rats. Presumably less testosterone means more inhibiting effects. Parlee (1972), however, contended that acetylcholine is a transmitter substance in the preganglionic (central) portion of the *sympathetic*, not the parasympathetic (cholinergic) nervous system as they stated. Hence, she argues that the factual basis of their hypothesized mechanism for the role of sex hormones in physiologic antagonism is false (Parlee, 1972). Broverman (1977), however, indicates that Parlee is mistaken since she is referring to peripheral effects, while the Broverman et al. theory deals with central effects. In any case, the simple antagonism being set up is not accurate and the complexities and lack of knowledge in this area make attempts to link acetylcholine to sex-related differences tenuous and speculative.

Estrogens Stronger Activators

No direct evidence of the greater activating effect in humans of estrogens compared to androgens was presented. The technical difficulties and possible confounding factors in providing adequate data for such an inference are considerable (Bleier, 1976). For example, the brain itself can convert androgen to estrogen (Ryan et al., 1972; Weisz and Gibbs, 1973). Because of this one cannot be sure that androgen effects are not estrogen effects. For example, an anti-estrogen (but not anti-androgen) drug blocked the effects which had been induced with androgen injections in ovariectomized female rats, for sterility (McDonald and Doughty, 1973/74), for acyclicity of gonadotrophin release (Doughty and McDonald, 1974), and for lordosis (Whalen et al., 1972). In the face of so much that is unknown, it is premature to draw conclusions about central nervous system effects of estrogen compared to androgen.

Empirical Findings cited by Broverman et al.

Broverman et al. (1968) cited many studies to indicate that drugs which activate/depress the sympathetic nervous system improve/depress performance on simple, well-learned tasks. This evidence seemed adequate. However, as Parlee (1972) has pointed out, the evidence cited in relation to complex, restructuring tasks was not at all adequate, having to do with rat performance, performance of mental defectives, and/or performance on tasks not clearly complex (counting backward, mirror tracing), nor were the reports of human studies numerous. There was also no discussion of the hypothesis of interfering effects of anxiety, an alternative hypothesis which could explain some of the few remotely relevant human studies they presented (Unger and Denmark, 1975). Some credible evidence was presented showing a relationship in human males between performance on simple, repetitive tasks and androgen level. This hardly suffices to support the theory. In fact, it presents the paradox that the most "masculine" men did better on the so-called female tasks than the more "feminine" men.

Much of the empirical data in support of the Broverman et al. (1968) theory is based only on male subjects, the clearest results being obtained with *adolescent* male subjects leading to the possibility that results may be confounded with level and/or rate of maturation effects. Most of the correlations between physical attributes and cognitive measures were not statistically significant and, of course, a certain number of correlations can be expected by chance. On the whole, because of these problems, these results can only be considered suggestive for males and do not apply at all to females or to sex differences (Broverman et al., 1964; Broverman and Klaiber, 1969).

Research of Petersen

PETERSEN LITERATURE REVIEW. Probably the study most relevant to the Broverman et al. theory is that of Petersen (1976). In addition to presenting her own research, she reviewed evidence relevant to hormones and cognitive functioning. Some of the evidence Petersen cited in support of the general proposition of a relationship between hormones and cognitive function is now irrelevant because of the disconfirmation of the X-linked hypothesis of the inheritance of space perception (see section on X-linked hypotheses). Data from persons with chromosomal/ hormonal abnormalities were also cited in support of the link between hormones and cognitive pattern, but data from these sources are not very strong, appropriate, or convincing. They will be discussed first. (See also discussion in last chapter.)

XY persons who look like females because their bodies cannot respond to their normal male levels of androgen were said to show a "female" performance on cognitive tests, i.e., higher performance on a "simple repetitive" task (Digit Symbol) compared to performance on a perceptual restructuring task (Block Design). While presumably one is to infer that lack of androgen response and unopposed estrogen leads to "female" type performance, there are many unconsidered points: (a) not mentioned is the fact that in the same study, XY "females" reared as males did not show the "female" performance (Masica, et al., 1969); (b) data consists of fifteen adults and children combined as one group, a dubious methodology; (c) even the XY "females" reared as females performed at normal or above normal levels on spatial tasks; and (d) there is no normal control group. Some groups of normal males *also* show a "female" pattern. The "female" pattern is a very relative finding.

Another finding Petersen (1976) cited in support of the hormonal-cognitive pattern link is a study of cognitive function in ten males physically feminized at a very early age by a kwashiorkor-induced endocrine dysfunction. Dawson (1967) interpreted the study as supporting the effects of socialization experience on cognitive patterning, but Petersen was impressed with the possibility that the results indicate the effects of estrogen on cognitive function. Compared to a normal control group, the kwashiorkor males showed significantly lower scores on two spatial tests and a significantly higher score on a verbal test. It should be noted that this was a *verbal* test, not a simple, repetitive task. It is sometimes said of this study that the kwashiorkor males showed a typical "female" pattern in supposedly having lower numerical scores. The difference of .9 points between the controls and the ten experimental subjects is hardly likely to be statistically significant.

It should be noted that kwashiorkor is a very serious protein deficiency disease and may well have caused brain injury and impaired spatial function partly or wholly as result. In any case, because of the small number of subjects, the confounding of hormonal and socialization effects, the use of a verbal rather than a fluency test, and the possibility of brain injury in the experimental subjects, it should be obvious that this study does not provide clear evidence that estrogen facilitates performance on fluency tasks while impairing performance on complex perceptual tasks.

Results of studies indicating that performance on both fluent production, simple perceptual tasks and spatial tasks declines with age were cited as indicating a link between cognition and sex hormones, since sex hormones also decline with age (Schaie and Strother, 1968; Schwartz and Karp, 1967; Witkin et al., 1967). It has been well-known that performance on such tasks declines with age, as it also does with cerebral deterioration. In fact, lower scores on such tasks, compared to performance on a task such as vocabulary, are routinely used to infer brain injury and cerebral deterioration (Wechsler, 1958). To infer that the performance decline can be attributed to decline in sex-hormones is unwarranted. It should also be noted that far from supporting the Broverman et al. theory, this fact is inconsistent with it. The Broverman et al. (1968) theory predicts that a decline in sex hormones should result in *improved* performance on spatial tasks. Obviously this is not the case. Rather than supporting the theory, these data contradict it.

PETERSEN DATA. Petersen (1976) analysed data from the files of the Fels Research Institute for thirty-five males and forty females at three successive ages: thirteen, sixteen, and eighteen. The measures of fluency were the Digit Symbol subtest of the Wechsler at ages thirteen and sixteen and the Primary Mental Abilities Word Fluency test for age eighteen. The Digit Symbol subtest is a dubious measure of fluency. It is not a "simple, overlearned" task. In fact, it has been classically recognized as a test of *new* learning. The Digit Symbol subtest did not form a single factor with the Word Fluency test. The measures of spatial skill, the complex, perceptual task, were the Block Design subtest of the Wechsler for ages thirteen and sixteen and the Space test of the Primary Mental Abilities test for age eighteen. Comparison of the sexes showed significant differences in favor of males for the two spatial tests and in favor of females for the Digit Symbol subtest, but not for the Word Fluency test. This latter finding contradicts the theory, since according to the theory, females should score higher than males.

Addressing the question of the hypothesized negative relationship between fluency and spatial skill, Petersen performed a principle components analysis for each sex. She used the scores for Block Design and Digit Symbol at ages thirteen and sixteen and then the scores from the same subjects at age eighteen on the PMA Space and Word Fluency tests. Use of so few measures does not make this a very adequate factor analysis or a very adequate test of the hypothesis. However, Petersen simply wished to see if she could demonstrate a negative relationship with her data (Petersen, 1977). The results showed a common, general factor for both sexes and a second factor in which, for males, the spatial tests loaded positively and the fluency tests loaded negatively. For females, however, contrary to the theory, the Word Fluency test loaded *positively* with the spatial tests. The results can be said to support Broverman and

Klaiber (1969) for males but not for females.

In order to study the relationship between cognitive performance and hormones, Petersen (1976) made ratings of physical characteristics from nude photographs of the subjects. Three of the physical measures were bipolar ratings from extreme feminine to extreme masculine. They were (a) amount of fat compared to muscle, (b) overall shape, e.g., shoulder breadth, and (c) size of breasts compared to size of genitals. These presumably reflect the relative influence of estrogens compared to androgens on physical development. Petersen notes that measures of estrogen effects for females may not have been very adequate, especially since breast size and fat can be influenced by nonestrogen factors. The fourth measure was of extent of pubic hair, a measure of androgen effect.

The Broverman et al. (1968) theory, however, dealt with the presumably greater activating effect of estrogens than androgens. This would seem to imply effects of blood circulating hormones, not effects of bound hormones, on body build. Hence the measures which Petersen used are probably not the most direct tests of the theory, though it is ambiguous. More direct tests would be measures of estrogens and androgens in the blood, though one would have no idea of what hormones, at what level, were effective in the brain. Even using measures of physical appearance, it would seem that some greater clarity could be achieved by separate measures of estrogen and androgen effects. One wonders what Petersen's androgyny measure means in terms of central nervous system hormone influences. Apparently we are to suppose that estrogens cancel out androgen effects so that there is *less* activating effect in androgynous males and females than in either high estrogen females or high androgen males. Thus one would conclude that high androgen or high estrogen, but not high estrogen and high androgen (as they cancel out), impairs spatial performance. This is a possible, but not a necessarily true, interpretation of the relationship of these hormones to each other.

The relationship between the cognitive and physical variables was tested by a canonical correlation calculated for each age and sex. The correlations were significant for both sexes at ages sixteen and eighteen but not at age thirteen. The nature of the relationship was that by age eighteen for males greater masculinity in physical characteristics, especially muscle development, was related to a pattern of better performance on the PMA Word Fluency test and worse performance on the PMA Space test. For females by age eighteen, greater masculinity in physical characteristics, especially in overall build, and greater androgen effect as indicated by amount of pubic hair, was related *only* to better performance on the PMA Space test; characteristics were not related to performance on the PMA Word Fluency test.

Just how to interpret these results is by no means clear. They are not accounted for by timing of maturation differences, since Petersen reanalysed her data and did not replicate the Waber (1976) findings of better spatial visualization in late maturers. The *male* results are consistent with some of the findings and contentions of Broverman et al. (1968)—physical masculinity related positively to fluency and negatively to spatial skill. The finding of no difference between the sexes in fluency at age eighteen was *not* consistent with the Broverman et al. theory, and the *female* findings were only partly consistent with it. The eighteen-year-old female spatial results are perhaps consistent with the Broverman et al. theory in that high masculinity, presumably low estrogenicity, related positively to spatial performance. These results, of course, are also consistent with other hypotheses, e.g., girls with more relative androgen effect gained more practice in male sex-typed spatial activities. The lack of relationship with fluency measures and the lack of negative relationships between cognitive skills are inconsistent with the theory. Petersen's results provide only partial support for the Broverman et al. theory and in any case, like their findings, the Petersen results are subject to other explanations.

Negative Data

If spatial performance is impaired and fluency facilitated by a high estrogen level, one would expect performance on these tasks to vary with phase of the menstrual cycle. Estrogen drops during the premenstrual phase of the cycle, remains low during menstruation, and rises again after menstruation. (For relevant literature review, see Sherman, 1971.) Many studies, however, have failed to demonstrate significant menstrual cycle effects on intellectual performance. Specifically, Englander-Golden et al. (1976) found no overall difference in performance on the Space Relations test of the Differential Aptitude tests between the premenstrual, menstrual, and mid-cycle (days seven to thirteen) phases. Moreover, contrary to what one would expect from the Broverman et al. (1968) theory, there was no menstrual phase difference in performance on the Digit Symbol subtest. Increased levels of estrogen did *not* improve performance on this perceptual fluency task. Zimmerman and Parlee (1973) also found no menstrual phase differences in digit symbol performance.

The results of these studies are totally contrary to the Broverman et al. (1968) theory (though this was not the focus of either study). They disconfirm the theory at least for estrogen effects in females and as an explanation of cognitive sex-related differences. It might be argued that menstrual cycle studies are not adequate to test the theory since direct measures of hormone levels were not taken. Since the subjects were all known to have menstruated, however, it would seem that sufficient estrogen variation should have been present through the cycles to generate the theorized effects on cognitive performance.

Conclusions Regarding Broverman et al. Theory

This theory attempts prematurely to relate cognitive and hormonal relationships cross species, intra individual, and between sex. Much of the data cited in support of the theory is based on males only and/or is otherwise inadequate or inappropriate. The statement of the theory includes conceptual and semantic usages that are confusing if not inaccurate. The differences between the sexes being accounted for comprise only a negligible part of the variance. Data contrary to predictions of the theory disconfirm it. The theory could not possibly account for cognitive differences between the sexes. Though there are some consistent findings in the male data of within sex variations with androgen, these data are insufficient to establish the point even for effects within males, and certainly are not sufficient to explain differences between the sexes.

Testosterone Effects on Attention

Rogers (1976) makes some suggestions about hormone effects on human cognitive differences between the sexes using work on chicks and using data from the Worcester group (Broverman et al., 1964, 1968; Klaiber et al., 1967). Andrew and Rogers (1972) have found that testosterone influences attentional behavior in chicks; male (but not female) chicks given testosterone increased goal-directed attention, behaving in a more single-minded, persistent fashion. Rogers finds parallels in human data from the Worcester group, e.g., reports that high androgen males do better on simple, overlearned tasks which required "sustained rapid volleys of the same responses to a limited set of stimuli."

Rogers noted that in humans, cultural effects may be present and that the effects of physique and circulating level of hormone are difficult to separate except in a pre-post design. One study, in which hormones were administered in a pre-post design (Klaiber et al., 1971) does support the hypothesis that it is testosterone, not some effect associated with physique, that improves simple, learned performance. Rogers notes several procedural problems with that study and wisely prefers to await further verification of such effects before drawing firm conclusions. Rogers (1976, p. 172) concludes that "we remain skeptical about androgenic effects on human cognition until we have the data in hand."

Rogers (1976) also attempts to explain sex-related differences in performance on a spatial task, e.g., embedded figures, with these ideas. He suggests that there may be an ideal level of androgen for maximal performance, such that high androgen males have too narrow a focus of attention but females typically have too broad a focus. While aware of some findings of no differences between the sexes in spatial performance, Rogers appears to have the impression that sex-related differences usually occur from age eight onward. As mentioned in Chapter Two, it seems likely that most persons attempting to explain differences between the human sexes in cognitive behavior are unaware of the small size of the effects and their unreliable nature.

Insufficient work has been done on Rogers's hypothesis to come to a firm conclusion about it. However, Rogers is accounting for a questionable fact (inherent sex-related cognitive differences) with another questionable fact (sex-related differences in attention in humans). The studies have been conducted only on chicks.

Prenatal Hormonal Effects on Cognition

The effects of prenatal hormones have been suggested as an explanation for cognitive sex-related differences (e.g., Petersen, 1976). It is known that humans, like lower species, pass through a critical period in prenatal development when the sex hormones "prime" or organize the brain for later sex-related behavior (Money and Ehrhardt, 1972). Petersen suggested that such prenatal organization might affect brain laterality and hence presumably spatial function. To account for her results, this view would require that the physical masculinity and cognitive performance of the males and females at age eighteen be related to prenatal organization of the brain. Let us consider some of the data relevant to this question.

There is evidence in lower animals that during a species-specific critical period very early in development, sex hormones differentially organize the brain for male or female behaviors (Money and Ehrhardt, 1972). Normally in humans a fetal androgenic substance is responsible for the sexual differentiation to maleness. Without this substance, a female form will develop. In lower animals, during the critical period, exogenous doses of androgens were found to increase certain behaviors such as aggression, but estrogen was also found to produce similar results (Edwards and Herndon, 1970; Payne and Swanson, 1972). The sex hormones are all closely related chemically and can change from one to the other in the body. As already mentioned, androgens can be converted to estrogens in the brain so what seems to be an androgen effect may, at another level, be an estrogen effect. This is the reason for many so-called paradoxical effects of sex hormones and for a certain amount of confusion among those reviewing and reporting research findings.

For example, Dalton (1968) found that the daughters of mothers who had received injections of natural progesterone during pregnancy (to guard against miscarriage) scored significantly higher than a group of controls on general aptitude tests. (Progesterone is one of the main hormones of pregnancy.) Ehrhardt and Money (1967) reported that fetally "androgenized" girls had unusually high IQs. These girls had been "androgenized" and masculinized by what are quintessential *female*, though artificially manufactured, hormones. The babies had external genitalia with male-like aspects. In some instances these data, including even the Dalton results, ended up being reported as showing that *male* hormones lead to high IQs. Since Baker and Ehrhardt (1974) found that the higher IQs of the fetally androgenized girls were also present in the normal sisters of the affected girls, it appears likely there was no true hormone effect. The high IQs were probably an artifact of the generally more sophisticated level of these families. The results of the Dalton study, however, still remain to be explained. If there is any true, replicable effect it may have to do with the *amount* of the sex hormones during the critical period rather than the *kind* of sex hormones.

One study has reported that prenatal exposure of exogenously administered estrogens and small amounts of progestins was associated with lower performance on the Embedded Figures Test, a spatial test (Yalom et al., 1973). That this effect can be attributed to the prenatal estrogen organizing the brain in some female way is highly unlikely for many conceptual, empirical, and statistical reasons: (a) At least half of the subjects received the hormones late in gestation, a time surely beyond the human critical differentiating period. (b) One would have no idea what the actual type or level of hormone action was in the brain as a result of these hormones. The implication that the hormones would organize the brain in a female way is speculative. (c) The subjects were the sons of severely ill diabetic women, so ill they required *daily* medical care. Such children are notoriously subject to brain injury and birth complications. The mothers received the hormones to help prevent miscarriage. (d) The nineteen experimental subjects were not significantly different from the fourteen subjects in the normal control group, but a borderline, $p<.10$, effect on a one-tailed test was demonstrated when the experimental group was compared with a group consisting of the normal subjects and eight children of diabetics whose mothers had not had hormone therapy. (These mothers had less severe diabetes.) The number of subjects was small and results did not reach an acceptable level of significance. (e) The result was not replicated with a sample of twenty six-year-olds whose diabetic mothers had received hormone therapy, compared with a sample of seventeen normals. In brief, because of use of abnormal subjects, too few subjects, inadequate probability levels, and failure to replicate, this study does not demonstrate any effect of prenatal female hormones on space perception.

The evidence for prenatal hormone effects on human intelligence is tenuous to say the least. There has been much more speculation and extrapolation than hard evidence.

CONCLUSION REGARDING HORMONES AND SEX-RELATED COGNITIVE DIFFERENCES

At this point, it is probably apparent that there is very little that can safely be concluded about "sex" hormones and intellectual functioning in humans. Very few effects have been demonstrated. While the Broverman et al. (1968) theory is clearly unsatisfactory, some relations have been demonstrated between androgen levels and cognitive performance. Effects that have been demonstrated need replication and ruling out of possible confounding effects, such as socioeconomic level and maturity. At such time as these effects are well-established, it will then be appropriate to devise a theory to explain them.

Chapter Six

BRAIN LATERALIZATION THEORIES

INTRODUCTION

 W HAT authors mean by "brain lateraliza-
tion" is often not precisely explained. For normal, right-
handed persons, the two hemispheres of the brain are thought
to specialize in somewhat different functions, the left hemisphere specializing in verbal, analytical tasks and the right hemisphere in spatial, gestalt tasks (Dimond and Beaumont, 1974;
Kinsbourne and Smith, 1974; Milner, 1971; Nebes, 1974). It is
also thought that each hemisphere may develop "program-
ming" favorable to its specific task (Kinsbourne, 1974a, 1974b).
Usually when authors speak of differences in "brain lateralization" they refer to the speed or completeness of the establish-
ment of left-hemisphere dominance for verbal, analytic
function, especially speech, though sometimes they mean dominance of the right hemisphere for spatial, gestalt function.
Unless otherwise specified, the reader should assume the discussion concerns right-handed persons.

Mathematics and Brain Lateralization

If verbal function is located in the left hemisphere and spatial function is located in the right hemisphere, which hemisphere handles math? While most accounts of lateralization of
cerebral function do not discuss localization of mathematics,
those that do locate mathematics in the left hemisphere with
verbal, analytic thinking. The only mathematical task identified as located in the right hemisphere is computation (Sperry,
1975), though this has not been clearly established (Dimond
and Beaumont, 1973; Milstein et al., 1977). Logically it would
appear that females should do as well as males in mathematics
since females are generally conceded to do as well as males on

verbal tasks. As previously noted in Chapter Two, however, complex and spatial skill, which is supposed to be a right-hemisphere function, can be very much involved in many types of mathematics achievement. Moreover some mathematical tasks may require use of both hemispheres. Bogen and Bogen (1969) suggest that "integrated use of verbal and visuo-spatial thought may depend on interhemispheric communication, including an important contribution from the corpus callosum" (p. 199). They cited examples from great thinkers, including Poincaré and Einstein, about the role of images, thoughts that are difficult to verbalize and unconscious thinking in creative mathematical work. They emphasized that lack of creativity may stem from "the inhibitory effect, on the appositional source (right-hemisphere), of an excess of propositional (left-hemisphere) thinking" (p. 201). Mathematics then probably involves important use of both hemispheres.

Studies of Mathematics and Brain Lateralization

There have been several studies of mathematics and brain lateralization, but unfortunately for various reasons the results are not easily interpreted. For example, Bakan (1969) reported that a predominance of right-eye movements (presumably left-hemisphere activity) is associated with majoring in a natural science and relatively better mathematical performance on the Scholastic Aptitude Test. The sex of the twenty-two subjects was not reported. Bakan (1971) made several statements about sex-related differences but presented no data to support his views.

Harshman and Remington (1976) cited studies to the effect that fewer right and more left lateral eye movements occur among women (Day, 1967; Weitan and Etaugh, 1974), though Duke (1968) and Etaugh (1972) found no sex-related difference. Moreover, the Weitan and Etaugh (1974) finding is a trend, $p<.10$, over responses to verbal, numerical, spatial, and musical questions (n = 24 females and 24 males). The theoretical meaning of such a difference, if replicated, is not clear since response to tasks believed to involve both hemispheres have been lumped together. A greater proportion of lateral eye movements was made to the right for verbal and numerical questions than for spatial and musical questions, $p<.01$. The numerical questions were computational. Right-eye movements presumably signal left-hemisphere involvement and left-eye movements, right-hemisphere involvement. Weitan and Etaugh (1973) reported that right-movers scored relatively higher on the Mathematics compared to the Verbal subtest of the Scholastic Aptitude Test (n = 15, sex unreported).

Milstein et al. (1977) investigated the influence of sex and handedness on performance of one-digit by one-digit multiplication problems tachistoscopically presented to one or both hemispheres. Subjects were right- and left-handed males and females (n = 40), ages fifteen to sixty. Though males were expected to perform at a superior level, a significant difference in favor of females was found. A significant interaction effect emerged, indicating that females were more accurate when the problems were presented to the right hemisphere while males, especially right-handed males, were more accurate when the problems were presented to the left hemisphere. Since computation was supposed to be better done in the right hemisphere, these findings are not consistent with previous ones (Dimond and Beaumont, 1972). The authors concluded that sex and handedness effects are independent, a conclusion also reached by Sherman (1978).

Kinsbourne (1974c) indicated that variations in experimental procedures can lead to varying results with lateral eye movement technique, so that some of the discrepant results are doubtless artifactual. At this point it is difficult to conclude anything about sex, laterality, and mathematics or spatial function from these studies.

Overview of Brain Lateralization Theories

There are several hypotheses of differences between the sexes in brain lateralization including those of Buffery and Gray, Levy, and Harshman and Remington. These hypotheses will first be briefly described and then the relevant evidence for each will be reviewed. A large number of studies have few female subjects, do not report sex of subjects, or use male and female subjects but do not analyse the results separately. For the most part these studies have not been included in this review.

Buffery and Gray (1972) hypothesized that dominance of the left hemisphere for verbal function is attained earlier in girls leading to less bilateral representation of spatial function. Buffery and Gray believe that bilateral spatial representation is beneficial to superior spatial functioning and hence lack of spatial bilaterality would account for poorer spatial performance. This theory has been sharply criticized by Marshall (1973) and Fairweather (1976).

Levy (Levy, 1972; Levy-Agresti and Sperry, 1968) hypothesized that females, like left-handed males, are more likely to have verbal function located in both hemispheres of the brain. It is hypothesized that maximal verbal and spatial function is attained when one hemisphere, usually the left, is specialized for verbal function and the other, usually the right, is specialized for spatial function. Since bilateral representation of verbal function would impair spatial development, females, like male left-handers, would have poorer spatial function. Initially, it was thought that verbal function was not impaired by bilateral representation because of the cultural importance it receives. Later, Levy (1974) suggested that bilateral verbal function confers an advantage to verbal performance. The Buffery and Gray and Levy hypotheses are in fundamental contradiction, for one proposes that less lateralization results in development of better spatial skill and the other that more lateralization results in development of better spatial skill. Yet these hypotheses are not direct opposites. Buffery and Gray hypothesized that because males have more bilateral *spatial function* they are better than females in performing spatial tasks. Levy hypothesized that because females are more bilateral in *verbal function*, the spatial function of the right hemisphere is interfered with, causing poorer spatial function.

Harshman and Remington (1976) suggested that because females mature earlier than males, at young ages females appear to be more lateralized (meaning clear left-hemisphere dominance in verbal function) than males. However, in their view, when males are fully mature they are more lateralized than females for both verbal, analytic and spatial, gestalt functions. They believe that this greater lateralization confers an advantage for spatial function. Similar views were expressed by Harris (1975). Now let us look at each of these theories in more detail.

BUFFERY AND GRAY HYPOTHESIS

The Buffery and Gray (1972) hypothesis states first that left cerebral dominance for verbal function is established earlier in girls than in boys. Secondly it assumes that because of this earlier left cerebral dominance, females have less bilateral spatial function and thirdly that this causes their spatial skill to be less poorly developed than is the case for males. Each part of this hypothesis will now be examined.

Theory Evaluation

Earlier Left Hemisphere Dominance in Females

That left cerebral dominance for verbal function is established earlier in girls is based first of all on data showing more precocious verbal development in females than in males. Although, as discussed previously, Maccoby and Jacklin (1974) have raised some questions, they, Harris (1977), and McGuinness (1976) concluded that girls are verbally precocious compared to boys. Fairweather (1976) cited data to this effect but also sounds a cautious note. Not having personally gathered data on this question I have accepted these conclusions, but with some sense of unease. Differences which I had been led to expect on the basis of the literature, have proven to be small and unreliable. Would the sex-related difference in verbal precocity likewise evaporate under close scrutiny? In any case the effect is apparently small.

In evaluating this question, it is well to keep in mind the possible consequences of the greater number of male children with language and physical abnormalities. An effect seems to be present in "normal" children, but thus far no one has sorted out these possible confounding factors. Fairweather (1976) has raised a further point of interest. He noted that the difference between the sexes in language deficits should always lead females to do better than males (in comparisons of truly randomly selected groups of male and female children that represent the total population). Why are not such differences always found? Obviously something is wrong somewhere. Let us consider possible explanations. Could it be that males do not more frequently have deficits? This seems unlikely since large consistent differences have been reported for years. Is it possible that language deficits do not affect test performance? It could be possible that some investigators have used tests that miss true differences, i.e., not enough "top" or complex items at the age tested. Is it possible that groups do not show differences because the male language deficits have been remedied? This undoubtedly accounts for part of the discrepancy between the cumulated reported findings and known deficits for subjects past the earliest years. Are males with deficits being excluded from the samples typically reported? This undoubtedly occurs. Is it possible that an early language deficit confers a later advantage? This is undoubtedly true in some cases, witness Demosthenes. Only further, careful research could untangle all these possible effects.

We will tentatively conclude that more girls than boys effectively use language at an early point. Note that the emphasis is on *effective use of language,* a concept which can include several measures. McGuinness (1976) also prefers to emphasize this point. It is the slight nature of this effect, occuring in the first years of life, that led me to dub it the bent twig effect (Sherman, 1967).

An additional source of evidence for the conclusion that left cerebral dominance is established earlier in females than in males, stems from tachistoscopic studies and studies of dichotic listening. Such studies take advantage of the fact that material presented in a hemi-field of space initially goes to the contralateral hemisphere. For example, the majority of right-handed adults identify tachistoscopically exposed, easily verbalized material more accurately when it is presented in the right visual hemi-field and hence initially to the left cerebral hemisphere, than when it is presented in the left visual hemi-field and hence initially to the right cerebral hemisphere. The reverse is found for difficult to verbalize (nonverbal) material. Buffery and Gray (1972) have concluded that there is a linguistic device in the left hemisphere which is more developed in the female than male human brain of the same age so that for females there is earlier and more complete lateralization.

Kinsbourne (1974a, 1974b) suggested that before age five, the dichotic superiority of the left hemisphere for speech sounds reflects a tendency to orient to the right with speech input and need *not* imply a greater left- than right-hemisphere facility in processing verbal material. If the attentional ascendency of the left hemisphere is accomplished with reciprocal inhibition of the right hemisphere, over time this inhibition will have a cumulative effect on the right hemisphere, i.e., reducing its competency for that particular material. If Kinsbourne is correct, the emphasis should be on the greater *attentional* ascendency of the left hemisphere, not on the greater competency of left-hemisphere verbal function of young females. It should also be noted that greater left- than right-sided auditory evoked response amplitude to syllables and words was found in a small sample of infants (Molfese et al., 1975). This suggestion of prelanguage lateralization cautions against simple equations between language and lateralization.

Moreover, not only may one question the existence of an earlier activated linguistic device in the left hemisphere of females, but one may also question whether left-hemisphere language dominance is established earlier in girls than in boys. Fairweather (1976) reviewed evidence from tachistoscopic and dichotic listening studies and concluded that the evidence was by no means clear. There are many negative findings and positive ones permit other interpretations.

Earlier Left Cerebral Dominance as a Cause of Less Spatial Bilaterality

Why should earlier left cerebral dominance, if true, cause less bilateral spatial representation in females and/or is there any evidence of less bilaterality of female spatial function? Buffery and Gray (1972) did not accept as relevant some findings that the left hemisphere is more important in female than in male spatial functioning (Lansdell, 1962, 1968). Other such evidence has emerged since (see review in following pages). On the whole, there is now a considerable amount of data which are inconsistent with their view. Their conclusion appeared to rest largely on some of Buffery's data that right cerebral dominance for visual-spatial function occurs later in males than in females. However, Witelson (1976) and Rudel et al. (1974) report the opposite. Even if it were true that right cerebral dominance for visual-spatial function occurs later in boys, it would not necessarily follow that this results in more bilateral representation of spatial function for males. Harshman and Remington (1976) suggest that for *adults* sex-related differences in lateralization could be quite different than for children and that more attention should be paid to data from mature persons. They think adult males are more lateralized than females. Buffery and Gray presented no solid evidence that males have more bilateral spatial representation than females.

Spatial Bilaterality Associated with Superior Performance

Buffery and Gray (1972) presented no independent evidence to indicate that bilateral representation of spatial function is associated with superior spatial function. Indeed, there is some evidence to the contrary (Waber, 1976). Furthermore, in the preschool ages, reported by Buffery and Gray as those when males have not yet established right cerebral dominance for spatial function, Coates (1974) demonstrated *female* superiority in spatial performance. If lack of laterality were an advantage, one would not expect instances of female superiority. While one can suppose that bilaterality is advantageous, there is no independent direct or indirect evidence that this is so and some to suggest it is not.

Conclusion Regarding Buffery and Gray Hypothesis

The assumptions of the Buffery and Gray (1972) hypothesis do not hold up under scrutiny. While girls may have a verbal headstart compared to boys, it is not clear that left-hemisphere dominance for verbal function is established earlier in girls than in boys. There is no evidence of a linguistic device in the left hemisphere. Right-hemisphere dominance for spatial function probably does *not* occur earlier in girls than in boys. If it does, there is no reason to believe later lateralization necessarily means less lateralization. Contrary to Buffery and Gray, bilateral spatial function is probably not favorable for spatial performance. The Buffery and Gray theory is clearly and consensually rejected (Fairweather, 1976; Marshall, 1973).

LEVY HYPOTHESIS

Levy has suggested (Levy-Agresti and Sperry, 1968; Levy, 1970) that maximal intellectual functioning is attained when one hemisphere (usually the left) is specialized for analytical, verbal functioning and the other hemisphere (usually the right) is specialized for gestalt, spatial functioning. She attributed the purported relatively poorer spatial function of left-handers to a greater frequency among them of persons with verbal function in both hemispheres. She hypothesized that this bilaterality interfered with optimal specialization of the hemispheres. Later, Levy (1974) reanalysed her data and found that among her Caltech male subjects, left-handers were superior to right-handers in verbal performance. She then hypothesized that left-handedness had conferred a verbal advantage to them.

Levy has explained her view of sex-related cognitive differences in these words:

> It is interesting that the [spatial] perceptual deficit seen in left-handers is also present in females in general . . . . It might be that female brains are similar to those of left-handers in having less hemispheric specialization than male right-hander's brains . . . . It is hard to reject the notion that a spatial perceptive deficit in women is a sex-linked, genetically

determined incapacity, an incapacity which possibly results from hemispheres less well laterally specialized than those of males (Levy, 1972, p. 174).

Levy Data Base

Levy (1970) began her work studying commissurotomy patients. These are persons who have had the connections between the left and right hemispheres of the brain surgically severed as a treatment for very severe epilepsy. With these persons, it is possible to test the function of the right hemisphere separately from that of the left hemisphere. These patients are few in number, most of them are male, and all of them have other brain injuries in addition to the surgery. Nonetheless, studies of these patients have proven interesting. The hypothesis that strong lateralization results in maximal cerebral organization was first generated by her work with Sperry with these patients.

Levy then sought to test this hypothesis. Since left-handers are known to be more frequently less well-lateralized than right-handers, she tested the hypothesis with them. Using a sample of California Institute of Technology male graduate students and postdoctoral fellows, Levy found that the performance of ten "left-handed or ambidextrous" males was significantly poorer on the Performance Scale of the Wechsler Adult Intelligence Scale than on the Verbal Scale and that their Performance Scale IQ was significantly lower than that of fifteen "fully right-handed" males. On the basis of these two lines of evidence, from male left-handers compared to male right-handers and from commissurotomy patients, Levy formulated her theory and extended it to sex-related cognitive differences. (See also Marshall, 1973 for an evaluation of the theory.)

Summary of Levy Theory

Basically the hypothesis is that because women have more bilateral representation of verbal function and because hemispheric specialization results in maximal cerebral organization, females perform more poorly on spatial tasks. Specifically, it was suggested that right-handed females would perform like left-handed males who are more likely to have bilateral verbal representation. Later, Levy (1976) extended the hypothesis to suggest hormonal mechanisms. Let us examine each of the major propositions in turn; the hormonal mechanism will be briefly discussed in the context of the 1976 paper.

Theory Evaluation

Evidence of Verbal Bilaterality in Females

Evidence cited in support of verbal bilaterality in females includes (a) evidence that women recover better from aphasia than men, (b) studies of temporal lobe surgery on epilepsy patients, (c) studies of women who received unilateral electroshock, (d) tachistoscopic studies, (e) anatomical studies, (f) studies of naturally occurring brain lesions, and (g) studies of commissurotomy patients. Evidence from each source will be considered in turn.

DIFFERENTIAL RECOVERY FROM APHASIA. The opinion that females are more verbally bilateral rests partly on observations that females recover from aphasia better than males. Presumably right-handed females becoming aphasic due to injury to the left cerebral hemisphere recover better than comparable males because they have more verbal capacity in the uninjured right hemisphere. This line of evidence is very indirect, even if one assumes that adequate numbers of matched males and females have been objectively compared to justify the opinion that females do recover better from aphasia than males. Verbal function is often better developed in females than in males and greater adequacy of performance *before* damage is associated with better recovery from aphasia. Therefore, the better development of verbal function in females before injury may account for more complete female recovery. This explanation seems more plausible than assuming there is more verbal capacity in the female than in the male right hemisphere. In any case the latter inference is not a necessary one from the apparent fact of better female recovery from aphasia.

TEMPORAL LOBECTOMY DATA. There are data available from studies of surgery on temporal lobe epilepsy patients. For these patients, part of the temporal lobe is excised in order to reduce the severity of their epilepsy. These studies are particularly valuable compared to studies of naturally occurring lesions since pre-post surgery performance can be compared, size and nature of brain injuries can be more exactly determined, and the time interval between the brain injury and intellectual evaluation can be more exactly controlled. It was from these studies that the first hint of sex-related differences in brain lateralization emerged.

Lansdell (1961) found that left temporal lobe surgery disrupted the performance of males, but not females, on Gorham's Proverbs Test. From this one might infer that females have more verbal capacity in the right hemisphere. However, two later studies by Lansdell do not provide even this slight support for the proposition of female verbal bilaterality. Lansdell (1962) found a decrement in verbal scores on the Wechsler Intelligence Scale following operation on the left hemisphere, but did not report any difference between the sexes in the decrement. Lansdell (1968) also did not find a sex by hemisphere interaction for the verbal comprehension factor. That is, verbal comprehension decrement following temporal lobe surgery was the same for males and females.

STUDIES OF UNILATERAL ELECTROSHOCK. There have been some studies of depressed women receiving electroshock therapy for their depression, in which the shock was applied to only one side of the brain at a time. Using this procedure, performance before and immediately after electroshock to either the left or right side of the brain could be evaluated in terms of its effects on intellectual performance. Cohen et al. (1968) examined the effect of unilateral electroshock on the performance of twenty-four right-handed, depressed women. Shock to the left hemisphere resulted in a decrement on a verbal paired-associates task of 16.7; shock to the right hemisphere resulted in a decrement of 2.5. In contrast, electroshock to the left hemisphere resulted in a decrement on a visuographic learning task of 4.8 compared to a decrement of 9.5 with shock to the right hemisphere. These data suggest some bilaterality of spatial function but very little bilaterality of verbal function in women. There was no male group so cross-sex comparisons cannot be made. Inspection of similar data for both left- and right-handed males and females reported by Warrington and Pratt (1973) did not show evidence of greater verbal bilaterality in females.

TACHISTOSCOPIC STUDIES. Hannay and Malone (1976b) compared tachistoscopic results of females with those of males from a previous study (1976a). The females showed right visual field superiority for verbal material for the five-second memory interval, $p<.05$, while males showed right visual field superiority for both the five second, $p<.01$, and the ten second interval $p<.05$. From the facts that males showed left cerebral dominance for verbal function in two experimental conditions and at a more stringent level of probability, it was concluded that females are less lateralized for verbal function than males. No direct statistical comparison of the two sexes was made. The authors' conclusion that their data showed less complete lateralization of linguistic function in females is not well supported by their data.

Harshman and Remington (1976) cited one tachistoscopic study in favor of the proposition of greater verbal bilaterality in females (Ehrlichman, 1971) and one not supporting it (Bryden, 1965). Lake and Bryden (1976) found no sex-related difference in lateralization on a verbal dichotic listening task for persons, regardless of handedness, without a family history of sinistrality. For those with a positive family history of left-handedness, males were more asymmetrical than females. These authors reviewed data relevant to the question of greater verbal asymmetry in males. They cited the studies of Carr (1969) and Bryden (1965) as finding no general sex-related difference but trends of interaction of sex with handedness. Some unpublished data were cited indicating greater lateralization among males, but insufficient detail was given to evaluate whether the differences were significant. Lake and Bryden (1976) unsuccessfully tried to support the case for greater verbal bilaterality in females with data from studies of aphasia. One of the best studies they were able to locate was that of Weisenburg and McBride (1935). Of the nineteen righted-women reported by them, none had aphasia as a result of right-hemisphere damage.

Harshman et al. (1976) evaluated dichotic listening data for evidence of adult sex-related differences in verbal lateralization. Data from three dichotic studies were reanalysed by sex of subject. Pooling results from the three samples, the mean right ear advantage for females was significantly less than for males. (They estimated roughly one half.) The authors noted that not all studies report such differences and suggested that "sex differences are obscured" when a short term memory load is added to the dichotic task by presenting multiple pairs of stimuli in a single item. Hence they believe that only the nonmemory verbal function shows sex-related differences in lateralization. They concluded that still other factors may be complicating the dichotic response behavior so that "no firm conclusions can be drawn concerning the conditions under which sex differences in dichotic listening will be found." Their caution seems to be well-founded.

ANATOMICAL STUDIES. Data regarding sex-related differences in brain anatomy were cited by Harshman and Remington in support of greater female verbal bilaterality. The fact that there were more adult female than male brains with larger cortical speech zones in the right than in the left hemisphere was cited as consistent with the proposition of more verbal bilaterality in females. The difference was not observable in infants (Wada et al., 1975). Overall, the total number of women with reversed asymmetry in the sample of 100 was 10, hence the percentage of women involved was small. Statistical assessment of all right-left ratios would have been helpful in evaluating the extent of differences between the sexes.

There is no way of knowing how the Wada et al. results related to other factors such as handedness. Furthermore, since females are more viable, it is possible that more female infants with injury to the left hemisphere survive and develop verbal function in the right hemisphere. Because of their greater viability and verbal facility and the lesser expectations placed on the female sex, these persons might be more likely than comparably damaged males to merge with the general population and never be detected as neurologically traumatized persons. Such an hypothesis could account for some of the interaction effects of sex with handedness, and would suggest that left-handed females in the general population may have a higher proportion of neurologically traumatized persons among them. Hence the source of the Wada et al. (1975) sex difference, if replicated, may be linked to sex only indirectly. (See also discussion of handedness later in this chapter.)

BRAIN DAMAGE STUDIES. Findings that males with left-hemisphere damage score lower on verbal tests than females with left-hemisphere damage are cited as evidence of greater female verbal bilaterality, but these data are not convincing since males may have had lower scores to begin with. More direct evidence for bilateral verbal representation in females would be findings that *right*-hemisphere damage has a more adverse effect on the verbal performance of females than males, but such was not the case in one study (McGlone and Kertesz, 1973), though findings were in that direction. Similarly McGlone (1976) reported that the Wechsler Verbal IQ of right-hemisphere damaged males was 106 compared to a Verbal IQ of 99 for right-hemisphere damaged females (n = 17) in each group. Even if one assumes that the groups are comparable, the results again are in the predicted direction but are probably not significant (test apparently not run). Males with left-hemisphere damage scored lower on Verbal IQ than females with left-hemisphere damage. Left-hemisphere damaged males scored lower on Verbal IQ than Performance IQ, $p<.01$, while this was not true for females. These facts, however, are less to the point. Citation of these two studies does not exhaust the possible relevant data from brain-injured persons, but results of earlier studies were often not analyzed separately by sex nor designed to test for sex-related differences (Sherman, 1974). These two studies, however, present some recent data and serve to illustrate the type of evidence used to support this point.

COMMISSUROTOMY STUDIES. Other kinds of data that have

been incorrectly cited to support the view of female verbal bilaterality include studies of commissurotomy patients. The data at issue concern the difference, $p<.01$, found between three male and four female commissurotomy patients on their A/P ratio (Bogen et al., 1972). The A/P ratio is the ratio of appositional (right-hemisphere) to propositional (left-hemisphere) thinking. Appositionality was measured by performance on the Street figure-completion test and propositionality by the Similarities subtest of the Wechsler Adult Intelligence Scale. The commissurotomy patients used only their left hemispheres to do the tests. The significantly different A/P ratio meant that, compared to males, females were able to achieve a relatively better score on the Street test (a presumably right-hemisphere task) using only their left hemispheres. From this the authors concluded that appositionality (spatial function) was less lateralized in the females before the commissurotomy operation. That *spatial* function is less well lateralized in females than in males is not necessarily evidence that verbal function is less well lateralized. Hence this result should not be cited to support the proposition that females are less verbally lateralized than males as was done by Harshman and Remington (1976).

SUMMARY OF EVIDENCE FOR VERBAL BILATERALITY IN FEMALES. Though it is possible that among left-handers, verbal bilaterality is more frequent or more pronounced in women, at the present time data do not support a conclusion that females have more bilateral verbal representation than males. Some of the data are subject to other interpretations; some have been inappropriately cited; some have not been firmly established; and some are frankly contradictory. The contention that females are more verbally bilateral because they recover faster from aphasia, even if true, is subject to other interpretations. The temporal lobectomy data do not clearly support the contention. Studies of unilateral electroshock provide no support while evidence from tachistoscopic and dichotic listening studies are equivocal. Evidence from anatomical studies requires replication, more adequate statistical tests, and the ruling out of alternative explanations. Data from studies of brain-injured persons are not clear-cut and data from commissurotomy patients were inappropriately cited. In summary, there is no clear evidence that females are verbally more bilateral than males.

Maximal Cerebral Organization Hypothesis

The second proposition of the Levy hypothesis is that cerebral hemispheric specialization maximizes intellectual functioning, meaning best development of both verbal, analytic and spatial, gestalt functions. This hypothesis, while plausible, is not so plausible as Kinsbourne's (1974a, 1974b) description of interhemispheric interaction. Portrayals of interhemispheric relationships have underestimated the extent of bilateral interaction (see also Smith et al., 1977). As indicated earlier, Levy (1970, 1974) tested her hypothesis by comparing the relative verbal-spatial performance of right- and left-handed males. Since left-handed males more frequently have bilateral verbal representation it was reasoned that this would interfere with maximum development of their spatial capacity. Therefore left-handed males should show lower spatial than verbal performance and lower spatial performance than right-handed males. This expectation was confirmed by Levy with a small, select male sample as already described and by Miller (1971) (sex of subjects not reported). However, neither Briggs et al. (1976) nor Sherman (1978) replicated this finding with larger, less select subject samples. The results of Newcombe and Radcliffe (1973) were also not consistent with the hypothesis.

McGlone and Davidson (1973) found a lower spatial performance of left-handers compared to right-handers only among those left-handers with presumed right-hemisphere dominance for linguistic function. This finding, as Levy (1976) noted, is not inconsistent with her hypothesis. McGlone and Davidson tested the Levy competition hypothesis by comparing subjects presumably using the same hemisphere, whether left or right, for both verbal and spatial function with those using either left or right hemisphere for verbal function and the other hemisphere for spatial function. The results did not show that spatial function was poorer among those presumably using different hemispheres for both functions as opposed to those presumably using different hemispheres for each function, and hence did not support the Levy hypothesis. Results were unfortunately not reported separately by sex. The test is certainly a stringent one for the Levy competition hypothesis and one that Levy (1976) did not consider appropriate.

Levy's rebuttal (1976) of McGlone and Davidson made many assumptions about unknowns when further empirical tests could presumably better resolve these questions. She analysed the findings of McGlone and Davidson to show that the results are not inconsistent with a model of the inheritance of handedness and brain dominance (Levy and Nagylaki, 1972). This model had not incorporated sex as a variable. However, Levy (1976) suggested that the hypothesized cerebral dominance gene is differentially expressed depending on the amount of sex hormones, ranging from a little estrogen in XO persons to more estrogen in XX persons to testosterone in XY persons. Note that Levy hypothesized testosterone as more powerful than estrogen while Broverman et al. (1968) hypothesized estrogen as more powerful than testosterone.

Levy hypothesized that variation in presumed hormone strength would be paralleled by differences in brain lateralization and effectiveness of spatial function. The greater the hormone effect, the greater the lateralization, the better the spatial function. As previously discussed, assumptions about the differential effects of "sex" hormones are hazardous indeed. Levy cited data from sex anomalous persons to support her viewpoint. However, studies of XO persons have not reported testing them for extent of lateralization of function. It would be interesting to know if they are less lateralized for verbal or spatial function than XX or XY persons. It seems unlikely that Levy's line of reasoning will prove to be completely valid since some of her assumptions are not congruent with data on persons of chromosome/hormone anomalies. Levy assumed that the XO "spatial deficit" could be attributed to lack of testosterone. However, XO persons can have as much natural testosterone from their adrenals as estrogens since they typically have no functional gonads of either sex. (Mosaics can be an exception.) The "spatial deficit" of the XY testosterone insensitive person has been exaggerated, and the XYY person, who typically has normal testosterone, has poor spatial function. (See section discussing persons with sex chromosome/hormone anomalies and Table II.) Sex hormones of some kind are doubtlessly needed for optimal development, but Levy's construction is unsupported.

Left-Handed Males Like Right-Handed Females

At this point it is appropriate to discuss the general question of sex and handedness since, according to the Levy hypothesis, the cognitive patterning of right-handed females should be like that of left-handed males because both groups more frequently have bilateral verbal representation. That aspect of the Levy hypothesis is inconsistent with another often reported fact, that females are more right-handed than males. That is, if right-handers are more lateralized than left-handers and females are more right-handed than males, then it seems unlikely that females are less lateralized than males.

Some studies have found females to be more right-handed than males and some have not (Sherman, 1978). In a representative sample of 9th grade students, mean scores of females were *not* more right-handed than males while a difference between the means of the two sexes appeared in more intellectually select samples of high school students (Sherman, 1978). This raises the possibility that selection factors may be confounding results. If there is an effect, it appears to be that more females are extremely right-handed than males, i.e. more females do everything with the right hand. Interpretation of this effect, if it is ever conclusively demonstrated, is complicated by two other possibilities which have not been full studied: (a) that *extreme* right-handedness is related to brain injury and (b) that right-handedness is more encouraged and enforced upon persons of less status. It is even possible that the true sex difference lies not in right-handedness per se but in response to cerebral trauma. It may be that more females than males become extremely right-handed in response to early cerebral trauma. All these possibilities are merely possibilities and are mentioned to illustrate the difficulty in drawing correct inferences on the basis of the limited nature of our current knowledge of handedness, cerebral trauma, and brain organization. From this discussion, however, it is also clear that the Levy hypothesis cannot be rejected on the basis that females are more right-handed than males since this fact has not been clearly established.

Let us return now to Levy's contention that females are cognitively organized like left-handed males. As already discussed, Levy (1974) reported left-handed males showing a markedly higher verbal than spatial performance, a pattern associated with females. Others have not replicated this finding and Sherman (1978) did not find such a pattern in students grades nine to eleven. If females are cognitively organized like left-handed males, their cognitive intercorrelations should be similar. However, the intercorrelations among cognitive factors were very different for right-handed females and left-handed males. The correlations between math achievement and vocabulary, math achievement and spatial visualization, and vocabulary and spatial visualization were similar for the two sexes although different for left-handers and right-handers. Correlations were all very different for right-handed females and left-handed males. Handedness, not sex, was the determining factor in cognitive patterning. Males and females of the same handedness tended to be alike in cognitive patterning while left-handers and right-handers were different. Right-handed females did not show a similar pattern to left-handed males. Since left-handers are known to be more verbally bilateral and since the cognitive patterning for females (right-handed) was not like the left-handed pattern, Levy's view that females are verbally bilateral like left-handers was not supported. These data strongly suggest that explanations of cognitive patterning associated with left-handedness will not suffice to explain any cognitive patterning associated with the sexes.

Conclusion regarding Levy Hypothesis

This hypothesis lacks empirical support and cannot account

for known data. Levy's statement of her hypothesis was based on inadequate evidence. In so far as handedness can provide an index of cerebral organization, evidence from handedness studies does not support her hypothesis. Left-handers do not necessarily show a spatial deficit and female cognitive performance was not like that of left-handed males. These findings argue against the view that females are more bilateral verbally, an assumption essential to her hypothesis. An overall review of relevant data also showed this assumption to be quite unproven. The Levy hypothesis is clearly unsupported and the extension of the hypothesis to include a hormonal mechanism is also unsupported.

GREATER MALE LATERALIZATION HYPOTHESIS

Harshman and Remington (1976) suggested that while females start out as more lateralized in language than males, this is only because females are on a faster maturational timetable. Males eventually surpass females and as adults are more lateralized for both verbal and spatial function than are females. This hypothesis assumes that lateralization is more favorable. This position is similar to that of Harris (1975, p. 6) who stated, "some brains are further specialized than others for spatial analysis, and these 'further specialized' brains are more frequently male than female. More specifically, the difference in specialization is presumed to lie in a difference between males and females in the. *extent* to which language and spatial-perceptual functions are lateralized to the left and right hemispheres, respectively, with the male brain being further lateralized than the female brain. The proposed result is that in females more than males language functions are bilaterally represented, with negative outcome for spatial ability."

Let us now discuss the key propositions of this viewpoint: that cerebral lateralization is intellectually favorable, that females are more verbally bilateral, and that they are more spatially bilateral.

Theory Evaluation

Lateralization as Intellectually Favorable

As already indicated it is not clear that being more fully lateralized is advantageous for all aspects of intellectual functioning, though there is some evidence to support this view for spatial function (Waber, 1976). Kinsbourne (1976a, 1974b) pointed out that strong lateralization is important for output, e.g., speech, but not necessarily for input nor internal behaviors (thinking?). Even Kinsbourne's view may be an oversimplification since the actuality of normal speech may depend on the complex coordination of both sides of the brain, each making its own contributions to speech, the left hemisphere being responsible for control of the right side of the face and lips and enunciation of consonant sounds, while the right side of the brain has control of the left side of the face and lips, resonance and vowel sounds (Smith, 1976). There is evidence from commissurotomy patients that the right hemisphere does a better job with spatial, gestalt tasks while the left hemisphere does a better job with verbal, analytic tasks (Bogen et al., 1972; Levy, 1970). Hence type of lateralization as well as extent of lateralization may be important. Degree of lateralization as a general concept is probably meaningless.

Females Verbally Bilateral

As discussed in connection with the Levy hypothesis, there is no convincing evidence that females are more verbally bilateral than males, and some of the data cited to support this view are inappropriate. The striking difference between the cognitive patterning of right-handed females and left-handed males also argues against this view (Sherman, 1978).

Females Spatially Bilateral

There are several converging lines of evidence indicating that for females more than males the left hemisphere is more likely to be involved in performing spatial tasks. This, however, is not necessarily the same as saying that females are more spatially bilateral, nor can one infer that the brains of normal members of the two sexes are organized differently. It may simply be that more females develop a preference for a left-brained, verbal, analytic approach — the bent twig (Sherman, 1967; 1974). Harris (1975) discussed this possibility as an alternative and/or supplement to the view that the sexes are actually different in degree of brain lateralization. The evidence of greater female left-hemisphere involvement in spatial function consists of (a) results of experiments in which electroshock was administered to a single hemisphere, (b) tachistoscopic and other studies, (c) studies of patients given temporal lobectomies, (d) studies of patients with naturally occurring brain lesions, and (e) studies of commissurotomy patients.

STUDIES OF UNILATERAL ELECTROSHOCK. As discussed previously, the effects of electroshock on women being treated for depression have been studied. Evaluating women before and after unilateral electroshock, the women showed more deficit in performance on the Rod and Frame Test, a test of spatial perception (see Chapter Three), when the electroshock treatment was applied to the left hemisphere than when it was applied to the right hemisphere (Cohen et al., 1973). In fact there was a paradoxical tendency for performance to improve after shock to the right hemisphere.

Could this improvement be the result of permitting total control by the left hemisphere, i.e., eliminating interfering competition from the right hemisphere (Kinsbourne, 1974a, 1974b)? If so, this may provide some clues to the benefits of more complete lateralization, though researchers would not ordinarily construe lateralization of spatial function to the left hemisphere to be a benefit since spatial function is "supposed" to be located in the right hemisphere. The evidence for the greater importance of the left hemisphere to female than to male spatial function would be stronger if the experiments were repeated on male subjects so that female results could be compared with male results.

TACHISTOSCOPIC AND OTHER STUDIES. Females more frequently than males have been found to be more accurate in enumerating dots tachistoscopically presented in the right visual field, suggesting that the left hemisphere is more frequently of greater importance to spatial function in females than in males (Kimura, 1969, 1973; McGlone and Davidson, 1973).

An incidental finding of the Sherman (1974) study was that the performance of female subjects was less accurate when the frame of the Rod and Frame Test was oriented to the subjects' right rather than to the left, while the opposite was true for males. For the second set of eight trials, the sex by frame orientation interaction was significant, $p<.05$, and the sum of chi-squares for the first three blocks of eight trials was significant, $p<.01$. This finding can be explained by the hypothesis that the left hemisphere is more involved in spatial function for females, while the right hemisphere is more involved for males.

Rudel et al. (1974) found that girls develop more slowly in the performance of right-hemisphere-dependent tasks and that girls more than boys depend on left-hemisphere mediation for such tasks. Moreover, both left- and right-handed women performed more poorly than left- and right-handed men respectively on a spatial task of right-left discrimination (Bakan and Putnam, 1974).

TEMPORAL LOBECTOMY STUDIES. With temporal lobectomy patients, Lansdell (1962) reported that left lobectomy impaired judgment of design in females while right lobectomy improved their performance; the reverse was true for males. The finding that right lobectomy in females *improved* spatial performance is consistent with the finding from unilateral electroshock studies that female spatial performance was improved with shock to the right hemisphere. That is, for females, spatial performance improved without the *right*-hemisphere contribution. For males, however, spatial performance improved without the *left*-hemisphere contribution. Lansdell (1968) found that after left-sided temporal lobe surgery, females had lower scores than males on the Block Design and Object Assembly subtests of the Wechsler Intelligence Scale (spatial tests), while in the case of right-sided surgery males had lower scores than females, $p<.05$. The temporal lobectomy data of Meyer and Jones (1957), analysed in Sherman (1974), are consistent with Lansdell (1968). For left-sided surgery there was more spatial deficit for females than for males, $p<.10$; for right-sided surgery there was more spatial deficit for males than females, $p<.05$. Presumably the interaction effect would be statistically significant. (It could not be calculated because of the absence of raw data.)

BRAIN DAMAGE STUDIES. As already indicated, there are many inherent difficulties in drawing inferences from studies of *naturally* occurring lesions, and many of the older studies did not test for sex-related differences and were not designed to evaluate such differences. Two recent studies already mentioned explicitly tested for sex-related differences (McGlone and Kertesz, 1973; McGlone, 1976). Males with right cerebral damage tended to show greater impairment on the Block Design subtest of the Wechsler Adult Intelligence Scale (WAIS) than did females with right cerebral damage, $p<.10$. However, females with left-sided damage did not show significantly greater impairment on the Block Design subtest than males with left-sided damage, though findings were in that direction. Block Design scores correlated .63 with scores on the Aphasia battery among the twenty-two females with left-sided damage, compared to a correlation of .23 for the thirty-two males with left-sided damage. This sex-related difference in correlation is not statistically significant, but the direction of the finding suggests the greater participation of the left hemisphere in female spatial functioning (McGlone and Kertesz, 1973).

In another study by McGlone (1976), there were no significant differences for either sex in WAIS Performance IQ, depending on whether the damage was left-sided or right-sided. One would expect right-sided damage to cause more deficit in PIQ. In males, however, mean Verbal IQ was lower than Performance IQ for subjects with left-sided damage, $p<.01$, while mean Performance IQ was lower than Verbal IQ for right-sided damage, $p<.01$. No such differences were found for females. McGlone interpreted these data to indicate greater laterality of function in males than in females. These data provide only slight support for the specific proposition that the left hemisphere is more involved in female than in male spatial functioning.

On the whole, variations in type of injury, time since injury, and the difficulty of estimating prior intellectual functioning in order to match groups, make data from studies of naturally occurring brain lesions more suggestive than convincing.

COMMISSUROTOMY STUDIES. The finding already discussed (Bogen et al., 1972) from commissurotomy patients, that the Street-figure completion test was performed significantly better by the left hemisphere of female rather than male patients, is, of course, striking evidence in support of the proposition that the female left hemisphere is more involved in spatial function than the male.

SUMMARY OF SPATIAL BILATERALITY DATA. The evidence on the whole supports the view that for human females the left cerebral hemisphere is more involved in spatial function than is the case for males and that males rely more on their right hemisphere for spatial function than do females. But is this evidence that females have more *bilateral* spatial function? Not necessarily since it could be that both sexes use both hemispheres, but that there are more females who rely on the left hemisphere especially. This would be consistent with evidence, if firmly established, that left-hemisphere dominance for verbal function is established earlier in females than males, while right-hemisphere dominance for spatial function is established earlier in males than in females (Rudel et al., 1974; Witelson, 1976). That is to say, the sexes could be equally bilateral in spatial function (or nearly so) but in different directions. The fact that male spatial performance improved after left temporal lobectomy suggests that this view may be more accurate since the improvement suggests the elimination of an interference effect.

Conclusion Regarding Greater Male Lateralization

Evidence of the greater bilaterality of verbal function in females is lacking and there is no clear evidence that lateralization per se is favorable. The kind of lateralization is also important. Females appear to use the left hemisphere, verbal-analytic mode more for spatial tasks than males. This may represent a preferred mode of function rather than any differences between the sexes in actual brain lateralization. Consistent with the bent twig hypothesis (Sherman, 1967), more females than males may establish preference for left-hemisphere use.

LATERALITY AND SEX-RELATED COGNITIVE DIFFERENCES: CONCLUSIONS

Theories relating laterality of brain function and sex-related differences in cognition, notably in space perception, have been the focus of considerable activity in the past few years. The theory of Buffery and Gray (1972) can definitely be rejected. The Levy theory (1972) that females are like left-handed males can also be rejected, and the hypothesis that females are more verbally bilateral than males is inadequately supported. There are sufficient ambiguities in findings, however, to reserve judgment on the latter point. There does appear to be evidence that females use the left hemisphere for spatial function more than do males. This would not necessarily make them more bilateral in spatial function, but could constitute a difference in problem approach. We will consider this point further in the next chapter.

Chapter Seven

SOCIAL DETERMINANTS
OF SEX-RELATED
COGNITIVE DIFFERENCES

INTRODUCTION

IN a period when environmental explanations have been supposed to dominate biological explanations, we have found that biological explanations are plentiful and vigorous. Those writers who championed a biological view, thinking they were redressing an imbalance in the literature, were mistaken in their perceptions. Perhaps many persons simultaneously took the same attitude and redressed the imbalance quite thoroughly. In any case, it is now the environmental view that has been neglected. While many people assume that cultural factors do fully account for cognitive sex-related differences; theories, hypotheses, and evidence as to how the culture has produced these effects are not plentiful. As a result, we will be able to say much less on this than on the topic of biological explanations for sex-related differences in cognition. Perhaps, too, the nature of socio-cultural questions does not lend itself easily to the technical laboratory manipulations which we most commonly think of as scientific. Cultural effects are difficult to isolate because the investigators are part of the culture. It is like trying to isolate the effects of various fluids while swimming in them.

In this chapter we will try to capture the reality of what has been called sex role as it affects sex-related differences in cognitive development. Far more elusive than test scores, the dynamics of cultural influence have been but poorly captured in experimental design. After some theoretical considerations, we will look at how the sex-role variable has been handled vis-à-vis cognition in the literature of academic psychology.

The important topic of sex-related differences in achievement will not be fully discussed here since it is only partly related to the question of sex-related differences in cognition. It is encountered at a broader level of discourse. The reader interested in questions of achievement in women should consult *Women and Achievement* (Mednick et al., 1975) and, regarding women in the sciences, *Women and Success: The Anatomy of Achievement* (Kundsin, 1974). Articles and whole issues devoted to the topic have appeared in the journals *Sex Roles* and *Psychology of Women Quarterly*. Numerous new texts on the psychology of women also contain sections on the topic. Our discussion of sex-role expectations will concentrate on white women of the United States; expectations for other groups differ. For example, as an integral part of their sex role, black women expect to work as well as to have children (Gump, 1978). Having a child sends a black woman into the work force while having a child takes a white woman out of the work force.

MALE AND FEMALE SUBCULTURES

Some Concepts and Definitions

From the age of two or three, children know what sex they are (Money and Ehrhardt, 1972), and by the age of five or six, children fully realize that they will always be the same sex (Kohlberg, 1966). Kohlberg thinks that, knowing this, children then value the same sex more and try to do and be what is appropriate for that sex. They figure this out for themselves. Certainly theories supposing that sex-role learning can be accounted for by direct teaching, identification, reinforcement, or modeling are implausible, though all these processes can be involved. (See discussion in Sherman, 1971.) In fact, the female world constitutes another culture in which the meaning and interpretation of most details of life are differently shaped from the earliest years. This culture is usually described as sex role.

A role can be defined as the behavior expected of an individual occupying a given social position, e.g., teacher, student; doctor, patient. There are two parts to the concept of role, the expectations including beliefs and cognitions, and the enactments or conduct (Sarbin, 1968). The conduct is prescribed by law, by custom, by tradition; it constitutes the norm of behavior. Violation of norms brings social rejection, censure, and even punishment. (A recent example: having refused to quit her job, a female construction worker had her fingers smashed with a hammer by two of her male co-workers.) Freeman (1971) has argued that the model most appropriate to explain the position of men and women in society is caste, not role or class. It is possible to adopt a different role, to move to a different class, but it is not possible to change caste and, Renee Richards aside, it is not possible to change sex. Moreover, Freeman argues that "caste" more accurately reflects the status differences between the sexes.

Transactional analysis (TA) describes individuals as living by a script. Each individual has ter individual script, but there are also cultural, banal scripts. Among these is a script for each sex (Berne, 1972; Wyckoff, 1971). The script cannot be violated without causing depression; it has a kind of superego function, to use a Freudian term. Power and permission are needed to act in ways contrary to the script. The script concept has the advantage that, in comparison to role, class, or caste, it points out the powerful way in which these standards become internalized. However, since sex role is the term most commonly used in the psychological literature, let us continue with this term, bearing in mind its limitations.

The norms of our culture have never been meticulously spelled out. They differ not only by sex but also by age within sex, but our present state of knowledge permits only a dim view of what they are and how they operate. It would be interesting to get objective measures of the extent of resistance to sex-role deviant behavior. How does such resistance compare to resistance to other nonconforming behavior? Do we, as scientists, know which behaviors are acceptable and which are not?

Sex-role Characteristics

The most important characteristic of the female sex role is

that it is of lesser status than the male role. As already discussed, females and female stereotypic characteristics are less valued than males and male stereotypic characteristics (see also discussion in Sherman, 1971). Margaret Mead has pointed out that although what is defined as important differs from culture to culture and from time to time, whatever is defined as important in a society tends to be in the hands of men (Mead, 1958). Great, original intellectual achievement is one of the most highly valued activities in our culture and is nearly totally dominated by males. Fewer women receive the requisite training, fewer receive the requisite positions. If they have the positions, fewer receive access to important equipment, personnel, and funds. If they should achieve significantly, their work is less likely to be recognized, and often it ends up being attributed to a male. The norms against intellectual achievement in women function most strongly against outstanding, creative achievement. Findings that females are *more* creative than males have been ignored (Helson, 1978). Women working to assist a man in his work are much less severely sanctioned. These norms are in the process of changing and more favorable conditions for women exist in some places than in others, but it would be a serious error to underestimate this fundamental point.

Mathematics, for example, is one of the most prestigious of intellectual activities. It is no accident that it is also an activity stereotyped for males. Math is an excellent subject to use for selection purposes. Many have observed that math courses tend to be conducted more like elimination trials than serious attempts to convey knowledge. The female taboo against mathematics is sufficient that Lynn Fox (1976) reported serious difficulty in getting even gifted girls to continue with the study of math. Females, having "naturally" not taken math courses, "naturally" cannot enter training programs, and "naturally" cannot take jobs with high prestige and salary. We will return to the case of mathematics in more detail later in our discussion.

Through careful study, researchers have attempted to delineate the characteristics of the male and female roles. Kagan

(1964) has described the female sex role in our culture in this way: Females are supposed to inhibit aggression and to inhibit the open display of sexual urges. They are to be passive with men, to be nurturant, to cultivate attractiveness, and to maintain an emotionally responsive, socially poised, friendly posture with others. In contrast, males are to be aggressive in the face of attack, independent in problem situations, sexually aggressive, in control of regressive urges, and suppressive of strong emotions, especially anxiety.

In a cross-cultural study of sex-related differences in socialization among 110 cultures, 82 percent expected girls to become more nurturant than boys, 87 percent expected boys to achieve more, and 85 percent expected boys to be more self-reliant (Barry et al., 1957). Block (1973) reported similar findings for the United States and Western Europe. She found that parents, especially fathers, emphasized different values in rearing their sons and daughters. For their sons, assertion, achievement, and self-aggrandizement were encouraged while their daughters were taught to control aggression, assertion, and self-extension. For girls, the emphasis in the parent-child relationship was on relatedness, protection, and support. Sex-typing in the United States was found to be more intense than in Europe.

Maccoby and Jacklin (1974) discounted the possibility that socialization practices are very different for boys and girls. That is, they questioned whether parents actually treat their sons and daughters very differently, or differently enough to account for much variance in sex-related differences in behavior. While, as already mentioned, sex role can and does have an enormous effect even if it is not directly taught or reinforced, the conclusion of Maccoby and Jacklin is defective even in the limited sense of being an adequate evaluation of the socialization literature. Block came to a very different conclusion. On the discrepancy between her findings and those of Maccoby and Jacklin, she commented, "By attending to child-rearing behaviors frequently ignored, by using more differentiated concepts, by assessing the socialization emphasis of parents when children are older, and by including fathers in our studies of child-rearing practices, it may be anticipated that we will establish more precisely the ways in which sons and daughters are differently socialized by their fathers and mothers" (Block, 1978). Block supports her case with a careful and lengthy analysis, presenting much original data.

Thus it seems clear that norms in the culture are different for males and females. These norms are expressed by parents in relationships with their children. Of the sex-role characteristics mentioned, the most relevant to cognitive development would appear to be the emphasis on achievement and independence in problem solving for males rather than for females. The links, however, between these descriptions of sex role and sex-typed treatment of children and their performance on cognitive measures are by no means well-established. We could continue with reviews of sex-related differences in treatment from parents interacting with infants, from teachers, and peer influences. Sex-role stereotypic messages are conveyed by the pure absence of females and facilities for females, by the way language is used, and by portrayals of men and women in textbooks, literature, and the media. These findings have been recently reviewed by several authors (e.g., Stewart, 1976; Tavris and Offir, 1977; Weitz, 1977). Data generally support the view that males and females are treated and portrayed differently, but how could these differences account for sex-related differences in cognition? Since these findings do not directly answer that question they will not be reviewed here. Instead, let us first look at the general evidence that sex role affects cognitive sex-related differences, and then at evidence from studies of more delimited variables. Lastly, we will examine some specific theories and hypotheses.

SEX-ROLE EFFECTS ON COGNITION: THEORY AND EVIDENCE

Evidence of Cultural Variation in Sex-Related Cognitive Differences

If sex-related differences in cognitive functioning vary systematically with the sex-role prescriptions of various cultures, it would be evidence that sex role affects cognitive sex-related differences. There are several examples of such findings.

In the verbal area, study after study has reported that girls learn to read earlier than boys. Such findings were so frequent that they stimulated speculation about the possible biological basis for such a difference. Johnson (1973), however, has shown that in countries with more male teachers and different cultural expectations, male children do not learn to read later than female children.

In the spatial area, sex-related differences in cognitive style have been found to vary with cultural attitudes (Irving, 1970). Among the Eskimo, who allow their girls to go out with the men and boys on hunts, the spatial performance of girls was as good as boys (Berry, 1966; MacArthur, 1967). It has been argued that Eskimos constitute a genetically different group than white people, and that the absence of a sex-related difference among them reflects not a different culture but a different gene pool. This argument becomes increasingly implausible as evidence has accumulated. For example, it has been found that Mexican boys and girls differ even more in spatial performance than typical United States' samples (Mebane and Johnson, 1970). In Mexico, sex-role divergence is more extreme than in the United States. In fact, the term "macho" derives from Mexico and similar South American cultures. The argument that lack of sex-related differences in spatial performance among the Eskimo can be attributed to genetic factors is a much less plausible explanation than that the variation in the size of the difference can be attributed to cultural factors related to sex role. Findings of sex-related differences in two high schools but not two other high schools in the same midwestern city can likewise not be plausibly accounted for by differences in gene pool (Fennema and Sherman, 1977).

An extensive international study of Husén (1967) found statistically significant differences between the sexes in mathematics performance in some countries but not in others. Differences between countries in mathematics performance were very much larger than differences between the sexes. Lower scoring girls of one country scored higher than the higher scoring boys of another country. As in the case of verbal and spatial differences, these results indicate strong cultural influences on sex-related cognitive differences.

These results in the verbal, spatial, and math areas do indicate the importance of cultural factors and some specifically indicate the importance of sex-role factors in sex-related differences in cognition. These findings cannot be plausibly explained by reference to genetic or other biological factors. They do not rule out biological influences on sex-related differences in cognition, but they suggest that biological influences, if present, must be very small in comparison to socio-cultural influences. In the next section we will look at specific demonstrations of sex-role effects on cognition.

Studies of Sex Role Effects on Cognition

Verbal Disposition

In the United States reading is considered a feminine activity (Stein and Smithells, 1969), and there has been evidence that females are better at reading than males. Are these facts related? Johnson (1973) suggested they are and more evidence comes from two other studies. Mazurkiewiez (1960) found that reading achievement test scores were higher for those boys who considered reading a masculine activity than for those boys who did not. Dwyer (1974) hypothesized that children's sex-role standards would predict achievement test scores. She studied 385 middle-class, white children in grades two to twelve. The Stanford Achievement Test was used through 8th grade and the Iowa Test of Educational Development for grades ten and twelve. Multiple regression analyses indicated that sex-role standards contributed significant variance to reading achievement scores. Sex-role standards about reading accounted for between 1 percent and 8 percent of the total variance in reading achievement test scores even when the effects of sex, IQ, and liking or disliking reading were partialed out. The effect held true at all grade levels but was strongest at grade levels six and above. The variance attributable to sex per se was negligible.

Space Perception

Space perception is sex-typed male (Stein and Smithells, 1969). Relationships between sex role and performance on spatial tasks have also been shown. Nash (1975) investigated spatial performance (Space Relations Test of the Differential Aptitudes Test), sex-role concepts, and sex-role preferences in 105 eleven-year-olds and 102 fourteen-year-olds. The degree to which subjects generally stereotyped sex roles did not relate to their spatial performance. Stereotyping of sex role related to intellectual competence was, however, related to spatial performance.

In addition, spatial performance was related to sex-role preference. As a sex-role preference measure, subjects were asked: (a) "Is it better to be a male or a female? Explain." (b) "Would you rather be a male or a female? (If you could have chosen your sex at birth, would you have chosen male or female?) Explain." Consistent with previous literature (Sherman, 1971), significantly more girls than boys preferred to be of the other sex. At 6th grade level, age eleven, 40 percent of girls compared to 9 percent of boys would have preferred to be of the other sex. At age fourteen, 9th grade level, the percentages were 15 percent for girls and none for boys.

No general significant sex-related difference in spatial performance was found at age eleven. A significant difference at age fourteen was found for the girls who preferred to be girls, but *not* for the girls who preferred to be boys. Even in the 6th grade, comparing boys who wanted to be boys and girls who wanted to be girls, there was a significant performance difference. The general difference between the two sexes emerged at the 9th grade apparently as a function of the fact that now fewer girls wished to be boys. In the two grades together, girls who would have preferred to be boys performed higher on the spatial test than other girls. This difference could not be accounted for by any overall difference in intelligence. In fact, male gender preference was positively related to spatial performance for both sexes.

Another study in the spatial area is that of Naditch (1976)

who investigated the performance of sixty-four subjects given the Rod and Frame Test either under the usual conditions or under conditions in which it was described as a test of empathy, a task stereotyped female. She obtained a highly significant sex by condition interaction. Males did better than females under the usual conditions, and females did better than males under the empathy condition. These results indicate that the sex-role appropriateness of the task influenced performance.

Castore and Stafford (1970), however, were not able to demonstrate any change in the performance of either male or female college students (n = 462) when a spatial test was presented as masculine, feminine, or neutral. The test was the same under all conditions but was presented on blue paper as a drafting aptitude test, on pink paper as a fashion design aptitude test, or on white paper as a pattern test, the neutral condition.

Problem Solving

Some of the earliest demonstrations of the relationship between sex role and cognition occurred in the area of problem solving. Carey (1958) was able to improve female problem solving performance by a pep talk stressing that problem solving is appropriate for females. Milton (1957) showed that sex-related differences in problem solving were at least partially accounted for by the subject's sex-role identity. In a subsequent experiment, sex-related differences in problem solving were reduced by altering the role appropriateness of the problem content (Milton, 1959). Milton stated that tasks conventionally used in psychological research are often stereotypically masculine and that problem solving tasks should be framed "in content appropriate to the sex role" (p. 707) if women are to perform at their best. On the contrary, Kostick (1954) found that males did better than females in deductive reasoning even on home economics problems.

However, if the entire activity, e.g., problem solving, is stereotyped as male, superficial changes (as in the Kostick study and that of Castore and Stafford) may not be effective. A series of studies at Educational Testing Service has shown some evidence that the content of items does affect how the sexes respond (Donlon, 1971; Hicks et al., 1976; Strassberg-Rosenberg, 1975). However, the authors noted that this effect is probably much less than the deeper effects of sex-role stereotyping, e.g., influencing courses of study. Indeed, in their most recent paper, the authors suggest that norms be established by educational background rather than by sex (Hicks et al., 1976).

While efforts to insure sex-fair testing are extremely important (Tittle et al., 1974), sex-role influences at a deeper level need emphasis and further investigation. Differences in performance between the sexes can probably be traced to differences in course of study more than to any other single factor. In the key area of mathematics this is a very important factor (Fennema and Sherman, 1977; Sherman and Fennema, 1977). The much less complete mathematical preparation that Lucy Sells (1973) found among Berkeley female students compared to male students was confirmed in Wisconsin and has been noted nationwide. Angoff (1971) provided data from the College Entrance Examination Board which showed that 73 percent of boys compared to 57 percent of girls taking the College Entrance Exam had had seven or more semesters of mathematics preparation (Donlon, 1971). In order to equalize opportunity more thought should be given to requiring both sexes to take important courses at least through high school (Wesley and Wesley, 1977).

Mathematics

As in the other intellectual areas examined, sex-role effects have also been demonstrated in mathematics (Fox, 1977). In the reading achievement study already discussed, Dwyer (1974) also attempted to predict mathematics achievement test scores. Her subjects were 385 white children grades two to twelve. Sex role standards about arithmetic still acounted for between 1 percent and 9 percent of the variance in arithmetic achievement scores, even when the effects of IQ, sex, and liking or disliking arithmetic were controlled. The variance contributed by sex per se was negligible. The only significant differences between the sexes were found for arithmetic achievement at grade two and for arithmetic, all subjects combined over age. For girls, IQ predicted reading achievement significantly better than math achievement while for boys the reverse was true. These differences can also presumably be attributed to sex-role effects.

The effect of sex-role influence on math achievement in high school age German girls has been demonstrated by Schildkamp-Kündiger (1974). As predicted, girls overachieving in mathematics, compared to girls underachieving in mathematics, were able to imagine successful achievement stories in response to female pictures rather than only in response to male pictures.

Previously mentioned in Chapters Two and Three were some of the results of the Wisconsin Study which simultaneously investigated cognitive performance in the verbal, spatial, and mathematical areas and eight affective factors related to sex role and mathematics. These studies are reported elsewhere in more detail. (See especially Fennema and Sherman, 1977, 1978.) Some of the analyses and discussions, however, are presented here for the first time. Discussion of the sampling can be found in the Appendix.

At the high school level, small but statistically significant differences in mathematics achievement were found at two schools but not at two other schools. When the affective factors were used as covariates, the difference between the sexes became nonsignificant. At the schools where significant sex-related differences in mathematics achievement in favor of males were found, significantly more positive affective influences were found for boys for five of the eight affective factors studied. This was not the case at the other two schools. (See Table III.) What are these affective factors and how do they relate to sex role and to mathematics achievement? Let us now look at these factors in more depth.

Affective factors are those which deal with feelings, interests, attitudes, values, and emotional sets or biases (Krathwohl et al., 1964). The affective variables chosen for study were those relating to sex role which might have a negative influence on girls' learning of mathematics. A careful look at these variables

TABLE III

SIGNIFICANT SEX-RELATED DIFFERENCES[a]

(N = 1133)

	School 1	2	3	4
Mathematics Achievement[b]	X	—	—	X
Verbal Ability	—	—	—	—
Spatial Visualization	—	X	—	X
Confidence in Learning Mathematics	X	—	X	X
Mother[c]	X	—	X	X
Father[c]	X	—	X	X
Teacher[c]	—	—	—	—
Attitude toward Success in Mathematics	—	—	—	X
Math as a Male Domain	X	X	X	X
Usefulness of Mathematics	X	—	—	X
Effectance Motivation in Mathematics	—	—	—	—

[a]Significant <.05. See Fennema and Sherman (1977) for complete discussion.
[b]In all instances except Attitude toward Success in Mathematics, males had higher scores, more positive attitudes. For Math as a Male Domain, males stereotyped math more as a male domain.
[c]Perceived attitude of mother, father, or teacher toward one as a learner of mathematics.

elucidates the links, the mediating factors, between sex role and cognitive behavior. The affective variables were confidence in learning mathematics, perceived attitudes of mother, father, and teacher toward one as a learner of mathematics, perceived usefulness of mathematics, effectance motivation in math (a kind of joy or interest in math problem solving), attitude toward success in mathematics, and perception of mathematics as a male domain. A highly reliable, five-point Likert type scale was devised to measure each of these variables (Fennema and Sherman, 1976).

All of these variables are not only plausibly associated with mathematics learning but also with sex role. Manifesting less self-confidence is associated more with the female than the male role. Females have been found to underestimate their ability to about the same degree that males overestimate their ability (Crandall, 1967). Parental pressures for achievement, as already discussed, are more associated with the male than the female role. Parental and teacher expectations are acknowledged to influence learning in children. Since it is thought, even among college students, that females are not as good as males in math and science (Rosenkrantz et al., 1968), one can anticipate that these negative expectations are communicated to girls. Most fields utilizing advanced mathematics actually are dominated by males; thus it should not be surprising if females as a group anticipated less use for mathematics in their adult life. Interest in problem solving, effectance motivation, has been linked to sex-role expectations (Carey, 1958; Kagan, 1964). Attitude toward success in mathematics is derived from the concept of fear of success hypothesized as a negative motivational factor relevant to achievement in women (Horner, 1972). Stereotyping math as a male domain is an obvious sex-role measure. Each of these variables will now be discussed in turn. A sample item for each scale will be presented to aid the reader in understanding what it is the scale measures.

CONFIDENCE IN LEARNING MATHEMATICS. (Sample item: I think I could handle more difficult mathematics.) The confidence dimension has been related to mathematics achievement (Aiken, 1972, 1974). The Confidence in Learning Mathematics Scale was significantly related to math achievement in middle school students and in high school students. Correlations between math achievement and Confidence in Learning Mathematics were moderately high. The correlations were nearly as high as those between math achievement and the general intelligence/verbal measure, and between math achievement and spatial visualization. The correlations between math achievement and the cognitive and affective variables are presented in Table IV. Sex-related differences in Confidence in Learning Mathematics in favor of males were significant at each grade from eight to eleven (Fennema and Sherman, 1978). Dornbusch (1974) has also found high school boys to be more confident of their mathematics ability than girls. Table IV and the question of causal inferences will be discussed more fully later.

The concept of math anxiety has gathered much popular attention (Tobias, 1976). Math Anxiety can be construed as the opposite of Math Confidence and like Confidence it probably relates primarily to sex role and not to inherent differences between the sexes. It does not appear that females are more inherently anxious or fearful than males, but they are more willing (and permitted) to display their fears (Sherman, 1971). A Mathematics Anxiety Scale was devised for the Wisconsin studies. (For example: Math doesn't scare me at all. Mathematics makes me feel uneasy and confused.) The scale is published in Fennema and Sherman (1976). It correlated -.89 with the Confidence in Learning Mathematics Scale and a pragmatic decision was made to drop the Anxiety Scale. It was judged that a construct such as confidence would be more suitable in the public schools than the more pathological sounding construct of anxiety.

TABLE IV

CORRELATIONS BETWEEN AFFECTIVE VARIABLES
AND MATH ACHIEVEMENT

	Grades 6-8		Grades 9-11		Grade 12	
	Math Concepts		Test of Academic Progress		Test of Academic Progress	
	F	M	F	M	F	M
	688	632	555	574	34	70
Verbal	.51†	.50†	.49†	.47†	.30	.19
Spatial	.59†	.51†	.45†	.51*	.37*	.28*
Confidence	.38†	.39†	.40†	.41†	.47†	.22
Math as a Male Domain	.45†	.31†	.21†	.07	.22	.08
Attitude toward Success	.15†	.27†	.09*	.13	.26	.36†
Mother	.20†	.20†	.28†	.20†	.42†	.23
Father	.24†	.19†	.24†	.23†	.21	.27*
Teacher	.31†	.24†	.38†	.36†	.38†	.09
Usefulness	.24†	.21†	.22†	.25†	.45†	.14
Effectance Motivation	.23†	.23†	.26†	.31†	.60†	.27*

* $p < .05$
† $p < .01$

MATHEMATICS AS A MALE DOMAIN. (I would trust a woman just as much as I would trust a man to figure out important calculations.) A high score on this scale means that math is not stereotyped as clearly male and a low score means that it is stereotyped as male. The extent to which girls stereotyped mathematics as a male domain ought to relate to their mathematics performance since achievement has been found to be related to one's perception of its sex-role appropriateness (Stein and Bailey, 1973). At every grade level from six to twelve and at every school, males reported mathematics as significantly more of a male domain than did females. Females denied that math is a male domain. Because of differences found in favor of males on the other affective variables and because of enrollment differences in mathematics classes, this expressed opinion of girls is clearly not fully integrated into behavior. Since the boys stereotyped math much more, one wonders about the negative effect on girls' motivation of being in continual relationship with peer males who are not wholeheartedly accepting of females in the math area. Such effects ought to have been assessed by the attitude toward success measure. As we shall see, however, this measure did not show powerful effects. (An additional pilot attempt to measure fear of doing better in mathematics than a boyfriend was even less fruitful.) Math as a Male Domain correlated significantly with mathematics achievement measures especially for girls and especially in middle school (.45 for girls). At the high school level, the scale correlated at a lower level with math achievement, but it was still significant for females.

For the high school data, a principle components analysis showed an intellectual and an affective factor for both males and females and a third factor for females only. This factor consisted of Math as a Male Domain and Attitude toward Success, clearly a specific sex-role factor. In the Middle School Study, Math as a Male Domain loaded on the intellectual factor for girls but not for boys. It was the only affective variable to load with the intellectual factor for girls. (See Tables VI and VII.)

ATTITUDE TOWARD SUCCESS IN MATHEMATICS. (I'd be proud to

be the outstanding student in mathematics.) One variable that has been hypothesized as specifically relevant to female achievement is fear of success (Horner, 1972). In the Wisconsin Studies, fear of success was given the more neutral label of attitude toward success to avoid accepting some of the theoretical implications of Horner's view, e.g., that it is a motive, that it is a *general* motive, established early, quite stable. None of these theoretical implications has been supported. (See for example: Condry and Dyer, 1976; entire September, 1976 issue of *Sex Roles.*) The conceptualization of fear of success was translated into an objective scale so that large numbers of subjects could be tested and so that a measure with reliable scoring could be used.

In the Middle School and High School Studies, Attitude toward Success showed no overall reliable differences between the sexes in favor of males at any grade level. In fact, in some statistical comparisons, females held more positive attitudes toward success in mathematics than males. Sex by school interactions suggested complex relationships between social class, sex role, and attitude toward success. Attitude toward Success in Mathematics did correlate significantly with mathematics achievement measures, but at a low level and lower than most other variables. Attitude toward Success does not appear to be a powerful variable in girls' learning of mathematics at the middle school or high school level, though anecdotal evidence suggests the advisability of keeping an open mind (Fox, 1974, 1976, 1977).

PERCEIVED ATTITUDES OF MOTHER AND FATHER. (My mother has strongly encouraged me to do well in mathematics. My father thinks I could be good in math.) The attitudes of significant others have long been acknowledged as important to motivation and development. Among these significant others, the parents have been regarded as the most important, especially the mother. However, theoretical developments stimulated by the theory of Talcott Parsons have eventuated in a growing focus on the importance of father for sex typing (Johnson, 1963; Sherman, 1971). Although Maccoby and Jacklin (1974) discounted the likelihood of the differential attitudes and behaviors of parents as being important to sex-typed differentiation in children, their evaluation of the literature, as already discussed, contained many conceptual and empirical errors and other limitations (Block, 1976a, b; Sherman, 1975). Data gathered by Block (1973, 1978) are among the most recent and comprehensive indicating that parents, perhaps especially fathers, treat the sexes differently. For example, parents, especially fathers, were found to emphasize achievement more for their sons than for their daughters. Spence and Helmreich (1978) have also found that fathers' attitudes were especially important in girls' achievement attitudes.

In life history studies of female mathematicians, fathers have been found to play an important role (Osen, 1974; Plank and Plank, 1954). Data from the Wisconsin Middle School and High School Studies generally confirmed these expectations (Fennema and Sherman, 1978). Boys always perceived their parents as being more positive toward them as learners of mathematics than did girls. These differences were statistically significant at the 7th, 9th, and 10th grades for the Father Scale, but only at the 9th grade for the Mother Scale. (See Table V.) Both girls and boys saw their fathers as significantly more positive toward them as learners of mathematics than their mothers. Father appears to be the family math expert. This is consistent with findings that father was the one to help with math homework (Ernest, 1976). Both the Mother and Father Scales correlated significantly with measures of math achievement.

TEACHER. (My teachers think I'm the kind of person who could do well in mathematics.) There has been speculation that teachers influence the sexes differently in the learning of mathematics. There is little direct evidence on this point. During a pilot testing ($n = 367$), high school students were asked to describe what had discouraged them most about the study of mathematics. One third of the girls compared to only one tenth of the boys specifically mentioned a teacher in connection with discouragement in the study of mathematics, a statistically significant difference by chi square test. Although differences between the sexes on the Teacher Scale were not so

TABLE V

SIGNIFICANT SEX-RELATED DIFFERENCES BY GRADE[a]

(*N* = 2463)

Variable Grade	6	7	8	9	10	11
Verbal	X	—	—	—	—	—
Space	—	—	—	—	X	X
Math	—	—	—	X	X	X
Confidence	—	—	X	X	X	X
Math as a Male Domain	X	X	X	X	X	X
Attitude toward Success	—	—	—	—	—	—
Mother	—	—	—	X	—	—
Father	—	X	—	X	X	—
Teacher	—	—	—	—	X	—
Usefulness	—	—	—	—	X	—
Effectance Motivation	—	—	—	—	—	—

[a]Significant *p*<.05; all differences favorable to males.

consistently large in favor of males as with some of the other scales, the importance of the variable should not be dismissed. Boys perceived teachers as being significantly more positive toward them as learners of mathematics than did girls at the 10th grade level. The 10th grade was a particularly crucial time in this sample since it marked the last year in which most girls would take mathematics. Perception of teachers' attitudes also related significantly and moderately to math achievement measures, especially for girls.

USEFULNESS OF MATHEMATICS. (I will use mathematics in many ways as an adult.) Differences between the sexes in perceived usefulness of mathematics was pinpointed by Hilton and Berglünd (1974) as crucial to the development of sex-related differences in mathematics performance. Haven (1971) found that girls who perceived mathematics as useful were more likely to continue its study. In the Wisconsin studies, boys from grade six through grade twelve had higher average scores on the Usefulness Scale; there was a significant difference at the 10th grade. Usefulness correlated significantly with math

Sex-Related Cognitive Differences

achievement, especially for 12th grade girls, .45.

EFFECTANCE MOTIVATION IN MATHEMATICS. (Once I start working on a math puzzle, I find it hard to stop.) The Effectance Motivation in Mathematics Scale measured effectance based on White's definition of effectance as "inferred specifically from behavior that shows a lasting focalization and that has characteristics of exploration and experimentation" (White, 1959, p. 323). The importance of studying this variable is derived from the hypothesis that females are not so involved as males in problem solving attitudes (Carey, 1958). Problem solving attitudes appear closely related to effectance. This measure did not show significant sex-related differences in favor of males at any grade level. In some statistical comparisons girls showed significantly more effectance motivation than boys. Effectance motivation related significantly to mathematics achievement, especially for 12th grade girls, .60. This variable, however, does not seem to be relevant for explaining sex-related differences in math achievement. There is no evidence that females are intrinsically less interested in mathematics.

TABLE VI

PRINCIPAL COMPONENTS ANALYSIS OF
COGNITIVE AND AFFECTIVE VARIABLES[a]

| | Factor 1 | | Factor 2 | | Factor 3 |
	FEMALE	MALE	FEMALE	MALE	FEMALE
Mathematics Achievement	.83	.86			
Quick Word Test	.73	.72			
Spatial Visualization	.72	.78			
Confidence in Learning Math			.79	.67	
Math as a Male Domain				.48	.74
Attitude toward Success in Math				.67	.68
Mother			.72	.73	
Father			.62	.64	
Teacher			.75	.76	
Usefulness of Math			.71	.77	
Effectance Motivation			.79	.68	

Note: Factor loadings ≥ .40 have been included.
[a]Analysis done using as Ss students in Grades 9-11 at all schools.

TABLE VII

PRINCIPAL COMPONENTS ANALYSIS OF ALL VARIABLES

	Female	Male	Female	Male
Mathematics Computation	.72			.71
Male Concepts	.84			.83
R-W Comprehension	.77			.76
R-W Application	.87			.90
R-W Problem Solving	.87			.85
Spatial Visualization	.72			.66
Verbal Ability	.64			.61
Confidence in Learning Math		.73	.72	.34
Math as a Male Domain	.39	.65	.54	
Attitude toward Success in Math		.59	.53	
Mother		.79	.80	
Father		.74	.67	
Teacher		.79	.79	
Usefulness of Math		.80	.76	
Effectance Motivation in Math		.72	.73	

Note: Factor loadings > .30 given

DISCUSSION OF RESULTS. Before summarizing these data, some observations about the data in the tables may be helpful to the reader. First of all, in Table III, note that the sex-related difference in mathematics achievement occurs in conjunction with sex-related differences favorable to males in socio-cultural factors. Notice also that this relationship is more pronounced than that between sex-related differences in spatial visualization and mathematics achievement. For example, while a sex-related difference in spatial visualization was found at School 2, it was not accompanied by a sex-related difference in mathematics achievement. This suggests that socio-cultural factors are more primary than spatial visualization in relationship to sex-related differences in mathematics achievement. Also, in the Wisconsin studies, looking at the data by grades (Table V), a sex-related difference in math achievement occurred before the difference in spatial visualization. Though spatial visualization is involved in producing sex-related differences in mathematics performance, sex-role, socio-cultural factors appear to be of primary importance. They are probably ultimately responsible for producing both the sex-related differences in mathematics and spatial visualization when they are found. This point will be further discussed later in the chapter.

In Table IV, note the large size of the correlations between spatial visualization and mathematics achievement. These data underscore the fact that spatial visualization is strongly related to academic performance. Its influence is by no means limited to the technical areas, yet this skill and its development have not typically been part of the goals of the education system. In fact, it has been widely believed that skill in spatial perception is untrainable.

The correlations between the Confidence Scale and mathematics achievement are very impressive. Math achievement correlations with the Teacher Scale were also moderately high. In fact, significant correlations between achievement and attitudes can be noted for all scales. Attitude toward Success in Mathematics correlated less with mathematics achievement than other scales. The correlations actually tended to be higher for males than females. This scale may tap an anti-intellectualism (fear of being considered brainy) which is not limited to females. It may vary not only with social class but also with more subtle socio-political orientations. Anti-intellectualism has long been a feature of our culture and endemic to our high schools (Coleman, 1963). The correlation of .36 between Attitude toward Success in Mathematics and math achievement among 12th grade, male math students suggests that this factor bears further study as one generally limiting the attainment of excellence in American youth.

The correlation of .45 between Math as a Male Domain and math achievement in middle school girls is dramatic direct evidence of a relationship between lack of stereotyping math as a male domain and performing well in mathematics. The positive correlations for males become more understandable when one remembers that this scale does not range from math being a male domain to math being a female domain, but rather it measures degree of considering mathematics as a *male* domain. Lack of stereotyping in males tended to cluster with positive affective scores and high cognitive scores lending some support to the view that more secure males tend to stereotype less

(Pleck, 1978). The incorrelation tables are presented in Fennema and Sherman (1976, 1978).

At the high school level, the difference between the Math as a Male Domain and math achievement correlates for the two sexes was statistically significant. It is not clear why correlations between Math as a Male Domain and math achievement are so much lower in high school than in middle school. There was a tendency for high school girls to deny that math is a male domain; scores had less variability. One suspects that, though at one level girls said math is *not* a male domain, at another level this belief was not fully integrated into behavior. For example, fewer girls than boys continued to enroll in math courses (Sherman and Fennema, 1977). At least one study has demonstrated a discrepancy between verbal report and behavior in the sex-role area. Weiss (1961) found that although girls claimed not to mind competing against boys, in fact, they tried less hard against peer males than peer females in a test of hand strength.

Because correlations for students in grade twelve were different from the others they have been presented separately, even though the numbers in each group were not large. The decline in the size of the correlations between cognitive variables and math achievement among 12th grade subjects is, of course, attributable to the greater homogeneity of the 12th grade students. These students are an intellectually select group. The differences between the sexes in correlation are of interest. In six of eight cases, mathematics achievement correlated higher with the socio-cultural scales for females than for males. This suggests that motivational factors play a greater role in female than male math achievement for seniors enrolled in such advanced math courses as advanced algebra or calculus. The high correlation between Effectance Motivation and math achievement attests to the importance of this variable even though females, in general, scored as high or higher on Effectance Motivation than males.

Combining Tables III and IV, one can infer that sex-related differences in socio-cultural factors do adversely affect female math achievement. Indeed covarying out the effect of either socio-cultural factors or spatial visualization eliminated significant sex-related differences in math achievement.

Table V adds information about sex-related differences considered by grade level. These data help in making causal inferences. There is one anomalous finding. The difference in favor of males on the verbal measure in the 6th grade is probably due to a sampling variation and therefore will not be interpreted further. Of more interest is the pattern of differences on the other measures. From 6th grade on, boys stereotyped math as a male domain more than did girls. From this we can infer that females are likely to receive messages from peer males that math is not feminine and not where they belong, beginning at least in the 6th grade.

While significant differences in math achievement did not appear until 9th grade, differences in confidence and perceived attitude of father toward one as a learner of mathematics, as well as differences in stereotyping, occurred *before* 9th grade. These data suggest that sex role, acting through mediating variables, negatively influences girls' mathematics achievement.

In interpreting Table V (and other results) it is well to keep in mind that the sample of students becomes progressively more select after 9th grade. Grade twelve was omitted in this table and in Table VI for that reason. Hence the apparently greater equality of attitudes between the sexes in grade eleven should not be generalized to 11th grade girls as a whole. Those girls with less positive socio-cultural influences had probably already dropped out of the sample (Sherman and Fennema, 1977). Tenth grade is a crucial point since in this population 85 percent of boys and 80 percent of girls took mathematics through 10th grade. Note that five of the eight affective factors were less favorable for 10th grade girls.

Table VI shows that Attitude toward Success in Math and Math as a Male Domain emerged as a separate factor for females but not for males. In Table VII one finds that Math as Male Domain is loaded on the Cognitive factor for females but not for males. These findings also contribute to the complex of findings leading to the inference of the importance of sex-role factors in girls' learning of mathematics.

VARIABLES AFFECTING SEX-RELATED DIFFERENCES IN MATH ACHIEVEMENT: SUMMARY. Several variables appeared to be especially relevant to sex-related differences in mathematics performance. These variables probably all serve as mediators of sex-role influences. These include (on the intellectual side) spatial visualization, and (on the affective side) confidence in learning mathematics, perceived attitudes of mother and father toward one as a learner of mathematics, and usefulness of mathematics. Less relevant variables were perceived attitude of teacher toward one as a learner of mathematics and attitude toward success. Effectance motivation was not a relevant variable.

Summary: Studies of Sex-Role Effects on Cognition

Several studies demonstrate relationships between sex-role factors and cognitive performance, in reading, space perception, and mathematics. There is also some evidence that sex-role expectations for females negatively influence their cognitive performance. This aspect of the research, i.e., inference of a causal relationship, is most likely to be challenged and surely a stronger accumulation of evidence will be required before one can expect consensual agreement from those now skeptical. While effects have been demonstrated, the relative importance of various factors, their timing and interrelationships, can only be guessed with the state of present knowledge.

Socio-Cultural Theories of Sex-Related Cognitive Differences

The research already described was, of course, based on theory, typically low-level empirical hypothesizing about sex-role effects on cognition. In this section, we will first discuss a general conceptual problem and then evaluate some more formally stated ideas about sex-related cognitive differences dealing with verbal, spatial, mathematical, and problem solving differences between the sexes.

Masculinity-Femininity and Cognitive Functioning

Research relating masculinity-femininity to cognitive performance assumes masculinity and femininity are important categories. Lest the reader wrongly suppose that I am arguing for a unisex viewpoint, let me quickly note that there are two sexes, a fact no one can change. To question the importance of masculinity and femininity is not to question the importance of maleness and femaleness. It is to ask if personal development and indeed even maleness and femaleness are served by stereotypic masculinity and femininity (Sherman, 1976b). The sexual linkage of many behaviors nonessential to one's sex creates unnecessarily limiting conditions. Parodoxically, even androgeny perpetuates sex-typing because inherent to the concept of androgeny is the assumption that some characteristics are male and some characteristics are female. The androgenous person is then believed to combine both male and female characteristics. (Freud expressed a similar objection to androgeny.) It is far better to simply desex behaviors and characteristics not essentially linked to sex. Otherwise one's sexual appropriateness becomes vulnerable for all sorts of irrelevant reasons.

Let us take an example from another culture. In former times Chinese women had their feet bound because this was considered feminine. But suppose a woman's feet were not bound? Would we wish to say she was masculine? In the same way, being dumb in mathematics can be considered feminine for contemporary women in the United States. But do we wish to say that being good or outstanding in mathematics is masculine? Using categories of masculine and feminine provides the opportunity to stigmatize people for behaviors that would be better considered sex-neutral. There are also other objections to masculinity-femininity research, such as the lack of validity of the measures, but less thought has been given to the inadvisability of dividing behaviors into masculine and feminine and the acceptance of that assumption which is endemic to this line of research.

Verbal

As previously discussed it appears that females have a slight advantage in verbal communication during the first years of life. This conclusion has been provisionally accepted subject to revision if more contrary evidence becomes available (see Maccoby and Jacklin, 1974). Aside from the explanation that female infants are more mature and hence master communication skills earlier than boys, a social explanation has been advanced. McCarthy (1943) suggested that girls' advantage over boys in language development results from the fact that the girl "more readily identifies with her mother." Studies of early mother-infant interaction have sought to verify whether or not some aspect of this interaction could be responsible for the female advantage. McGuinness (1976) examined this question and came to a negative conclusion. Here is her assessment of early sex-related verbal differences and their development.

> No sex differences are apparent for the total amount ot vocalization, but there are qualitative differences. Males and females show similar rates of early babbling (Moss, 1967; Lewis, 1972), but over a period of time a much higher rate of vocal interchange develops between mothers and daughters (Goldberg and Lewis, 1969; McCall, 1972; Messer and Lewis, 1972). Lewis' study (1972) suggests that this occurs because of a complex interaction between the vocal behavior of the infant and the behavior of the mother; girls receive much less physical attention from the mother (supporting the finding of Moss, 1967), and they appear to be more comforted by "distal" stimulation, whereas boys require physical comfort, rather than speech. Although the sexes did not differ in their amount of vocalization, Lewis found that mothers actually reinforced more of the boys' vocalizations than those of girls. When he examined his data in terms of the mother's response to the infant's vocalization, he found that 50 percent of male, but only 37 percent of female vocalization elicited a maternal response. However, 67 percent of female vocalizations occurred in *response* to maternal behavior (despite the lower level of reinforcement which would follow these responses).

Mothers do not appear to speak more "effectively" to one or the other sex: in a complex series of experiments Phillips (1973) could find no difference in the number and complexity of words each time the mother spoke to male and female infants aged 8, 18 and 28 months.

McGuinness concluded, "In general there is little support for the idea that differential reinforcement by the mother could be responsible for the female's greater language ability."

Spatial Perception

DEPENDENCY. Building on the work of Witkin et al. (1962), Maccoby (1966) postulated that girls score more poorly on field articulation tasks because of their greater conformity and dependency. At that time there was very little evidence of an association between field articulation and dependence among females. Maccoby, however, thought that females were more passive and dependent than males, a view she has since changed (Maccoby and Jacklin, 1974). As mentioned in the methodological discussion of the Rod and Frame Test in Chapter Two, the procedure involves the subjects telling the experimenter to adjust the rod until it is vertical. This procedure could permit confounding effects related to personality and/or role factors. Persons who are either not assertive or who are in roles in which assertiveness is not expected, might not want to bother the experimenter enough to get the rod accurately adjusted. Thus an association between dependency and Rod and Frame performance may not have quite the meaning attributed to it, being essentially artifactual.

Evidence cited in favor of the dependency hypothesis comes from a cross-cultural study in which the sexes were compared for field independence between the Temne of Africa, a society in which females are treated as dependent, and the Eskimos of Canada, where women are in no way treated as dependent. Berry (1966) found no significant sex-related differences in embedded-figures tests among the Eskimos, in contrast to the Temne samples which showed significant sex-related differences favoring males. These variations in results can be subject to other interpretations, e.g., differences in spatial practice were not ruled out.

Other evidence that has been cited in support of both the dependency and practice hypotheses are studies showing that children who range farther from their homes have better spatial skill than those who do not (Munroe and Munroe, 1971; Nerlove et al., 1971). The authors interpreted the findings (as I do) as indicating that greater exploratory experience develops greater spatial skill. In view of the authors' interpretation and in view of obvious confounding with practice, it would seem unwise to attribute the results to differences in dependency. The finding is interesting since females do not range as far from home in many cultures. Actual documentation of "home range" for males and females of different ages in the United States is not available, but large differences would surely be found probably beginning sometime in the middle childhood. Also, differences in ranging have been such a clear aspect of sex role that attributing these differences simply to dependency, a personal characteristic, is also unwise. In any case "dependency" is such a catchall trait that its value as a scientific concept is severely limited, a point brought out in the research to be described next.

Sherman (1974) studied the relationship between field articulation and dependency in twenty-five male and twenty-five female college psychology students. Field articulation was measured by the Rod and Frame Test, the Group Embedded Figures Test (Witkin et al., 1971), and the Draw-A-Person Test (Witkin et al., 1954). Dependency was measured by the Succorance Scale of the Edwards Personal Preference Schedule (Edwards, 1959) and the Kessler Passive-Dependency Scale (Merenda et al., 1961; Merenda et al, 1960). Underscoring the problem with supposed traits, the dependency measures did not correlate well with each other and the field articulation measures correlated less well with each other than they did with a measure of spatial visualization. Females did not score lower than males on any of the field articulation tasks, nor were they significantly more dependent than males. (See comment regarding this research in Chapter Three.) For males, the two dependency measures correlated significantly, .54, and both measures related in a low negative, nonsignificant way with the field articulation measures. For females, the dependency measures were not significantly correlated, .13. Need for Succorance correlated significantly with the Rod and Frame Test performance, .51; the more need for Succorance, the poorer the performance. For females, Need for Succorance correlated near zero with Embedded Figures and Draw-A-Person. Passive-Dependency was weakly and nonsignificantly associated with better field articulation performance.

Data certainly did not provide convincing evidence that greater female dependency *causes* poorer female performance on field articulation measures. Any relationship that does exist, e.g., the fairly high correlation between Need for Succorance and Rod and Frame Test performance found for females, .51, may well be attributable to confounding effects of the particular procedure rather than attributable to an actual relationship between spatial skill and dependency per se. A relationship between dependency and spatial skill would seem to require some plausible mechanism of operation. It is difficult to imagine how simply being dependent would interfere with spatial skill, assuming of course that the dependency is not of such an extreme form as to qualify as inertia. If dependency is more than an artifactual factor, it may be through the limitations of relevant experiences. My colleague Corinne Koufacos commented that if a Greek man were lost in the forest, he would look for the way out; if a Greek woman were lost in the forest, she would look for a man to show her the way out. Certainly extreme passive-dependent habits would not develop cognitive skills. In the next section we will consider practice as a more adequate explanatory mechanism.

PRACTICE. In 1967, Sherman proposed that cultural sex-role expectations result in different experiences for the two sexes and that these experiences affect the development of visual-spatial skills. The hypothesis does not propose a relationship between femininity and spatial performance as has been incorrectly stated. This is not to deny the possibility of motivational decrements in dealing with a sex-inappropriate task. The primary focus, however, was on practice and relevant experience as an important, direct causal variable. Femininity or passivity (dependency, conformity) may be correlated with lack of relevant experience. In their extreme forms, they can be related to spatial performance in terms of motivation. In their extreme and less extreme forms they could be more distal parts of the causal chain, e.g., avoidance of performing tasks seen as sex inappropriate. Hence dependency and/or femininity could lower motivation or relevant practice, but would not directly cause lower spatial skill.

Note also that the hypothesis does not predict that males will always perform better than females in performance of spatial tasks. Whether they do or not is dependent on the general equivalence of the two groups and, most pertinent to this discussion, their equivalence in terms of relevant spatial practice. The finding of Coates (1974) that preschool girls (ages three to five) perform better than boys on a spatial task (Preschool Embedded Figures Test) does not necessarily contradict the hypothesis. As Coates herself suggested, the results might be accounted for by greater female maturity. In any case, sex differentials in practice would presumably be in process of development at this early age.

Coates made use of Maccoby's (1966) hypothesis of a curvilinear relationship between maximal intellectual performance and degree of passivity-aggression to explain the results. A medium amount is supposed to be most beneficial. The idea was that females are more likely to be intellectually limited by too much passivity while males are more likely to be limited by too much aggression. Coates (1974) suggested that at ages three to five both sexes are in the phallic stage and thus at this age females are more maximally aggressive while males are too aggressive for maximal performance.

Presumably all the rest of their lives until old age, females are not sufficiently aggressive to score as well as males on spatial tasks. In later years, the sexes have been reported as showing no difference in spatial performance (Schwartz and Karp, 1967; Cohen, 1975). Presumably in old age, females become sufficiently more aggressive to score as well as males on the tasks. The Maccoby curvilinear hypothesis is flexible enough to cover most circumstances, but while parsimony is much to be admired, accuracy is even more admirable. The variations in sex-related differences with age may not necessarily be validly explained by one hypothesis. Also, as Maccoby herself realizes, much more precision of definition and measurement will be needed to make this dimension scientifically useful (Maccoby and Jacklin, 1974).

The sex-typed practice hypothesis is hard pressed to account for either female superiority from ages three to five or the absence of sex-related differences in old age. While the hypothesis of sex-typed practice cannot account for all apparently valid data, as we shall see the curvilinear hypothesis cannot either. Let us now determine if the practice hypothesis can be demonstrated relevant to the development of male advantage in the spatial area. There are several aspects of the hypothesis to consider: (a) Can space perception be learned? (b) Do the sexes actually differ in spatial practice? (c) Could these differences in relevant spatial experiences account for findings of male superiority in spatial performance?

Space perception can be learned and improved with practice, though this fact has been widely ignored. This happened partly as a function of the historical accident that much of the investigation of space perception has occurred within the tradition of Gestalt psychology which stressed innate factors. Gibson (1953) made the general point that perceptual learning does occur. Since that time much work in remedial education has amply demonstrated the point. For some while, however, under the influence of Herman Witkin, performance on certain spatial tasks (field articulation) was thought to be uniquely different, measures of a special cognitive dimension.

Witkin erroneously believed that performance on these tasks was unmodifiable and uninfluenced by practice and teaching. Since that time, field articulation has been shown to be modifiable and practice effects have been demonstrated on the Rod and Frame Test (Kato, 1965; Sherman, 1974) and on the Embedded Figures Test (Goldstein and Chance, 1965; Chance and Goldstein, 1971). Body balance and spatial orientation training have been demonstrated to have significant positive effects on spatial performance, including Rod and Frame Test, for nursery school students (Gill et al., 1968).

Moreover, if sex-related differences disappear after practice, this is evidence that while males were at or near the asymptote of their ability, this was not the case for females. Such a finding would support the view that males typically have received more spatial training. Such findings have been reported by Goldstein and Chance (1965), Chance and Goldstein (1971), Johnson (1976), Connor et al. (1977), and Connor et al. (1978).

The Connor et al. (1978) study investigated 104 1st graders given a pre-test and a post-test on half the items from the Children's Embedded Figures Test. Half of the children were randomly assigned to a training condition and received a brief training procedure on visual-spatial disembedding prior to the administration of the post-test. Control children received no training. The performance of girls improved significantly more from pre-test to post-test than the performance of boys. Boys and girls showed similar beneficial effects of training in addition to the benefit of direct practice. The pre-test tendency of boys to perform better than girls was not evident on the post-test. The training did not significantly generalize to performance on another spatial task, Folding Blocks Test, though the effect was close to significant for girls ($p < .10$). However, pre-test score on the Children's Embedded Figures Test predicted the Folding Blocks Test score significantly better for girls in the control group than in the training group. This was not true for boys. Altogether these findings argue for greater change in female than male spatial skill. Further, the lack of stability of individual differences in performance argues against views of high heritability (Vandenberg, 1975).

An extremely interesting study by Coates et al. (1975) related play and sex-related differences in performing field articulation tasks in preschool children ($n = 54$). The original hypothesis was that field articulation would relate to amount of social play; however, the amount of time spent playing with blocks appeared to be the more crucial variable. As suggested (Sherman, 1967), boys were found to play significantly more with blocks than girls. For girls, the more they played with blocks, the better their performance on field articulation tasks. This was not the case for boys. Possibly the boys had already reached the asymptote of their skill.

Moving to an older age level, more data are accumulating

about the effects of different courses of study on spatial skill. Blade and Watson (1955) had reported large gains in spatial skill after one year of engineering study. De Russy and Futch (1971) found that a college student's success in locating the embedded figures was related to ter major subject of study — those majoring in science performed better than those majoring in liberal arts. Fennema and Sherman (1977) found that the sex-related difference in spatial visualization scores found in students at two schools was eliminated when one covaried out differences between the sexes in number of space related courses taken, e.g., drafting, design courses.

The study of Johnson (1976) demonstrated the effect of course of study on spatial performance, particularly for females who are less likely to be at the asymptote of their ability. Students in liberal arts scored significantly more poorly on the Embedded Figures Test than students in drafting or mathematics. At the beginning of the drafting course, males were significantly superior to females on the spatial task, but no significant difference was found after six weeks. At the beginning of the courses, women in drafting, liberal arts, and mathematics did not differ in spatial skill. After six weeks, women in drafting performed significantly better than other women. Presumably these women had not changed in their passive-dependency, aggressiveness, social orientation, or sex-typing during this six week period.

If relevant practice is the crucial variable, improvement in female spatial functioning can be attained by providing appropriate educational experiences. This approach is much more feasible and avoids excess meanings, i.e., improving female spatial skill (or mathematical skill) can be seen as just that, not as making women asocial, cold, independent, or masculine. It will be unfortunate if discussions of what "we know" about the basic nature of the sexes continue to promote these confusions (Lewis, 1976).

SPATIAL SUMMARY. Evidence is slowly accumulating that practice and training do affect spatial performance, that females are more likely than males to lack relevant spatial experience, and that females are more likely than males to be farther from the asymptote of their ability. These findings have profound implications for education and for entrance tests to various advanced and professional schools. Spatial items are included in many of these tests. The scores women receive on these items may well not represent their true potential.

Mathematics

Fox (1977) examined a theory common for many years: that boys and girls who identify with their fathers or a generalized masculine sex role are either better at mathematics than those who have a feminine identification, or at least are better at mathematics than in verbal skill (Aiken, 1970, 1975, 1976; Elton and Rose, 1967; Plank and Plank, 1954). Studies to test such an idea are difficult to devise because of the ambiguity of the concepts and difficulties of translating theory into testable designs. There is also confounding of various factors — "permission" from father to participate in activities not usually considered female and practice and training can all be confounded with identifying with father or masculine role, yet they are conceptually distinct processes. Identification theory, in general, as presented by Freud is poorly supported for females (Sherman, 1971). As Fox pointed out, identification with the father (whatever that means) does not necessarily lead to a masculine rather than feminine identification and conversely, high scores on masculinity scales do not necessarily mean identification with the father (Block, 1973; Constantinople, 1973; Heilbrun, 1974).

Empirical studies provide no support for the masculine identification hypothesis. Creative women mathematicians did not score high on the masculinity scale of the California Personality Inventory (Helson, 1971). Female math majors in college scored *higher* on the femininity scale of the Minnesota Multiphasic Personality Inventory (MMPI) than did female education majors (Lambert, 1960).

Carlsmith (1964) found that boys and girls whose fathers were absent from home during early childhood years had higher verbal than mathematical skill, presumed to be a feminine pattern. They have also been shown to have decreased quantitative scores (Landy et al., 1969). However, Landy et al. suggested not lack of identification as an explanation but decreased opportunity to interact with father. Ferguson and Maccoby (1966) emphasized that father absence creates stress and tension, lowering math compared to verbal scores for both sexes. Nelson and Maccoby (1966) did not get clear results in favor of either hypothesis. Thus Fox (1977) concluded that there is no "overwhelming" evidence to support the masculine identification hypothesis, an assessment which understates the lack of support for the hypothesis.

In the Wisconsin High School Study, data indicated that compared to mothers fathers were perceived as significantly more positive toward *both* their sons and daughters as learners of mathematics. Boys perceived fathers as significantly more positive toward them than did girls in grades seven, nine, and ten while mothers were so perceived only at grade nine (Fennema and Sherman, 1977, 1978). Of the parents, in some ways father's attitude toward learning mathematics appeared more important than mother's.

While father may play a special role in the learning of mathematics by girls, the collective data seem better accounted for by an explanation other than those previously presented. As will be recalled from the discussion of script, power and permission are needed to violate a script. In TA theory the cross-sex parent has unusual power in the formation of a script. A view emphasizing father's role of giving permission to violate the sexual script places a very different interpretation on the role of father vis-à-vis his daughter's learning of mathematics than the traditional Freudian view. In TA terms, father would be important in conveying the message "It's OK to learn math." and also very likely in conveying information "Here's how." Father's message would not be "Be like me" or "Be a man."

Problem Solving

Lynn (1969, 1972) has suggested that boys are more analytical than girls (assuming this to be the case) because the process of identifying with the abstract, culturally defined masculine role requires a more analytical method of learning sex role than does learning the female role through direct identification with the mother. Lynn marshalled a good deal of argument and evidence to support his thesis but does not deal with alternative interpretations or contrary evidence. At least one piece of evidence directly contradicts his thesis. According to Lynn's hypothesis, there should be higher correlation between cognitive development and sex-role development (presumably traditional sex typing) for boys rather than girls. However, Kohlberg and Zigler (1967) did not obtain this result. In general, Lynn's hypothesis appears increasingly implausible and framed in an outdated context.

SUMMARY: SOCIAL DETERMINANTS OF COGNITIVE SEX-RELATED DIFFERENCES

There is a good deal of evidence to support the theory that sex role directly and indirectly affects sex-related cognitive differences. This evidence does not rule out biological influences, but indications are strong that if there are direct biological influences, they are not incorrigible and they are less powerful than the sex-role factors. Much more research will need to be done before we fully understand sex-role influences.

Chapter Eight

AN INTEGRATIVE
THEORETICAL STATEMENT

PROBABLY the most striking conclusions emerging from this review are the trivial and fragile nature of sex-related differences in cognition and the flimsy quality of the theories of biological influence. Indeed, the cogent question appears to be not "Are women as intelligent as men?" but "Do we want women to be as intelligent as men?"

Nevertheless, it could be argued that though sex-related differences are small, some truly biologically based cognitive differences between the sexes do exist. If such a difference exists, the most plausible would appear to be female verbal precocity based on some aspect of the accelerated maturation of females. This precocity, if reliably valid, could bend the twig toward verbal, left-hemisphere approaches to problem solution. The bent twig hypothesis relies on the law of primacy: that which is established first is preferred and more firmly set. It is hypothesized that males catch up in verbal skill as they mature and as they are exposed to heavy educational intervention in verbal training. Much of this verbal training may be less to the point for females or even counterproductive, further emphasizing in them verbal, left-hemisphere skills. The history of education is thus seen as basically the history of how to educate males.

Since the bent twig hypothesis has been misrepresented, it may be well to state explicitly what it does *not* mean. The bent twig hypothesis (Sherman, 1967, 1971) does not mean that females have a preference for auditory compared to visual stimulation (Maccoby and Jacklin, 1974). It does not mean that because a left-hemisphere preference develops, the right hemisphere does not or cannot develop, as wrongly implied in Maccoby and Jacklin (1974), first printing. (Their method of testing the hypothesis was also inappropriate; see Chapter Two.)

The bent twig hypothesis suggests that verbal skill may be

sex preferred for more females than males. In addition to whatever bent may be initially acquired in favor of verbal skill, there are other important negative influences on the development of female spatial skill. Visual-spatial skills have been sex-typed male; they have been part of the historic male role which has commonly involved the tasks which require ranging far from home. As such, visual-spatial skills have been thought to be "naturally" acquired. Visual-spatial skills have been given very little attention in education or in research. However, these skills are probably maximally acquired only by males participating in relevant activities sex-typed male (and by those females who one way or the other manage to acquire the relevant experiences).

Thus, without awareness, and because of historic, cultural reasons based in biology, the male subculture has included activities which develop spatial skill. These include blocks, construction toys and kits, models, aiming games, and later chess. Males travel farther by foot, bike, and car. When traveling with a female, the male typically drives and/or leads, e.g., finds the way. Some school courses do involve spatial perception, e.g., geometry, drafting, art, and technical courses. More males than females take these courses, including those which emphasize visualization in the service of intellectual problem solution. The difference in course of study widens with more advanced training. Some evidence relevant to these points was presented in the last chapter.

Of the historic, cultural reasons based in biology, the most fundamental difference between the sexes is the greater physical size and strength of the adult male. This has allowed him to dominate. The second fundamental difference, one which no longer operates in the same manner as in the past, is the difference in reproductive duties of the two sexes. Historically these characteristics have also helped to shape the differences in the male and female cultures in that activities ranging far from home have fallen to the male.

There are many biologically based reasons for the development of that custom. In times past most women were either in a menstruating phase, pregnant, nursing, or dead. That is, few persons lived long. Far away from home, women in reproductive phases were a danger to themselves, their offspring, and even the group. The smell of blood attracts wild animals. One can imagine how welcome a menstruating woman would be in a hunting party. Most of the victims of unprovoked bear attacks in Yellowstone Park in recent years have been menstruating women. There have been good reasons, then, for the development of male and female cultures as they are, but they are clearly no longer maximally functional. Exactly how and to what degree these cultures should and can be changed is, of course, a salient contemporary question.

If there is a direct biological influence on sex-related differences, it is seen as fundamentally stemming from verbal precocity which bends the twig and is combined with many cultural and educational processes which, without our conscious awareness, shape the cognitive development of the two sexes. But what about the case of mathematics? Mathematics also involves the symbolization of spatial relationships, and it too is sex-typed male. Females are subtly and not so subtly discouraged and warned away from mathematics. Mathematics learning in females is adversely affected not only by the sex-typed practices which apply to mathematics but also indirectly through the lack of relevant spatial experiences for females. Mathematics is a fundamental subject which is *not* picked up at home and it is sequential. Losing out in mathematics education means losing out on many career opportunities.

"Aha," it might be argued, "You have picked the explanation that pleases you, but the fact is there are simply more male than female geniuses in mathematics." That there appear to be more male math geniuses is certainly true. Whether this is actually the case and/or would be the case under different cultural conditions is another question. As previously discussed, when careful studies have been made of genius, the conclusions have been that there are no true differences between the sexes. This fact, combined with the strong, negative cultural influences against female learning of mathematics, argues against the view that there are inherently more male geniuses in mathematics. Trying to produce a crop of girls precocious in math is like trying to get roses to bloom in a Wisconsin winter. In any case better mathematics literacy for females can surely be achieved whether or not they become geniuses. Perhaps here is an example of the need to change the script "one line at a time."

Yet another counterargument might be "But what of differences between the sexes in brain lateralization? Don't these differences point to a biological basis for sex-related differences in cognition?" Recent advances in neuropsychology have been extremely exciting. In hard fact, however, differences between the sexes in verbal lateralization are quite unproven. As reviewed in Chapter Six, it appears that females do use the left hemisphere for spatial function more than do males. In addition to evidence previously discussed, some additional support for the importance of verbal function (left-hemisphere) compared to spatial function (right-hemisphere) for females may be found in the factor analytic study of McCall (1955). He reported that verbal function was more important to female than to male intellectual performance. More involvement for females of verbal, analytic function in problem solving has been reported by Meyer (1976) and Schonberger (1976). Allen (1974) reported that though most women and men used the same strategies in approaching spatial tasks, more women than men relied on strategies that were "less mentally 'spatial.'"

Findings of female preference for left-hemisphere approaches, even if they prove valid and reliable, do not necessarily point to a biological difference in the brains. Females may use the left hemisphere more than males for spatial and problem solving tasks because the left hemisphere has become sex-preferred by the bending of the twig and by the culturally induced and enforced divergence in experiences and training already discussed. These serve to strengthen further the verbal, left-hemisphere approach and neglect the spatial, right-hemisphere approach.

Waber's (1976, 1977) research suggesting that later maturation favors both brain lateralization and spatial, as opposed to verbal, development carries a potential alternative or additional explanation for male supposed superiority in spatial skill. This explanation would also essentially rest on the female accelerated timetable of maturation.

Waber (1976, 1977) studied the comparative verbal-spatial performance of early and late maturing boys and girls. Girls were selected from ages ten to thirteen, boys from ages thirteen to sixteen. The final sample of eighty included ten early and ten late maturing boys and girls at both age levels. Waber found that within individuals and regardless of sex, early maturers scored better on verbal than spatial tasks and late maturers scored better on spatial than verbal tasks, $p<.01$. In the older group, but not the younger group, late maturers showed greater lateralization than early maturers. Waber argues that sex-related cognitive differences reflect differences in the organization of cortical function that are related to differential rates of physical maturation. Verbal performance was not related to maturation rate while spatial performance was, leading to the conclusion that sex-related differences in verbal and spatial skills "may have very different etiologies and cannot be explained by a common set of causes" (1976, p. 573). Waber is essentially saying that males are better at spatial tasks than females because males tend to mature later than females. Later maturation leads to greater brain lateralization and better spatial performance.

There are several questions and cautions in regard to Waber's work. Waber selected her early and late maturation groups from girls ten to thirteen and boys thirteen to sixteen. While this procedure would be adequate if one could assume no differences in maturation rate for verbal and spatial skills from ages ten to sixteen for the two sexes, her own data show that there are certain differences and these differences may have distorted some of the findings. Using only data for thirteen-year-olds to equate for age, verbal-spatial differences scores were related to maturational rate, $p<.05$. Nonetheless, it would be well to repeat the study including fully mature persons.

The Waber study is being cited as showing a relationship between degree of lateralization and rate of maturation. However, this relationship was not found among all subjects, only among the older subjects. The relationship was *not* with degree of lateralization of verbal function to the left hemisphere, but the absolute degree of lateralization without regard to direction. This fact makes the interpretation of the finding more difficult, and its meaning must await replication and further research.

There are also problems about the tasks Waber used. The three verbal tasks—Digit Symbol, PMA Word Fluency, and Stroop Color Naming—did not form a single factor. These tasks are presumed to be left-hemisphere tasks, but there is so much automatization in these tasks that one wonders how reliably they engage the left hemisphere. One would be more comfortable had a marker test such as Vocabulary been included.

Most serious of all however, *Waber did not find a significant difference between the sexes in spatial functioning.* What then is being explained? Moreover, Petersen (1976) did not replicate the relationship between rate of maturation and spatial as opposed to verbal skill. Perhaps some confounding factor accounted for the apparent relationship.

In addition, the timing of frequent occurrence of significant sex-related differences in spatial skill is not so favorable to adolescent hormonal explanations (the presumed explanation of the Waber findings) as has commonly been thought. The Wisconsin study did not show any difference between the sexes in spatial visualization until nearly age sixteen (Fennema and Sherman, 1977). Moreover, differences, when found, were associated with course of study. Strauch (1976) found no increase with age in spatial test score differences between the sexes which would be consistent with a hormonal explanation.

In summary, Waber's hypothesis is not firmly supported and seems unlikely for several reasons. It can certainly be regarded as unproven. While anything is possible and there may indeed be life on Mars, it behooves us to preserve an active skepticism with regard to such a socially important matter as inherent cognitive differences between the sexes. As scientists, teachers, counselors, and government policy makers, we must reserve judgment in instances of social risk to minority groups until evidence is very clearly established. A long history of pseudo-scientific abuse argues for the necessity of this viewpoint.

A thorough understanding of the cognitive development of the two sexes will surely await much more definitive research than has been reviewed in this book. While firm conclusions cannot be drawn, it may be worthwhile to consider the implications of the theoretical stance outlined which integrates existing knowledge into a coherent framework. That framework provides for a biological bending of the twig accompanied by cultural augmentation.

This theory suggests that research be directed toward a deeper understanding of how spatial skill develops in the two sexes. Development of training methods in spatial perception and their conscious introduction into the educational system are logical steps. Right-hemisphere training may be particularly valuable.

The viewpoint of "teaching to strength" is ill-advised. Such a view might suggest that girls be taught mathematics by a verbal approach. The opposite is being recommended. That is, girls (and others) should have more opportunity to develop their spatial, right-hemisphere skills. When learning to swim better, sometimes one uses only the arms and not the legs in order to strengthen the arms. Likewise, not using the left hemisphere and using the right hemisphere might be very beneficial to female development. One would not suggest that a swimmer with weak arms, neglect the arms, and swim only with the legs. Likewise, one should work toward strengthening female spatial function rather than merely expecting females to rely on part of their potential.

If the theory as outlined is correct, females are not inherently less cognitively able than males. Differences in experience and courses of study can, however, lead to performance differences between the sexes. These differences have been created in non-obvious ways and appear to be natural. If we wish equality for the sexes, equating relevant experiences for the sexes will be very helpful. This may mean requiring both sexes of comparable intellectual potential to take the same basic core of important courses at least through high school. Of these courses, mathematics is of particular importance. Requiring courses would leave less room for the operation of anti-intellectual peer pressure and lack of knowledge of the importance of the subject.

The theory also suggests that women do not need to become masculine to be successful in spatial and mathematical skills, they need only learn and practice the skills. The theory does suggest the advisability of desexing spatial (e.g., drafting) and mathematical skills. The desexing of behaviors not essential to maleness and femaleness makes possible a broader range of options for personal development.

At the beginning of this chapter it was suggested that the more cogent question is not "Are women as intelligent as men?" but "Do we want women to be as intelligent as men?" If this answer is in the affirmative, it is hoped that the theoretical position outlined in this chapter will point the way toward that end.

Chapter Nine

ANNOTATED BIBLIOGRAPHY

THE main theoretical articles, literature reviews, sections of books, and empirical research relevant to each hypothesis were annotated. Only the most widely cited, important, and relevant work was included. It was often possible to use the author's own abstract or summary. Where this was not possible the study was summarized by the reviewer or in some cases, the abstract is from another bibliography. In these instances numbers were appropriately rounded; probabilities > .05 were not regarded as significant, and probabilities were only given at .05, .01, and sometimes .10 levels. The citation was given first and then the material was factually summarized with any evaluative comments which seem warranted in the last paragraph. Evaluative comments vary in extent and thoroughness. All articles were discussed in the accompanying text. The bibliography was divided roughly by chapter content into the following sections: (a) sex-related differences in the variability of intelligence and X-linked hypotheses, (b) chromosome/ hormone anomalies, (c) metabolic explanations, (d) laterality, and (e) social determinants and bent twig hypothesis. Readers who wish to locate a particular entry may check the index.

VARIABILITY OF INTELLIGENCE
AND X-LINKED HYPOTHESES

Bock, R. D.: A family study of spatial visualizing ability. *American Psychologist*, 22:571, 1967. (Abstract)

A marked sex difference in ability favoring males is consistently observed for the first space factor. To test the hypothesis that this difference is due to sex linkage, the distribution of spatial ability among parents of index cases selected for high and low spatial ability were examined. Data for forty-five families revealed six families in which daughters of high ability had both parents of low ability. Unless attributed to misclassification of genotypes, this result contradicts the hypothesis of sex linkage. The data are consistent with the hypothesis that the trait is due to sex-influenced gene with frequency about .7 and 50 percent expressivity in females (author abstract).

Too little detail to evaluate.

Bock, R. D. and Kolakowski, D.: Further evidence of sex-linked major-gene influence on human spatial visualizing ability. *American Journal of Human Genetics, 25*:1-14, 1973.

A test of spatial visualizing ability was administered to parents and offspring in a sample of 167 families from a midwestern suburban community. Correlation of age-corrected data among family members identified by sex showed the pattern expected for a recessive sex-linked gene of intermediate frequency. The correlations, when combined in a weighted average with results reported in earlier studies by Stafford and by Hartlage, significantly reject an autosomal model for the inheritance of spatial ability. Nor are they readily explained by an environmental, or sex-limited, shift-of-dominance model. In addition, the spatial score distributions for a sample of 727 11th grade students exhibited a marked sexual dimorphism which could be attributed to homoscedastic Gaussian components representing proportions of 49:51 in males and 80:20 in females. These proportions are consistent with the hypothesis that spatial ability depends in part upon a recessive, sex-linked gene with frequency approximately .5 in this population. The magnitude of the familial correlations suggests that approximately 46 percent of the score variance is attributable to genetic variation from this source. A mechanism more complex than sex linkage may need to be posited, however, because spatial proficiency in Turner's syndrome and testicular feminization syndrome has been observed to be typically female. If substantiated for testicular feminization syndrome, this would suggest that the gene for spatial ability is both sex-linked and testosterone-limited in its expression. Also, the expectation that directional dominance is positive for an adaptive trait might not hold for a sex-linked trait if selection pressure were primarily on males (author abstract).

Bock and Kolakowski's statement that "spatial proficiency in Turner's syndrome . . . has been observed to be typically female" is the kind of inexact statement that is to be avoided. Since persons with Turner's syndrome often perform at a mentally defective level on spatial tasks and have been described as suffering from "space-form blindness," the Bock and Kolakowski statement could be readily misinterpreted to mean that such performances are typically female.

Bouchard, T. and McGee, M. G.: Sex differences in human spatial ability: Not an X-linked recessive gene effect. *Social Biology,* in press, 1977.

Spatial visualization scores were obtained on the members of 200 families. Large sex differences favoring males were found in both parents and offspring. Familial correlations, however, did not order themselves as predicted from the theory that human spatial visualization is under the control of an X-linked recessive gene. The results are compatible with a sex limitation and/or socialization theory of ability acquisition (author abstract).

Corah, N. L.: Differentiation in children and their parents. *Journal of Personality, 33:*300-308, 1965.

Witkin and his colleagues have presented data which demonstrate the degree of relationship between level of psychological differentiation in boys and their mothers. The present study attempted to extend these findings to include girls and fathers. In all, thirty boys and thirty girls between eight and eleven years of age were studied in relation to their parents. Embedded-figures tests and the figure drawing sophistication scales were the measures of differentiation used. In addition, verbal intelligence was assessed and controlled.

The results indicated that level of differentiation in boys is significantly related to that of their mothers but not to that of their fathers. Conversely, level of differentiation in girls was significantly related to that of their fathers but not to that of their mothers. Implications of the role of the opposite-sexed parent for fostering differentiation in the child were discussed (author abstract).

Level of differentiation refers to performance on a type of spatial task, embedded-figures, related to but not quite the same as spatial visualization. "Differentiation," also known as field independence or analytical cognitive approach has been considered a skill favoring males. While it was not mentioned in the summary, clear sex-related differences were not found in this study. In fact, some findings favored females. There was no difference between boys and girls on the Embedded-Figures Test and girls did better than boys on the figure drawing, $p<.05$. Fathers scored higher than mothers on embedded-figures, $p<.01$, while there was no difference between mothers and fathers on figure drawing. Actual intrafamilial correlations for the Embedded-Figures Test which have been cited as supporting the X-linked hypothesis (though not by Corah) were: Mother-son, .31; father-daughter, .28; mother-daughter, .02; father-son, .18. As can be seen, correspondence to prediction is very approximate; the mother-daughter correlation is too low and the father-son correlation too high. The way in which the summary neglected to mention sex-related differences favoring females and the failure to find differences favoring males, provides a small illustration of how bias enters the research literature. Probably because these findings were not in the summary, other investigators did not notice them. They are not reported in Maccoby (1966), for example. Occurrences such as these have helped researchers to overestimate the extent and reliability of differences between the sexes in space perception. It is also to be noted that the findings in support of the X-linked hypothesis are very weak and that the author interpreted the results as suggesting cross-sex socialization effects.

DeFries, J. C.; Ashton, G. C.; Johnson, R. C.; Kuse, A. R.; McClearn, G. E.; Mi, M. P.; Rashad, M. N.; Vandenberg, S. G.; and Wilson, J. R.: Parent-offspring resemblance for specific cognitive abilities in two ethnic groups. *Nature, 261*:131-133, 1976.

Investigated familial factors in mental ability for fifteen cognitive variables, various environmental indices, blood group, and enzyme systems. Only results relevant to the X-linked hypothesis are summarized here. 739 American families of European ancestry and 244 American families of Japanese ancestry in Hawaii were studied. Children included were thirteen or more years of age. Data were age corrected by a z-score banding technique. The results of correlations involving individual test of spatial ability (mental rotations, "lines and dots," card rotations, hidden patterns, paper form board), the spatial factor scores, and progressive matrices did not support the hypothesis that spatial ability is influenced by an X-linked gene.

Guttman, R.: Genetic analysis of analytical spatial ability: Raven's Progressive Matrices. *Behavior Genetics, 4*:273-283, 1974.

The Raven Progressive Matrices test was administered to members of 100 families, including parents, children, and first cousins. Scores varied with age and sex; males' scores were consistently higher than females'. Midparent:child correlations of scores were zero for subtests A and B, 0.19 for C, 0.30 for D, 0.22 for E, and 0.41 for the total test score. Between-mate correlations ranged from zero to 0.30 on the different subtests. Full-sib intraclass correlations were 0.14, 0.09, 0.19, 0.18, 0.30, and 0.22; first-cousin correlations were lower but had the same relative order of size. In an analysis of the thirty-six individual items of subtests C, D, and E, correlations were found to increase with difficulty. Twelve items gave parent:offspring correlations of 0.2 and higher. Of these, one item, E-8, had a father:son, father:daughter, mother:son, mother:daughter correlational pattern in accordance with a hypothesis of X-linkage. Differences in levels and/or patterns of intrafamily correlations may sometimes discriminate between items that test different aspects of the problem-solving process. It is suggested that a genetic analysis of a battery of items which are especially designed to test specific elements of this process could lead to the definition of specific abilities and to an elucidation of the mode of inheritance of some of these abilities (author abstract).

This paper is misleadingly titled and cited. Raven's Progressive Matrices is not primarily a spatial measure as it loads primarily on the verbal factor. The intent of this paper is to *use* the presumably established X-linked inheritance of spatial ability to differentiate items of greater or lesser heritability. The finding of one of sixty items with correlations conforming to X-linked predictions capitalizes on random error and in no way constitutes positive evidence for the X-linked hypothesis.

Hartlage, L. C.: Sex-linked inheritance of spatial ability. *Perceptual and Motor Skills, 31:*610, 1970.

100 Ss, representing 25 families containing all combinations of father-son, father-daughter, mother-son, and mother-daughter pairs were administered the space section of the Differential Aptitude Test (DAT; Bennett, Seashore, & Wesman, 1947). Minimum age was sixteen years and maximum age was fifty-six. Correlations were computed between scores on the DAT for all father-daughter, father-son, mother-son, and mother-daughter pairs.

Mean DAT space scores were sixty-one for fathers, fifty-four for sons, fifty for daughters, and forty-eight for mothers. Highest Pearsonian rs occurred between mothers and sons ($r = .39$, $p<.025$) and fathers and daughters ($r = .34$, $p<.05$). Lower and nonsignificant values were obtained between mothers and daughters ($r = .25$) and between fathers and sons ($r = .18$). These figures are similar to Stafford's estimates, .31 for father-daughter and mother-son pairs (author abstract).

Lehrke, R.: A theory of X-linkage of major intellectual traits. *American Journal of Mental Deficiency, 76:*611-619, 1972.

It was hypothesized that major genes relating to intelligence are located on the X-chromosome. Apparently these genes relate to certain verbal abilities and to perception of spatial relationships. X-linkage of such traits would result in the greater male variability, which has long been noted. This, in turn, can explain several puzzling situations, including the substantially greater numbers of males with mental retardation and learning disorders. It could also explain, at least in part, why more males than females are found in occupations requiring the highest levels of intellect. Deleterious alleles of these genes can result in mental retardation that is obviously transmitted as a sex-linked recessive; or, in less extreme form, they can be an important element in cultural-familial (multiple-gene) retardation. It was estimated that 25 to 50 percent of all retardation is due to X-linked genes (author abstract).

Hypothesis of X-linkage for verbal and/or spatial abilities does not have empirical support. Lehrke (1974) contains more detail about X-linkage of mental deficiency in some families.

Maccoby, E. E. and Jacklin, C. N.: *The Psychology of Sex Differences.* Stanford, California, Stanford U Pr, 1974, pp. 114-120.

Authors noted the difficulty of assessing sex-related differences in variability in partially self-selected groups such as used by Terman in his studies of genius. They cited an earlier conclusion of Miles, Terman, and Tyler to the effect that there is no consistent tendency toward a higher incidence of gifted boys, and that the sex ratio in the gifted range depends on the content of the test. Recent studies of specific cognitive skills were surveyed for evidence of differences in variability. For verbal ability, it was concluded that "the studies do not provide firm support for the hypothesis that males are more variable, although the trend is in that direction for subjects 12 years or older." On the other hand they found "some evidence for greater male variability in numerical and spatial abilities." They presented evidence to indicate that there may well be many more male mental defectives than female because of greater male vulnerability. At least in respect to mathematics, however, they concluded that there were not only more males at the low end of the distribution, but also, relying on the work of Stanley, Keating, and Fox at Johns Hopkins, at the high end of the distribution. Reviewed evidence related to X-linked hypothesis of spatial ability concluded, "there is at least some degree· of sex-linked genetic control over spatial ability" (p. 121).

This conclusion was premature. X-linked hypothesis of mathematical problem solving was not mentioned. While Maccoby and Jacklin recognized the possible role of selection factors, they unfortunately have not applied this insight to their own analysis of the research literature. The data they have used to evaluate the variability hypothesis are not appropriate because of likely biases in selection factors.

Sherman, J. and Fennema, F.: Distribution of spatial visualization and mathematical problem solving scores: A test of Stafford's X-linked hypotheses. *Psychology of Women Quarterly,* in press, 1978.

This study investigated distribution of spatial visualization scores (Space Relations test of the Differential Aptitude Test) and mathematical problem solving scores (Mental Arithmetic Problems) obtained by 161 male and 152 female, 9th grade, white students for fit to the distributions predicted by the X-linked hypotheses of recessive inheritance of these skills. Data did not support the X-linked hypotheses. No significant sex-related differences were found between mean scores of tests of spatial visualization or mathematical problem solving (author abstract).

Stafford, R. E.: An investigation of similarities in parent-child test scores for evidence of heredity components. Doctoral dissertation, Princeton, Princeton University, 1963. *Dissertation Abstracts International, 11*:4785-4786, 1964. (University Microfilms, No. 64-2713.)

The general hypothesis of this study states that certain psychological traits which have their scores distributed continuously may actually have an underlying genetic dichotomy which is masked by various other effects. To be more precise, three specific hypotheses state for each variable that: (1) there is a similarity between parents and their children unexplained by similarity between parents; (2) this similarity may be explained by hereditary components; and (3) these hereditary components are of the discrete or segregated type of inheritance.

The population, consisting of 104 fathers and mothers and their teenage sons or daughters, was given eight psychological tests; Symbol Comparison, Word Association, Mental Arithmetic, Pitch Discrimination, Letter Concepts, Spelling, Identical Blocks, and English Vocabulary. Self-reports of height and weight were also obtained. These data were analyzed both by correlational methods and dichotomic analysis. The latter is a new method designed for this study.

Parent-child correlations have previously been inadequate for investigating the presence of hereditary components in mental tests, because it is impossible to assess the degree to which the correlations are due to environmental effects. However, the transmission of a trait determined by a gene located on the X chromosome results in a unique pattern of family correlation coefficients.

Dichotomic analysis is essentially an arbitrary quartering of a bivariate distribution of parent-child scores by a successive series of artificial divisions in the continuous distributions. The frequencies observed by these arbitrary quarterings may be compared to the theoretical expected genetic frequencies by a series of chi-square goodness-of-fit tests. Should a "good fit" be found at one of the artificial divisions in the bivariate distribution of the father-son scores and at approximately the same artificial division in the bivariate distribution of the mother-daughter scores, then an underlying dichotomy would be assumed.

To test the first hypothesis stated above, correlations between family members for each variable in the study were obtained from standard scores which partialed out the age differences in the raw scores. From these correlations, it was observed that there was only one variable, word association, which did not show a significant similarity between at least one of the parents and one of their offspring. Two of the variables, English vocabulary and height, showed a highly significant correlation between fathers and mothers which negated the second part of the first hypothesis.

The second hypothesis was accepted because two variables, spatial visualization as measured by the Identical Blocks Test and a general reasoning ability as measured by the Mental Arithmetic Test, showed a unique family correlation pattern which indicated that they have a sex-linked recessive hereditary component. Although the two tests have some variance in common, inspection of the mothers' and sons' test scores suggested that each test has an independent hereditary unit on the X chromosome.

To test the third hypothesis, each variable was subjected to dichotomic analysis. Only the Symbol Comparison Test of perceptual speed and the Pitch Discrimination Test, a measure of musical aptitude, gave clear evidence of fulfilling the requirement that the best fit to the genetic model was approximately the same hypothesized dichotomy for the father-son distribution of scores as it was for the mother-daughter distribution of scores. The Letter Concepts Test of inductive reasoning showed a possiblity of having an underlying dichotomy, but none of the remaining variables showed any evidence of an underlying dichotomy for both father-son and mother-daughter distributions (author abstract).

The obtained correlations were said to conform to those expected with a gene frequency of .20. Later Bock and Kolakowski (1973) found them consistent with a gene frequency of .50. Tests of significance between correlations were not reported. The dissertation contains the most complete account of Stafford's procedure and data.

Stafford, R. E.: Spatial visualization and quantitative reasoning: One gene or two? Paper presented at the meeting of the Eastern Psychological Association, Atlantic City, New Jersey, April 1965.

Presented data from 1963 dissertation of intrafamilial correlations for Mental Arithmetic test and Identical Blocks test. Also compared performance on these tests of fifty mothers with their teen-age sons. Mothers and sons who were above average on one ability were not above average on both, hence the conclusion that the abilities are independent, manifested by two genes. Correlations for monozygous twins among PMA Number, Kohs Blocks, and PMA Space were presented. Correlations between the latter two were higher than between PMA Number and either of the spatial tests. This finding was interpreted as supporting the likelihood of two separate genes on the X chromosome, one affecting spatial visualization and the other affecting quantitative reasoning.

Neither data nor rationale was presented in sufficient detail to evaluate. Author did not adequately support his case.

Stafford, R. E.: Bimodal distribution of "true scores" by twins on the Differential Aptitude Tests. *Perceptual and Motor Skills, 23*:470, 1966.

The Differential Aptitude Tests, Form A, were administered to 111 pairs of monozygotic twins as part of a larger study. Age differences were partialled out by using standard scores. The standard scores for each pair of monozygotic twins were averaged and their distribution plotted. Bimodality was also seen for mean monozygotic standard scores for Verbal Reasoning, Space Relations, and somewhat less clearly for Spelling, Language, Clerical Speed, and Accuracy. There was no discernible bimodality for scores on Abstract Reasoning, Numerical Ability, or Mechanical Reasoning. It appears that this evidence supports the idea that certain traits have an underlying dichotomy, possibly dependent upon a single pair of genes (quote from article).

Without presentation of more data and/or statistical tests, it is impossible to evaluate this report.

Stafford, R. E.: Hereditary and environmental components of quantitative reasoning. *Review of Educational Research, 42*:183-201, 1972.

Reviews relevant evidence and concludes that "there is an underlying hereditary component for a proficiency in quantitative reasoning which fits the sex-linked recessive model fairly well. . . . We . . . cannot discount the very important interaction effects of the environment (such as home life, choice of school, adequacy of teacher, proper attitude, and family support) with genetic endowment which result in students with varying degrees of quantitative reasoning ability."

The evidence for this hereditary component is not supported by statistical tests which reach an acceptable level. One study (Garron, 1973) cited as supporting the X-linked hypothesis, in fact challenged it.

Williams, T.: Family resemblance in abilities: The Wechsler scales. *Behavior Genetics, 5*:405-409, 1975.

This note reports data on parent-child and spouse resemblance on the Wechsler intelligence scales, the WISC and WAIS. Test data on parents and one male ten-year-old child from fifty-five Canadian families are used to estimate father-son, mother-son, midparent-son, and father-mother correlations on eleven comparable subscales and on the verbal, performance, and total IQ aggregates. Heritabilities for these same scales are estimated as the regression of offspring on midparent values (author abstract).

Correlations were not consistent with the X-linked hypothesis. Arithmetic subtest correlation for father-son, .31, was significant $p<.05$. Similarly the correlation for the Block Design subtest, a spatial measure, for father-son, .28, was significant, $p<.05$. Father-son correlations should be zero according to X-linked hypotheses. The assumption of assortative mating seems to have been met.

Wittig, M. A.: Sex differences in intellectual functioning: How much of a difference do genes make? *Sex Roles,* 2:63-74, 1976.

An X-linkage theory of inheritance of genes controlling sex differences in major intellectual traits is critically examined. A review of the research suggests that the mechanism of inheritance of differences in spatial visualization ability is X-linked recessive and its expression is probably testosterone-limited. However, the evidence concerning inheritance of differences in IQ does not support an X-linkage theory. Several characteristics of heritability estimates are discussed, including their specificity to a particular population at a certain point in time, their fluctuation with changes in amount of environmental variation, and the necessity of unconfounding sex and treatment in order to better determine the relationship between heritability and changeability of sex differences in specific intellectual trait expression (Author abstract).

Conclusion that "Spatial Visualization is X-linked recessive and probably testosterone-limited" no longer has empirical support.

Yen, W. M.: Sex-linked major-gene influence on selected types of spatial performance. *Behavior Genetics,* 5:281-298, 1975.

Four paper-pencil spatial tests, measuring two- and three-dimensional spatial visualization and spatial orientation, were administered to 2508 Caucasian (sic) high school students. Sibling correlations and within-sex score distributions were examined for the influence of a major sex-linked gene. Sex-linked influences were most clear on the test of two-dimensional visualization and on an average of the standard scores on all the tests. For those tests best fitting the genetic model, estimates of the frequency of the recessive gene (contributing to good performance) were near 0.45. There was evidence of sex limitation and a small amount of assortative mating, but no evidence of incomplete dominance in females. Environmental or non-sex-linked genetic factors influenced spatial performance but did not systematically improve performance with age (author abstract).

Part of results supported the X-linked hypothesis, but most did not. Failure to find an improvement in test scores from grade nine to twelve casts doubt upon the methodology.

CHROMOSOME/HORMONE ANOMALIES

McKerracher, D. W.: Psychological aspects of a sex chromatin abnormality. *The Canadian Psychologist, 12:*270-281, 1971.

A sample of 147 special security patients with no demonstrated chromosome abnormality and with no evidence of brain damage or psychosis, was compared with two groups of genetically abnormal patients, evincing an XXY or XYY chromosome pattern. The XXY patients were significantly lower in verbal and performance ability than were the patients in the other two groups. They were also more defensive in answering a personality questionnaire, but this was shown to be partly a function of their lower intelligence. Both of the genetically abnormal groups contained a higher proportion of subjects with significantly depressed verbal abilities than in the control group, though the trend was similar for all three groups. Approximately two-thirds of both genetically abnormal groups had commited some form of sex crime. It was suggested that this might indicate a specific genetic-based lag in mental aspects of sexual maturation in addition to the already demonstrated general social instability (author abstract).

Masica, D. N.; Money, J.; Ehrhardt, A. A.; and Lewis, V. G.: IQ, fetal sex hormones and cognitive patterns: Studies in the testicular feminizing syndrome of androgen insensitivity. *Johns Hopkins Medical Journal, 124:*34-43, 1969.

Fifteen patients with the syndrome of androgen insensitivity (testicular feminization), ranging in age from six to twenty-eight years tested with a mean Full IQ of 108. The difference between Verbal IQ 112 and Performance IQ 102 was statistically significant, $p<.01$. Applying the z test, the sample mean Full IQ was not significantly different from the Wechsler norms of standardization. Analysis of Wechsler subtest scores showed that the disparity between the specific factors of Verbal Comprehension (M = 12.18, S.D. = 1.78) and Perceptual Organization (M = 9.87, S.D. = 2.82) was statistically significant, $p > .01$. These clinical findings correlate well with published social psychological surveys that imply that the norms for females show a slight verbal superiority over those for males whose strengths lie more in mechanics, mathematics, and spatial relationships. If there is some specific male pattern of intellectual functioning, such as superior visual-perceptual organization, normally expressed directly or indirectly by the 44+ XY male karyotype, such a specific male pattern of intellect was lacking in patients with the complete form of testicular feminization. Their feminine test scores pattern may be, analogously to their phenotypic differentiation, primarily attributable to androgen insensitivity during fetal life and beyond; or it may be a secondary effect of sex assignment and rearing as a female; or it may be a product of both factors (author abstract slightly revised).

Note small n and inclusion of children with adult subjects, a weakness of many of these studies.

Money, J.: Two cytogenetic syndromes: Psychologic comparisons 1. Intelligence and specific factor quotients. *Journal of Psychiatric Research*, 2:223-231, 1964.

Thirty-eight patients with Turner's syndrome (XO) and twenty-three with Klinefelter's syndrome (XXY) have been studied. In each syndrome, IQs ranged from the grossest mental defect to very superior. Wechsler Intelligence Test results, from the majority of cases were complete enough to permit a comparison between the three specific cognitional factors of Cohen: Verbal Comprehension, Perceptual Organization, and Freedom from Distractibility. Specific-factor scores in Klinefelter's syndrome were not noteworthy in their difference from one another. By contrast, in Turner's syndrome, there was a marked discrepancy between Verbal Comprehension and Perceptual Organization (M. Diff. = 3.71, t = 6.7) significant at the < 0.001 level. There was also a discrepancy, less marked, between the Verbal Comprehension and Freedom from Distractibility (M. Diff. = 2.7, t = 6.9) significant at the < 0.001 level. Both chromatin-positive and chromatin-negative cases obeyed the trend. It is suggested that a degree of space-form dysgnosia and a degree of dyscalculia may be characteristic symptoms of Turner's syndrome (author abstract slightly altered).

Money, J. and Granoff, D.: IQ and the somatic stigmata of Turner's syndrome. *American Journal of Mental Deficiency, 70*:69-77, 1965.

Forty-six patients with Turner's syndrome have been studied. IQs within the syndrome ranged from the grossest mental defect to superior. The full sample was subdivided into groups based on the presence or absence of three somatic anomalies associated with the syndrome: (1) webbing of the neck; (2) cardiac anomalies; (3) epicanthal folds, and also on the basis of having many or few of twelve possible anomalies. No statistically significant differences in intellectual functioning, taken on the basis of intelligence testing, could be found between the groups with and without the three specific physical anomalies, nor between groups having many or few anomalies. Certain trends are noted suggesting a clustering together of the various somatic anomalies. This clustering is more apparent in chromatin-negative patients than in those with chromatin-positive chromosome constitutions. Moreover, the clustering of physical anomalies appears unrelated to the incidence of mental deficiency in the syndrome, and to the incidence of the specific cognitional disability of space-form blindness, so-called (author abstract).

This is a larger sample than reported in Money (1964).

METABOLIC HYPOTHESES

Broverman, D. M.; Klaiber, E. L.; Kobayashi, Y.; and Vogel, W.: Roles of activation and inhibition in sex differences in cognitive abilities. *Psychological Review, 75*:23-50, 1968.

A hypothesis that known sex differences in cognitive abilities reflect sex-related differences in physiology is offered. Females surpass males on simple, overlearned, perceptual-motor tasks; males excel on more complex tasks requiring an inhibition of immediate responses to obvious stimulus attributes in favor of responses to less obvious stimulus attributes. It is hypothesized that these sex differences are reflections of differences in relationships between adrenergic activating and cholinergic inhibitory neural processes, which, in turn, are sensitive to the "sex" hormones, androgens, and estrogens. Studies of the effects of drug and hormone administrations on these behaviors, and of sex hormones on adrenergic and cholinergic neuro-transmitters are examined. Implications for cross-sectional correlative analyses of cognitive organization are discussed (author abstract).

This article contains too many misconceptions and too much misinformation to recount here.

Broverman, D. M.; Klaiber, E. L.; Kobayashi, Y.; and Vogel, W.: Reply to the "Comment" by Singer and Montgomery on "Roles of activation and inhibition in sex differences in cognitive abilities." *Psychological Review, 76*:328-331, 1969.

Singer and Montgomery state that the hypothesis that certain sex differences in cognitive abilities may reflect sex differences in physiology lacks supporting evidence. This statement lacks substance since they do not consider the evidence reported in support of the hypothesis. The issues with which Singer and Montgomery are concerned are either problems of definition or are peripheral to the hypothesis (author abstract).

Englander-Golden, P.; Willis, K. A.; and Dienstbier, R. A.: Intellectual performance as a function of repression and menstrual cycle. Paper presented at the convention of the American Psychology Association, Washington, D. C., 1976.

Performance on complex (Space Relations and Verbal Reasoning) and simple (Digit Symbol) tests was investigated as a function of Byrne's Repression-Sensitization (RS) dimension, phase of menstrual cycle and premenstrual-menstrual (PM) symptomatology in a group of females not taking oral contraceptives. Two control groups, consisting of males and females taking oral contraceptives, were included. Equivalent tests were given at two sessions two weeks apart. Analysis of the Space Relations Test as a function of menstrual phase and Repression-Sensitization indicated the predicted interaction effect of phase by RS with poorest performance for the menstruating repressor group ($p < .02$), but the predicted deterioration by the premenstrual repressor group was not observed.

Similar analysis for the Verbal Reasoning Test yielded an interaction effect of phase by RS ($p < .03$) and a main effect for phase ($p < .05$). As predicted, differences on the Digit Symbol test did not reach significance. Substituting PM symptomatology for RS, a significant effect was obtained only for phase on Verbal Reasoning Test ($p < .05$). Results were interpreted as indicating a reactive nature of repression, so that during menstruation, repression may interfere particularly with performance on complex tasks. The three subject groups did not differ significantly on any of the three tests; however, trends in the present data corroborated those quoted in the literature (author abstract).

Maccoby, E. and Jacklin, C.: *The Psychology of Sex Differences.* Stanford, California, Stanford U Pr, 1974, pp. 42-53, 98-105, 122-125.

Authors reviewed the literature and concluded there is no evidence of sex-related differences in the learning of simple tasks in conditionability nor in the inhibition of responses. They concluded that the dichotomization of tasks into those which do and do not emphasize restructuring is an inaccurate description of sex-related cognitive differences. They noted the factual errors in the Broverman et al. (1968) theory and the inadequate empirical support for the theory.

Mikkelson, W. M.; Dodge, H. J.; and Valkenburg, H.: The distribution of serum uric acid values in a population unselected as to gout or hyperuricemia. *American Journal of Medicine, 39*:242-251, 1965.

Serum uric acid determinations were made for 6,000 study subjects from the Tecumseh Community Health Study, Tecumseh, Michigan, 1959-1960. These 6,000 subjects represent a natural population without prior selection for either hyperuricemia or gout.

Male subjects, of whom there were 2,987, had serum uric acid values ranging from 1.0 to 13.6 mg per 100 ml with an arithmetic mean of 4.9 mg per 100 ml and a standard deviation of 1.40 mg per 100 ml. Female subjects, 3,013 in all, had serum uric acid values ranging from 1.0 to 11.6 per 100 ml with an arithmetic mean of 4.2 mg per 100 ml and a standard deviation of 1.16 mg per 100 ml. The sex specific distribution curve for male subjects is broad and slightly skewed to the high value end of the scale. The curve for female subjects, by contrast, is narrow, peaking sharply at a value well below that of the curve in male subjects and is somewhat more skewed toward the upper end of the scale.

The age-sex specific mean serum uric acid values for both sexes are lowest in the four-year-olds with rising trend of values in the five to nine and ten to fourteen year age groups. At about puberty the curves begin to separate. The curve for male subjects continues to rise to a peak at ages twenty to twenty-four years; it then falls slightly and plateaus at a level of about 5.2 mg per 100 ml. For female subjects, there is a slight rise in serum uric acid values beyond puberty but the curve shortly falls again and plateaus at a level of about 4.0 mg per 100 ml until the age of menopause, when it rises gradually to approach closely that of male subjects in the early fifties.

The data with reference to relative distribution about arbitrarily defined cutting points suggest that these points, commonly used in clinical medicine to define "hyperuricemia," are unrealistically low and, in addition, fail to take into account important differences associated with age. The observed serum uric acid level for each individual subject has been adjusted or standardized to that of the appropriate age-sex group. The distribution curves of the present data show no suggestion of bimodality and suggest genetic polymorphism (author abstract).

Because gout is regarded as a male disease, gout is sometimes not suspected in women with consequent unnecessary tissue damage. Urate levels that are not pathologic for males may have health implications for females.

Mueller, E. F.; Kasl, S. V.; Brook, G. U.; and Cobb, S.: Psychosocial correlates of serum urate levels. *Psychological Bulletin,* 73:238-257, 1970.

A series of recent studies strongly suggest that uric acid, the end product of purine metabolism in men, or its precursor is related to social class, achievement, and achievement-oriented behavior. Furthermore, there is evidence that serum uric acid levels change in response to socially and psychologically stressful situations. The present review gives a short introduction to the problems of uric acid metabolism and reviews the main variables affecting urate levels in the blood. The possibility that uric acid or its precursors act as stimulants of central nervous system activity is considered and the research problems most relevant to future progress in this area are discussed, especially the need to clarify the causal relations between uric acid, behavior, and environmental stimulation (author abstract).

Note modesty of conclusions.

Parlee, M. B.: Comments on "Roles of activation and inhibition in sex differences in cognitive abilities" by D. M. Broverman, E. L. Klaiber, Y. Kobayaski, and W. Vogel. *Psychological Review,* *79*:180-184, 1972.

The hypothesis of D. M. Broverman, E. L. Klaiber, Y. Kobayashi, and W. Vogel that "known sex differences in cognitive abilities reflect sex-related differences in physiology" is criticized on the grounds that (a) their review and classification of the literature on sex differences in cognitive abilities is inadequate because it is selective and arbitrarily characterizes those facts which it does include, (b) the pharmacological studies cited in support of their thesis involve behaviors which are at best tangentially related to human cognitive abilities and rely for their relevance on some dubious cross-species analogies, and (c) the authors have made, and defended, a factual error in citing evidence for an important part of their proposed mechanism by which "sex" hormones might affect autonomic activity (author abstract).

Petersen, A. C.: Physical androgyny and cognitive functioning in adolescence. *Developmental Psychology,* *12*:524-533, 1976.

This study investigated the relationship of physical manifestations of sex hormone influence to cognitive functioning in a longitudinal sample of adolescent males and females. The results suggest that, in males, relatively less masculine (androgynous) physical characteristics are positively related to spatial ability and negatively related to fluent production. Similarly more masculine physical characteristics are positively related to fluent production and negatively related to spatial ability. Fluent production is unrelated to physical

characteristics in females. Less feminine (androgynous) physical characteristics are related to spatial ability. Possibilities
for the development of these relationships are discussed
(author abstract).

Study does not contain most recent information on X-linked
inheritance.

Singer, G. and Montgomery, R. B.: Comment on "Role of activation
and inhibition in sex differences in cognitive abilities." *Psychological
Review,* 76:325-327, 1969.

The hypothesis of a relationship between sex-based differences in physiology and sex differences in cognitive abilities
proposed by Broverman, Klaiber, Kobayashi, and Vogel is
criticized on the grounds of either a lack of supporting evidence, or supporting evidence which is contrary to the pres-
ently known facts (author abstract).

LATERALITY

Bakan, P.: Hypnotizability, laterality of eye-movements and functional brain asymmetry. *Perceptual and Motor Skills,* 28:927-932,
1969.

The direction of lateral eye-movements upon inward direction of attention or reflection is related to hypnotizability and
also with humanistic interests, relatively poorer mathematical
performance on the Scholastic Aptitude Test and clearer im-
agery. Results are discussed in terms of functional asymmetry
of the brain (author abstract).

Results cannot be interpreted because of failure to analyse by
sex.

Bakan, P. and Putnam, W.: Right-left discrimination and brain lateralization: Sex differences. *Archives of Neurology,* 30:334-335, 1974.

To determine whether there is a sex difference in the ability
to make right-left discriminations, a group form of the Culver
Lateral Discrimination Test was administered to 400 university undergraduates. Subjects looked at slide projections of
right or left body parts and were required to identify the body
part as right or left. Performance of right-handed women was

significantly poorer than that of right-handed men, and the same trend was found for left-handed subjects. There was no significant difference between right- and left-handed subjects on the test. The results are discussed in terms of a sex difference in degree of functional asymmetry between the right and left cerebral hemispheres, and it is suggested that the female brain has less hemispheric functional asymmetry (author abstract).

Bogen, J. E.; DeZure, R.; Tenhouten, W. D.; and Marsh, J. F.: The other side of the brain IV. The A/P ratio. *Bulletin of the Los Angeles Neurological Societies, 37*:49-61, 1972.

Two kinds of data are presented: (a) on varying cultural groups, 49 rural Hopi, 73 rural White, 270 urban Black women, 224 urban Black men, 277 urban White women, 327 urban White men and (b) on 11 comissurotomy patients. Subjects were given the Street figure completion test to measure appositionality, right-brained, spatial, gestalt thinking and the Similarities subtest of the Wechsler Adult Intelligence Test to measure propositionality, left-brained, verbal, analytic thinking. The ratio of performance on these two tests, the A/P ratio, is taken as an index of hemisphericity. Results showed that the Street test does depend more on right-hemisphere functioning. Significant cultural variations were found in hemisphericity, but no differences were found between the sexes in hemisphericity. Among the comissurotomy patients who could only use their left hemispheres for the tasks, four females performed differently than three males, $p<.01$, males attaining a higher A/P ratio. This was interpreted as support for the view that the left hemisphere of females participates more in appositional thinking (solving spatial-gestalt tasks) than is the case for males.

Finding of no sex difference in A/P ratio in normal populations was not expected by authors. Very interesting study. Miscited as evidence for bilateral propositionality in females.

Briggs, G. G.; Nebes, R. D.; and Kinsbourne, M.: Intellectual differences in relation to personal and family handedness. *Quarterly Journal of Experimental Psychology*, in press, 1976.

Right, mixed and left-handed college students were given

the complete WAIS and a series of cognitive factor tests. Results showed left and mixed-handed individuals to have a significantly lower full scale IQ than right-handers. There was no difference between the mixed and left-handers and no significant sex by handedness interactions. In all three handedness groups, subjects with a positive family history of sinistrality had a lower full scale IQ than did subjects without left-handed relatives. Neither handedness nor family history differentially affected the Verbal or Performance subscales, nor did they have a significant effect on scores in the other cognitive tests. Authors state, "Our findings . . . support neither Levy's original data, nor her model's predictions."

Buffery, A. W. H. and Gray, J. A.: Sex differences in the development of spatial and linguistic skills. In Ounsted, C. and Taylor, D. C. (Eds.): *Gender Differences: Their Ontogeny and Significance.* Baltimore, Williams & Wilkins, 1972.

Reviews evidence in animals and humans and concludes that males are superior to females in visuo-spatial abilities. Thinks that, as with sex differences in emotionality, male superiority in visuo-spatial abilities is linked to genetic and endocrine control. Reviews evidence regarding linguistic skills and concludes that females are at least more verbally fluent than males. From evidence of asymmetry of cerebral function, concludes that left cerebral dominance for language is developed earlier and is frequently more lateralized in the human female than male brain. They hypothesize that this leads to greater bilateral cerebral representation of spatial function in males. They believe this to be an advantageous cerebral organization.

Evidence not consistent with their views is not fully considered and little positive independent support for their hypothesis is adduced. Out of date, especially regarding sex-linked inheritance of spatial skill.

Carr, B. M.: Ear effect variables and order of report in dichotic listening. *Cortex,* 5:63-68, 1969.

This paper described an experiment designed to investigate the possibility that performance on a dichotic listening task would vary between sexes; that overall accuracy in reporting the digit presentations would improve as the test progressed; and that there would be a preference to report all digits of one ear before reporting any digits from the opposite ear. The results of this experiment confirmed earlier evidence that subjects are more efficient at recalling digits presented to the right ear than to the left. Since the left cerebral hemisphere is dominant for speech, it seems reasonable to accept the contention of stronger contralateral than ipsilateral auditory nerve pathways. As was expected, there was no difference between the sexes on the test, presumably because cerebral dominance is well-established for all normal adults. Although there were exceptions, the subjects as a group did not progressively improve in overall proficiency at reporting the digits they heard. Finally, in spite of an earlier finding to the contrary, no statistically significant order of report preference was found in this study. It was theorized that if such a preference does exist under certain conditions, it may be due to the same factors which cause the right-ear effect (author abstract).

Subjects were sixteen male and sixteen female right-handers.

Cohen, B. D.; Berent, S.; and Silverman, A. J.: Field-dependence and lateralization of function in the human brain. *Archives of General Psychiatry, 28*:165-167, 1973.

Rod and Frame Tests were administered before and after a single electroconvulsive shock treatment (ECT) delivered either to the left or right cerebral hemisphere of neurologically normal patients being treated for depression. A third group was also tested twice but with no intervening ECT. All twelve left-ECT patients showed more field-dependence (larger errors) on the second test; all twelve right-ECT patients showed less field-dependence. The findings were discussed in terms of a model in which two cognitive control processes, field articulation and scanning are localized in the left and right brain hemispheres, respectively. Also, implications were drawn regarding the possibly special role of shock to the right hemisphere in the treatment of depression (author abstract).

"Field dependence" and "field articulation" refer to performance on certain spatial tasks most commonly the Rod and

Frame Test, an Embedded Figures or Hidden Figures Test, also Block-Design, figure drawing. Measures are strongly related to spatial visualization. Only female subjects were used.

Cohen, B. D.; Noblin, C. D.; Silverman, A. J.; and Penick, S. B.: Functional asymmetry of the human brain. *Science, 162*:475-477, 1968.

Verbal and nonverbal memorization skills were tested before and after electroconvulsive shocks to the left, right, or both cerebral hemispheres of neurologically normal females. As predicted, decrements for the left-hemisphere-shocked group were larger on the verbal than nonverbal tasks, while the reverse was true for the right-hemisphere-shocked group. Largest decrements on both tasks were shown by the bilaterally shocked group (author abstract).

Fairweather, H.: Sex differences in cognition. *Cognition, 4*:231-280, 1976.

Sex differences in cognitive skills, grouped into three areas — motor, spatial, and linguistic — are assessed in the context of current notions of cerebral lateralization (Buffery and Gray, 1972). There are few convincing sex differences, either overall, or in interactions with (putative) functional localization. There are several qualifying criteria (nature of further interactions with age, birth order, culture, sex of experimenter, sex-role pressure) which would have to be met, but these are as yet inadequately documented. Serious caution is urged on the proliferating number of researchers in this area (author abstract).

Hannay, H. J. and Malone, D. R.: Visual field effects and short term memory for verbal material. *Neuropsychologia, 14*:203-209, 1976a.

The role of memory in the usual right visual field superiority for verbal material reported with normal subjects was investigated. Nonsense words were presented vertically in either the left or right visual field. The exposure duration, which was individually determined for each subject to produce about 75 percent correct responses, ranged from 5 to 25 msec. After a delay of 0, 5, or 10 sec the subject decided whether or not a nonsense word exposed in central vision was the same as the stimulus word.

With males, the results suggested that the right visual field superiority represents left-hemisphere specialization for retention of verbal material and hemispheric equality in reception. With females no visual field superiority was found perhaps indicating that both hemispheres receive and retain verbal information equally well. The findings support the concept of less-complete lateralization of linguistic and spatial functions in females (author abstract).

Results due to lack of control of familial handedness. See Hannay & Malone, 1976, in *Cortex*.

Hannay, H. J. and Malone, D. R.: Visual field recognition memory for right-handed females as a function of familial handedness. *Cortex*, 12:41-48, 1976b.

Right-handed females with only right-handed family members demonstrated right visual field superiorities indicative of a slight left-hemisphere specialization for memory but not for reception of verbal material. Field superiorities obtained for right-handed females with a left-handed parent or sibling were not significant.

In general, less complete lateralization of linguistic function in females was indicated and the importance of familial handedness in cerebral asymmetry of function was confirmed (author abstract).

Authors based their conclusion of less complete lateralization of linguistic function in females on a comparison of results of females from this study with males from a previous study. No statistical comparison of the two sexes was made. Data are weak to support the conclusion of a sex-related difference because direct statistical comparisons of the two sexes were not made. Familial right-handed females showed right visual field superiority at five seconds in this study, $p<.05$, compared to right visual field superiority for familial right-handed males for the five second memory interval, $p<.01$, and the ten second interval, $p<.05$, from the Hannay & Malone (1976) study in *Neuropsychologia*.

Harshman, R. A. and Remington, R.: Sex, language and the brain, part I: A review of the literature on adult sex differences in lateralization. Unpublished manuscript. Los Angeles, Phonetics Laboratory, University of California, 1976. See also *UCLA Working Papers in Phonetics*, *31*:86-103, 1976.

While it is known that men and women differ in relative performance on verbal and spatial tasks, the cause of this difference has not yet been determined. There is evidence, however, that both cultural and biological factors are involved. One possible biological factor is brain organization. A review of clinical and experimental data indicates that the brains of men and women tend to show differences in hemispheric specialization for language and spatial functions, with men showing a greater average degree of lateralization than women. This conclusion is supported by several different types of evidence; clinical studies of the effects of unilateral brain damage or commissurotomy on verbal and spatial tasks; anatomical studies of cerebral asymmetries in language-related cortical areas; electro-physiological studies comparing right and left hemispheres during stimulation or behavioral tasks; tachistoscopic perceptual studies of right and left visual field advantages to verbal and visuo-spatial stimuli; and other, indirect evidence. Data on lateralization of children must be considered separately, because of complexities in interpretation arising from boys' developmental lag relative to girls (author abstract).

This review is already outdated especially in treatment of behavioral genetics. Brings together material from disparate sources. Case for greater lateralization of male spatial function seems adequate, but case for greater lateralization of verbal function is much weaker.

Kimura, D.: Spatial localization in left and right visual fields. *Canadian Journal of Psychology*, *23*:445-458, 1969.

A series of single dots was presented tachistoscopically in either the left or the right visual field, the subject's task being to locate the dot on a spatial map depicting all of the dot locations presented. For men, localization of the dot was more accurate in the left visual field than in the right visual field, under all testing conditions. Women showed the left-field superiority under some testing conditions; under others they showed no difference between fields. There was no sex difference in over-all accuracy of performance, and simple detection of a dot was not found to be more accurate in one field than another for either sex. The results are discussed in terms of a probable "spatial co-ordinate" system in the right hemisphere of the brain (author abstract).

Lake, D. A. and Bryden, M. P.: Handedness and sex differences in hemispheric asymmetry. *Brain and Language, 3*:266-282, 1976.

A study was designed to assess the contributions of the factors of sex and familial history to cerebral dominance, where cerebral dominance was inferred from laterality on a dichotic listening task. The 144 subjects were selected from a larger sample on the basis of handedness, sex and familial history-of-sinistrality, and tested on a task involving the dichotic presentation of CV syllables. Analysis of the data indicated that in female subjects, the presence of familial sinistrality increased the likelihood that they present atypical left-ear superiorities, while in males the converse was the case. Moreover, there was a significant sex difference overall, such that males were more clearly lateralized than females. A review of other dichotic listening studies provided support for the reliability of this sex difference for dichotic tasks using verbal material. A review of the clinical literature indicated that the hypothesis of a sex difference is at least tenable and merits further investigation. However, the possibility that there is a sex difference in the cognitive strategy used in dichotic listening cannot be ruled out (author abstract).

The overall finding that males were more lateralized was due to the group with family history of sinistrality. Right-handed males and females without a family history of sinistrality were not significantly different. Familial sinistrality rather than indicating left-handed heredity may be a sign of family history of neurologic insult.

Lansdell, H.: A sex difference in effect of temporal-lobe neurosurgery on design preference. *Nature, 194*:852-854, 1962.

Twenty-two patients with temporal-lobe epilepsy were tested on the Graves design judgment test before and after undergoing unilateral temporal-lobe surgery for the relief of their epilepsy. Performance of males (n = 8) with right-sided surgery declined, while that of females (n = 5) improved. Performance of females with left-sided surgery (n = 2) declined while that of males (n = 7) improved; the interaction of sex, side and pre-post measures was significant, $p<.01$. Subjects were also given the Wechsler Bellevue Intelligence test and showed a drop, $p<.05$, in verbal scores after operation on the left hemisphere. No interaction with sex was reported for the verbal material.

Lansdell, H.: The use of factor scores from the Wechsler-Bellevue Scale of Intelligence in assessing patients with temporal lobe removals. *Cortex, 4*:257-268, 1968.

 After temporal lobe surgery, females with left-sided surgery (n = 8) had lower scores on the Block Design and Object Assembly subtests of the Wechsler than males (n = 11), while males with right-sided surgery (n = 13) had lower scores than females (n = 20). The sex by side interaction was significant, $p<.05$. A significant, $p<.05$ interaction was also found for seven "nonverbal" tests. No such sex by side interaction was found for the verbal material, though the verbal comprehension factor did not show a side effect either.

It is not clear that the sex by sidedness groups were equivalent on relevant variables such as age, previous education.

Levy, J.: Lateral specialization of the human brain: Behavioral manifestations and possible evolutionary basis. In Kiger, J. A. (Ed.): *The Biology of Behavior*. Corvallis, Oregon U Pr, 1972.

 "It is interesting that the perceptual deficit seen in left-handers is also present in females in general. Using the Porteus Maze Test, Porteus . . . found, in testing dozens of cultures all over the world ranging from that of Australian aborigines to that of French school children, girls were significantly inferior to boys. MacFarlane Smith . . . , in his book *Spatial Ability*, has also pointed out that females show a specific spatial disability. It might be that female brains are similar to those of left-handers in having less hemispheric specialization than male right-hander's brains . . . . It is hard to reject the notion that a spatial perceptive deficit in women is a sex-linked, genetically determined incapacity, an incapacity which possibly results from hemispheres less well laterally specialized than those of males. That the sex chromosomes do participate in determining spatial ability is given strong support by the finding that girls with Turner's syndrome, and XO condition, have profound defects in spatial perception."

The Levy hypothesis is not frequently spelled out in print. These quotations most clearly and briefly present her views. Note that the hypothesis of a "spatial" sex-linked "incapacity" has been disconfirmed. Her interpretation of Turner's syndrome data are also open to question.

Maccoby, E. and Jacklin, C.: *The Psychology of Sex Differences.* Stanford, California, Stanford U Pr, 1974, pp. 125-127.

Authors presented Buffery and Gray (1972), Levy (1972) and bent twig hypothesis (Sherman, 1967). Account is now out of date. The Levy hypothesis was erroneously presented since it is only verbal function which Levy hypothesized as bilateral in females as in left-handed males. The Buffery and Gray hypothesis was contrasted with the Levy hypothesis in a misleading way. The bent-twig hypothesis was misrepresented since it was not related to brain laterality in 1967 or 1971 and has never assumed that the female right hemisphere is "shut off." The authors contradicted themselves by saying that there are no early sex-related differences in verbal vs. spatial thought whereas elsewhere they indicated that females have a verbal edge on males. Their recommendation of a test of the bent twig hypothesis does not follow logically. From the statement early verbal acceleration in females leads to a preference for a verbal approach to problem solving, it does not follow that "boys who talk late have better spatial ability in late childhood than boys who talk early." The converse of a true statement cannot be assumed to be true.

McGlone, J.: *Sex differences in functional brain asymmetry.* (Research Bulletin #378 Department of Psychology) London, Canada, University of Western Ontario, July 1976.

Investigated comparative intellectual performance on the Wechsler Adult Intelligence Scale of eighty-five right-handers, ages fifteen to seventy, with unilateral brain injury, admitted consecutively to the University Hospital in London, Ontario from 1973 to 1975. There were no significant differences between males and females with left or right hemisphere lesions in age, education, or length of illness. Analysis of variance showed a significant side of lesion by sex by task (Verbal versus Performance IQ) interaction, $p<.01$. Verbal and Performance IQs respectively for left-damaged females were 99,99; left-damaged males 83,94; right-damaged females 99,95; right-damaged males 106,93. Men with left-sided lesions obtained significantly lower Verbal IQ scores than all other groups. Women with left-sided lesions did not differ in Verbal IQ score from women with right-sided lesions or men with right-sided lesions. Performance IQ did not differ significantly according to sex or laterality of the lesion. In men, left-hemisphere damage impaired Verbal IQ more than Performance IQ ($p<.01$) and right hemisphere damage lowered Performance IQ compared to Verbal IQ ($p<.01$). These relationships were not found for women. McGlone concluded that these results suggest the adult male brain is more asymmetrically organized than the female brain for both verbal and nonverbal abilities.

Data from naturally occuring brain lesioned persons are often hard to interpret since there is no way of adequately providing controlled comparisons either in terms of pre-post injury data or in comparison of matched groups. The observed data are consistent with the author's conclusions, but may be artifactual and/or interpreted in other ways. For example, a point that is not in contention is that the right hemisphere is important to spatial function in males. If these data are valid and the groups comparable, why is it that right-hemisphere damaged males performed as well as left-hemisphere damaged males on the Wechsler Performance Scale?

McGlone, J. and Davidson, W.: The relation between cerebral speech laterality and spatial ability with special reference to sex and hand preference. *Neuropsychologia, 11*:105-113, 1973.

Left- and right-handed normals of both sexes completed two visuo-spatial tasks along with a dichotic words test and a tachistoscopic dot enumeration test. The latter two tests yielded measures of verbal and nonverbal cerebral dominance, respectively. Contrary to earlier reports not all left-handers were poorer than right-handers on spatial tasks. Such impairment was associated only with left-handers showing higher left-ear scores on the dichotic test (i.e., presumed right-hemisphere speech). Competition effects between verbal and nonverbal functions subserved by the same hemisphere, however, did not adequately account for these spatial deficits. Compared to males, females showed poorer spatial ability and a higher incidence of right-field superiority on the dot enumeration test, suggesting that left-hemisphere mediation of nonverbal ability may be disadvantageous (author abstract).

Probability of the last effect was < .10. This study is sometimes miscited as showing greater bilaterality in verbal representation when it rather suggests greater left-hemisphere involvement in spatial function for females.

McGlone, J. and Kertesz, A.: Sex differences in cerebral processing of visuo-spatial tasks. *Cortex, 9*:313-320, 1973.

Subjects were seventy-eight right-handed neurological patients with unilateral brain damage. Groups were matched on Raven's Coloured Progressive Matrices, but not entirely matched for age. Subjects were given an Aphasia battery and the Block Design subtest of the Wechsler Bellevue Intelligence Scale. Testing was mostly done within a month of hospital admission, but groups were not entirely equated in this regard. Patients with left-hemisphere lesions obtained lower scores on the Aphasia battery than did patients with right-hemisphere lesions, $p<.01$; conversely patients with right-hemisphere damage scored lower on Block Design, $p<.01$. There were no main effects of sex or interactions of sex with side of lesion. Males with right-hemisphere lesions did most poorly on Block Design, $p<.10$. This was interpreted to support the view that spatial ability may be more unilaterally represented in the right hemisphere of males than in females. While correlations between Block Design and the Aphasia battery for seventy-two patients was .12, the correlation for twenty-two females with left-hemisphere lesions was .63. This was interpreted to indicate that following injury to the left hemisphere the degree of language impairment is to some extent predictive of visuo-spatial disability in women, but not in men.

Inferences about normal persons from patients with naturally occurring brain injury are difficult for many reasons including the large number of factors to be controlled and the unknown variables. Many relevant variables were controlled in this study, but some were not fully controlled. Results to support the theoretical point that males are more lateralized in spatial function were weak and not statistically significant. Proper statistical tests for differences between correlations were not run. Also, rather than compare the correlation between Block Design and the Aphasia battery for the entire group, .12, with that of left-damaged females, .63, the more appropriate comparison would have been with left-damaged males, .23. This comparison is not significantly different. Results though weak are consistent, however, with McGlone's interpretation.

Rudel R. G.; Denckla, M. B.; and Spalten, E.: The functional asymmetry of Braille letter learning in normal, sighted children. *Neurology*, *24*:733-738, 1974.

Eighty right-handed children (40 boys, 40 girls) ages seven to fourteen were taught to read twelve Braille letters by palpatation, using a paired associates method. Forty learned six letters with their left hand and then six other letters with their right; the left-right order was reversed for the remaining forty. Although language is involved, the tactile-verbal paired associate learning ultimately is better accomplished by the left hand. The results are discussed in terms of other demonstrations that (1) the left hand may be superior to the right on spatial tasks that exclude vision, (2) girls develop more slowly in the performance of left-sided (right-hemisphere-dependent) tasks, and (3) girls depend more than boys on left-hemisphere mediation (author abstract).

Sherman, J.: Cognitive performance as a function of sex and handedness: An evelution of the Levy hypothesis. *Psychology of Women Quarterly*, in press, 1978.

Investigated incidence of left-handedness and nonrighthandedness in a sample of 9th grade students (n = 313). In comparison, incidence among undergraduates is underestimated. Girls were not significantly more right-handed than boys in the 9th grade sample but were significantly ($p<.01$) more right-handed than boys in a sample of math students, grades nine to eleven (n = 1097). Handedness did not affect math achievement (Test of Academic Progress), verbal (Quick Word Test) or spatial (Space Relations Test of the Differential Aptitude Test) performance in the 9th (n = 108) or 10th (n = 75) grade students. For 11th grade students (n = 98) a significant sex by handedness by measures (verbal-spatial) interaction was found ($p<.05$). Results did not support the hypothesis that left-handedness decreases spatial performance and benefits verbal performance, nor did the results support the further hypothesis that the cognitive pattern of higher verbal than spatial performance often considered characteristic of females, can be attributed to more bilateral cerebral verbal function in females as in left-handers.

Waber, D. P.: Sex differences in cognition: A function of maturation rates? *Science, 192*:572-574, 1976.

Regardless of sex, early maturing adolescents performed better on tests of verbal than spatial abilities, the late maturing ones showed the opposite pattern. Those maturing late were more lateralized for speech than those maturing early. Sex differences in mental abilities, it is argued, reflect differences in the organization of cortical function that are related to differential rates of physical maturation (author abstract).

Subjects were selected from girls ages ten to thirteen and boys ages thirteen to sixteen. This procedure is adequate if one assumes that both verbal and spatial skills develop at the same rate for both sexes during this period. Otherwise, confounding of effects due to differential maturation rates could occur. It would seem wise to repeat this study on fully mature persons. Author indicates that those maturing late were more lateralized for speech, regardless of hemisphere. Combining lateralization results over hemispheres obscures interpretation.

Wada, J. A.; Clarke, R.; and Hamm, A.: Cerebral hemispheric asymmetry in humans. *Archives of Neurology, 32*:239-246, 1975.

Morphological asymmetry of the frontal operculum and temporal planum becomes measurable at the 29th week of gestation. There is evidence of subsequent differential development of the planum in favor of the left, with the left planum larger than the right. While both the frontal operculum and left planum were always present, the right planum ranged in size from absent (10 percent) to larger than the left (about 10 percent). Females predominated ($p < .05$) in the latter group.

The findings suggest that (1) a higher percentage of persons may have right-sided cerebral speech dominance or bilateral cerebral representation for speech than has been assumed previously, (2) a predetermined morphological asymmetry contributes to establishing the ultimate pattern of cerebral speech representation following an early insult to a predisposed hemisphere, and (3) it is necessary to scrutinize clinical material for the differential organization of hemispheric development between sexes (author abstract).

Weitan, W. and Etaugh, C.: Lateral eye-movement as a function of cognitive mode, question sequence, and sex of subject. *Perceptual and Motor Skills, 38*:439-444, 1974.

Verbal and numerical questions elicited significantly more lateral eye-movements to the right than did spatial and musical questions for forty-eight college students. These results are consistent with the hypothesis that lateral eye-movement is related to the functional organization of the cerebral hemispheres. Contrary to expectations, asking the questions in homogeneous sets as opposed to a mixed list did not produce more eye-movements in the predicted direction for each cognitive mode. Males tended to make more right-movements than females on all four types of questions (author abstract).

The finding that males make more right eye-movements than females was not significant, ($p < .10$). Even if it were significant, its meaning is obscure since response to questions supposedly involving different hemispheres have been combined.

Witelson, S. F.: Sex and the single hemisphere: Specialization of the right hemisphere for spatial processing. *Science, 193*:425-427, 1976.

Specialization of the right hemisphere for spatial processing was studied in 200 normal boys and girls between six and thirteen years of age. Boys performed in a manner consistent with right-hemisphere specialization as early as the age of six. Girls showed evidence of bilateral representation until the age of thirteen. The results suggest a sexual dimorphism in the neural organization underlying cognition during a major period of childhood. The results, which have implications for reading instruction, are discussed in terms of a possible sex difference in neural plasticity during development and the clinical consequences of such a difference (author abstract).

SOCIAL DETERMINANTS AND BENT TWIG HYPOTHESIS

Aiken, L. R., Jr.: Non-intellective variables and mathematics achievement: Directions for research. *Journal of School Psychology,* 8:28-36, 1970.

This study reviews empirical research on attitudes, anxiety, interests, sex and masculinity-femininity, family factors, socio-cultural background, and teachers (attitudes, understanding, motivation cues related to student achievement) and how these factors affect achievement in mathematics.

Attitude toward mathematics measures do relate to mathematics achievement but attitude measures may be used more efficiently as moderator variables in predicting achievement from ability test scores. In college-women positive attitudes toward mathematics are relative to intellectual and social maturity, self control, and theoretical values. Anxiety can have both positive and negative effects. Attempts to desensitize students to negative anxieties have been made but long term effects have not been established. Interest in mathematics is correlated with achievement. Attempts to relate personality inventory results to achievement in mathematics have generally dealt with few variables and small samples. The weight of evidence indicates a greater interest and achievement in mathematics by males at the high school level and beyond. Some studies based on Masculinity-Femininity Scales show masculine characteristics identified with mathematics achievement. Studies on identification with parents and fathers in particular, as it affects mathematics ability, are reviewed as are the effects of socio-economic status of the family and parental over-protection. Studies related to teacher attitudes and motivational cues and student mathematics performance are also discussed.

Aiken recommends additional studies on the non-intellective variables which may be related to mathematics achievement (from Tobin et al., 1976).

Allen, M. J.: Sex differences in spatial problem-solving styles. *Perceptual and Motor Skills, 39*:843-846, 1974.

University student volunteers, forty-seven women and forty-six men, took a battery of six spatial tests and checked for problems in a parallel form of each test a list of possible problem-solving strategies. Significant sex differences on reported strategy used for three of the tests were found. Evidence suggests that the women were less efficient than the men in their use of frequently used strategies and used more guessing and concrete solution styles (author abstract).

Block, J. H.: Conceptions of sex role: Some cross-cultural and longitudinal perspectives. *American Psychologist, 28*:512-526, 1973.

This article discusses socializing influences as they impinge on the development of sexual identity. The author finds that the socialization process appears to have differential effects on males and females. Males are encouraged along a more androgynous sex role definition since some traditionally feminine concerns are emphasized along with the traditionally masculine traits. For women the socialization process tends to reinforce the submissive, docile aspects of the traditional female role and discourages those traditional masculine qualities such as self-assertiveness, achievement orientation and independence. Thus the socialization process expands men's options but limits women's options (from Tobin et al., 1976).

Carey, G. L.: Sex differences in problem-solving performance as a function of attitude differences. *Journal of Abnormal and Social Psychology, 56*:256-260, 1958.

The purpose of the study was to investigate whether sex differences in problem-solving performances (which do not result from differences in general intelligence, special aptitudes or information) are caused by attitude toward problem solving.

An attitude toward problem solving scale was constructed and that and a series of ten problems were given to groups of three men and three women each. Then a discussion, the intent of which was to promote a more favorable attitude toward problem solving, was held. After the discussion, another form of the attitude scale and a different set of problems were given to the group. A group that did not participate in the discussions acted as the control.

The attitude scale evidenced some internal validity and men had higher scores than women. Attitude scores had a positive relationship to performance scores. After the discussion, women's performance increased while men's did not change. The findings tend to support the hypothesis of sex differences in problem solving as a function of sex differences in attitude (from Tobin et al., 1976).

Carlsmith, L.: Effect of early father absence on scholastic aptitude. *Harvard Educational Review, 34*:3-21, 1964.

This study investigated the effects of temporary father absence on scholastic aptitude in males. Both length of absence and child's age at onset of absence were considered. Subjects were 881 Harvard freshmen in the class of 1963, 307 freshmen in the class of 1964, and 137 male and 135 female seniors at three Massachusetts public high schools in 1961. All subjects were born during the war years, 1941-45, were from intact families, and had taken the college entrance Scholastic Aptitude Test. According to questionnaire data from the college students and the parents of the high school students, approximately one third of the subjects' fathers had served overseas during the war from three months to five years. To control for subjects's general level of ability, the difference between each subject's mathematical and verbal scores was taken as the indicator of aptitude. An additional analysis of the effects of father-absence versus father-presence was made for a Harvard class of 1964 subsample, matched on age, ordinal position in family, private or public education, parents' age, and father's education and occupation.

For all three samples, early and long separation from the father resulted in relatively greater ability in verbal areas than in mathematics, and no separation produced relatively greater ability in mathematics. A late and brief separation appeared to produce an extreme elevation in mathematical ability relative to verbal ability. In relating these findings to sex-identification theory, it was suggested that the relative superiority of math or verbal aptitude is a single measure of conceptual style or approach to problem solving. Development of a masculine analytic approach, as opposed to a feminine global approach, is apparently associated with a boy's relationship with his father during certain early periods of his life. The possibility that aptitude differences in father-present and father-absent boys could result from such variables as anxiety is also discussed (from Astin et al., 1975).

Chance, J. E. and Goldstein, A. G.: Internal-external control of reinforcement and embedded-figures performance. *Perception and Psychophysics, 9*:33-34, 1971.

Male and female Ss were tested in an extended series of sixty-eight embedded figures. Rate of decrease in discovery time was related to Ss' attitudes about locus of control of reinforcing outcomes. Results confirmed those of an earlier study, showing that practice dissipated sex-related performance differences observable in early trials (author abstract).

Coates, S.: Sex differences in field dependence-independence between the ages of 3 and 6. *Perceptual and Motor Skills, 39*:1307-1310, 1974.

The present study analyzed sex differences in field dependence-independence between the ages of three and six years, using the Preschool Embedded Figures Test. Results indicated that at age five girls were significantly more field-independent than boys (author abstract).

Coates, S.; Lord, M.; and Jakobovics, E.: Field dependence-independence, social-non-social play and sex differences in preschool children. *Perceptual and Motor Skills, 40*:195-202, 1975.

The present study investigated the hypothesis that preschool children who spend more time in social play than in non-social play would be more field-dependent than their field-independent counterparts. Overall the hypothesis was supported by the results. Although the social-non-social dimension appeared to account for most of the findings, correlations between individual play activities and field dependence suggested that this single dimension could not adequately account for all of the findings. The dimension of perceptual-motor demand required in some of the activities may have been involved as well. Discussion focused on the complexity of the play preference, cognitive findings, and on sex differences as well (author abstract).

Cohen, D.: Sex differences in the organization of spatial abilities in older men and women. Doctoral dissertation, Los Angeles, University of Southern California, 1975. *Dissertation Abstracts International,* in press. (University Microfilms, No. 75-15, 522.)

The objective of this study was to examine the hypotheses that older men and women will differ in level of performance on tests of spatial ability, and that the cognitive structure of spatial abilities reflected in the interrelationships among the performance scores will be different. One hundred four women (average age, 70.2) and ninety men (average age, 69.0), equated in education, were administered a psychological test battery with nine subtests: vocabulary, word reasoning, word fluency, space, close-ups, circle continuations, match problems, hidden figures, making objects.

Whereas there was insufficient evidence to conclude that sex effects in level of performance existed to a significant degree, age effects occurred for three spatial tests and one verbal task when a 4(age) x 2(sex) ANOVA was performed.

Statistical comparison of the intercorrelation matrices and principal component factor analysis revealed that the organization of spatial abilities is different in men and women, arguing against the hypothesis of cognitive identity for the sexes. Three factors were extracted for both men and women.

A 4(age) and 2(sex) ANOVA was performed which matched the most highly correlated factors for men and women. This analysis evaluated factor scores which could be generated for both populations from the two "genotypic" correlation matrices. One set of spatial factors matched across sexes was clearly not the same, while another set of figural factors appeared to be similar. The third set (a verbal dimension) differed in factor saturation. The nature of specific differences in cognitive structure in spatial abilities remains to be rigorously tested (author abstract slightly changed).

Conner, J. M.; Schackman, M; and Serbin, L. A.: Sex differences in response to practice on a visual spatial test and generalization to a related test. *Child Development*, in press, 1978.

Ninety-three first graders (mean age 6.5 years) were given a pre-test and a post-test on half of the items from the Children's Embedded Figures Test. Half of the children were randomly assigned to a training condition and received a brief training procedure on visual-spatial disembedding prior to the administration of the post-test. Children in the control condition received no training. The performance of girls improved significantly more from pre-test to post-test than the performance of boys. Boys and girls showed similar beneficial effects of training in addition to the benefit of direct practice. The tendency that was observed for boys to perform higher than girls on the pre-test ($p<.10$) was not evident on the post-test. Scores on the pre-test predicted scores on a different measure of visual-spatial ability only for children in the control group. The results are interpreted in terms of current theories of sex differences in visual-spatial perception (author abstract).

Donlon, T. F.: Content factors in sex differences on test questions. Paper presented at the meeting of the New England Educational Research Organization, Boston, June 1971.

This study examined item analysis data for the SAT population of May, 1964. (N = 55,717 boys and 47,082 girls on SAT-M and SAT-V.) Because of the large N, most items yielded significant differences. Following Coffman's focus (1961), analysis of extreme items was made. For the total test, there was no difference between men and women on the verbal, and boys were superior on the mathematical. A practical criterion of .07 (percent passing the item) or greater was chosen to identify items differing between men and women. Eight items favored men, and eleven items favored women on the verbal. In analyzing the sixty items of the mathematical test, seventeen had references to real world things: magazines, pulley wheels, etc. Donlon comments, "There seems to be a masculine tenor to the contents of the seventeen items. No girls are agents in this world. We meet 'a boy,' 'John,' 'a man' . . ." (p. 9). Women did better than men on only two items; one seemed to be accounted for in terms of content, but the other was an algebra question. Analysis of items by content (algebra, geometry, etc.) led to the conclusion that "the approximate forty-point difference between the sexes on this test in scale scores is a function of the content formula. . . . If the content were limited to algebra, the difference could diminish to about twenty points" (p. 10). These analyses do not rule out the possibility that items on which either men or women do well may have some other property in common, other than the apparent masculine or feminine content (from Tobin et al., 1976).

Dwyer, C. A.: Influence of children's sex role standards on reading and arithmetic achievement. *Journal of Educational Psychology,* *66*:811-816, 1974.

The relationship between sex role standards and reading and arithmetic achievement was examined. It was hypothesized that children's sex role standards, assessed by checklist, would predict their achievement test scores. Subjects were 385 middle-class Caucasian children in grades two, four, six, eight, ten, and twelve. Multiple regression analyses indicated that sex role standards contributed significant variance to reading and arithmetic achievement test scores. This effect was stronger for males than females. The results suggest that reading and arithmetic sex differences are more a function of the child's perception of these areas as sex-appropriate or sex-inappropriate than of the child's biological sex, individual preferences for masculine or feminine sex role, or liking or disliking of reading or arithmetic (author abstract).

Ekstrom, R. B.; Donlon, T. F.; and Lockheed, M. E.: The effect of sex biased content on achievement test performance. Paper presented at the annual meeting of the American Educational Research Association, San Francisco, California, April 1976.

The purpose of the study was to find out whether sex bias in the content of achievement tests is a determiner of sex differences in performance on these tests. Four tests were analyzed; California Achievement Tests (Level 5 Form A), Iowa

Test of Basic Skills (Levels 11 and 14 Form 6), Metropolitan Achievement Test (Grade Level 12, Form F) and Sequential Tests of Educational Progress (Grade Level 10, Series II). Content analysis of each item was performed and item analysis based on the norming samples was conducted separately by sex of respondent.

Males outnumber females in the language of achievement tests but for younger children this did not seem to make a difference. At the tenth-grade level, more significant relationships are evidenced. Reading items are easier for girls, regardless of the sex of the references, and mathematics items are easier for boys. However, in general, having more females in items did not make them easier for girls nor did having more males in items make them easier for boys. There were sex differences in response to achievement test items and these may be related to differences in some process which is sensitive to socialization effects (from Tobin et al., 1976).

Elton, C. F. and Rose, H. A.: Traditional sex attitudes and discrepant ability measures in college women. *Journal of Counseling Psychology, 14*:538-543, 1967.

The purpose of this study was to investigate the hypothesis that girls avoid mathematics because of its masculine character. To test this hypothesis, they attempted to ascertain if girls with superior English aptitude and average mathematical aptitude exhibit feminine interests on a measure of masculinity-femininity and if girls with average English aptitude and superior mathematical aptitude exhibit masculine interests on a measure of masculinity-femininity.

The subjects were students at the University of Kentucky who were divided into low, middle, and high English aptitude groups and low, middle, and high mathematical groups on the basis of scores on the American College Test. In addition, scores on the Omnibus Personality Inventory (OPI), which is routinely administered to all entering freshmen, were analyzed.

The results confirm the hypothesis. The high aptitude mathematics—low aptitude English girls exhibited masculine interests, while the high aptitude English—low aptitude mathematics girls exhibited feminine interests on the OPI. The authors suggest that the girls whose masculine role interests are lower have developed their English skills at the comparative expense of their mathematical skills while girls whose masculine interests are higher have developed their mathematical skills at the expense of their English skills. Implications for counseling are suggested (from Tobin et al., 1976).

Fennema, E. and Sherman, J.: Sex-related differences in mathematics achievement, spatial visualization and affective factors. *American Educational Research Journal, 14*:51-71, 1977.

This study investigated (a) mathematics achievement (Test of Academic Progress) of 589 female and 644 male, predominantly white, 9th-12th grade students enrolled in mathematics courses from four schools, controlling for mathematics background and general ability (Quick Word Test); (b) relationship to mathematics achievement, and to sex-related differences in mathematics achievement, of spatial visualization (Differential Aptitude Test), eight attitudes measured by the Fennema-Sherman Mathematics Attitudes Scales, a measure of Mathematics Activities outside of school, and number of Mathematics Related Courses and Space Related Courses taken. Complex results were obtained. Few sex-related cognitive differences but many attitudinal differences were found. Analyses of variance, covariance, correlation, and principal components analysis techniques were used. The results showed important relationships between socio-cultural factors and sex-related cognitive differences (author abstract).

Fox, L. H.: Sex differences in mathematical precocity: Bridging the gap. In Keating, D. P. (Ed.): *Intellectual Talent: Research and Development.* Baltimore, Johns Hopkins, 1976, pp. 183-214.

A special summer accelerated algebra I program for seventh-grade girls was designed to improve their competence in mathematics, accelerate their progress in mathematics, and increase their awareness of career opportunities in science and mathematics. The class was designed to appeal to the girls' social interests. Not all the girls enjoyed the class or benefited from it. This class, however, did appear to be more successful for girls than either of two coeducational classes conducted by the Study of Mathematically Precocious Youth (SMPY). The impact of participation in an accelerated class on the girls was compared with the effect of taking algebra I in a traditional class on girls and boys of similar ability. The major finding was that failure to attend to the social interests of girls in planning special educational experiences in mathematics could lead to a widening of the gap between the sexes with respect to high-level mathematical achievement (author abstract from Tobin et al., 1976)

Gill, N. T.; Herdtner, T. J.; and Lough, L.: Perceptual and socioeconomic variables, instruction in body-orientation, and predicted academic success in young children. *Perceptual and Motor Skills,* 26:1175-1184, 1968.

Perceptual differences were investigated at the first-grade level among Negro and white lower-class children and middle-class white children; and nursery, kindergarten, and first-grade, middle-class, white children. Half of the nursery school children had been given special exercises to enhance bodily awareness. A rod-and-frame test, the Frostig test, and the Metropolitan Achievement test were the criterion measures. Lower-class children were less effective; race was not a significant factor; special exercises were beneficial; and perceptual performance was more highly correlated with predicted academic success for girls (author abstract).

Goldstein, A. G. and Chance, J. E.: Effects of practice on sex-related differences in performance on embedded figures. *Psychonomic Science,* 3:361-362, 1965.

Men and women Ss were tested in an extended series of sixty-eight Embedded Figures. The initial significant sex-related mean difference in discovery times was reduced to almost zero by the final trials. All Ss showed improvement with practice (author abstract).

Helson, R.: Women mathematicians and the creative personality. *Journal of Consulting and Clinical Psychology,* 36:210-220, 1971.

An empirical study of the personality, research style, and background characteristics of women mathematicians was designed to contribute to the understanding of creativity and to appraise women's creativity and potential for scientific accomplishment. It also tested the notion that creative women mathematicians must be "abnormal." Subjects were from forty-one to forty-seven women who had obtained a Ph.D. in mathematics between 1950 and 1960 and were referred by their graduate institution or fellow mathematicians. Age range was twenty-four to sixty-four; two-thirds of the sample were married; and most came from Jewish or Protestant backgrounds. The creativity of each subject was rated by mathematicians in her field of specialization, and subjects were categorized into creative comparison groups based on these ratings. The creative group was believed to constitute virtually all creative women mathematicians in the United States at the time. Assessment procedures included a variety of tests and measures in several areas: Intelligence, personality characteristics, interests, cognitive and esthetic abilities, mathematical style, and personal and professional history.

Findings showed that the women classified as creative were performing at a higher level of professional achievement than the comparison subjects. Results offered no support for the idea that creative women mathematicians differed greatly from other women Ph.D.s in mathematics in cognitive abilities or for the idea that they might be more masculine on the type of measures used. However, many large differences were found between the creative and comparison subjects in background and personality. The traits most characteristic of the creative women were rebellious independence, narcissism, introversion, and a rejection of outside influence; strong symbolic interests and a marked ability to find self-expression and self-gratification in directed research activity; and flexibility, or lack of constriction, in general attitudes and in mathematical work. These traits also appeared stronger in the creative women mathematicians than in creative men mathematicians tested in another study. The creative women sought and, despite obstacles, attained more integration and simplification of life than comparison women. The present study did not investigate why so few women in this country pursue the study of higher mathematics, but the extent of foreign birth and parentage in the sample and the degree to which the creative women were found to reject outside influences suggest that countervailing social pressures are a major factor (from Astin et al., 1975).

Hicks, M. M.; Donlon, T. F.; and Wallmark, M. M.: Sex differences in item responses on the Graduate Record Examination. Unpublished manuscript. Princeton, Educational Testing Service, 1976.

This study explores the scope and nature of sex differences in the December, 1974 aptitude tests of the Graduate Record Examination. It does so by determining individual test items which differ from the other items in terms of the magnitude of the difference in item difficulty for the sexes. The method is used in earlier studies by Angoff and Stern (1972) and by Strassberg-Rosenberg and Donlon (1975). In general, limited evidence of sex differences was established (author abstract).

Hyde, J. S.; Geiringer, E. R.; and Yen, W. M.: On the empirical relation between spatial ability and sex differences in other aspects of cognitive performance. *Multivariate Behavioral Research, 10*:289-309, 1975.

The hypothesis that sex differences in field independence and mental arithmetic can be accounted for by sex differences in spatial ability was supported for a group of forty-six female and thirty-five male undergraduates. Sex-typing does not appear to be strongly related to spatial ability for either sex. There is a possibility of the existence of a field-independence trait independent of spatial ability, particularly among females; however, if such a trait does exist there do not appear to be significant sex differences with respect to it. Factor analysis indicates that tests of spatial ability, field independence, and mental arithmetic emerge together in a spatial ability factor. Sex differences in the factor structure of nine measures, most of which typically display sex differences (spatial ability, field independence, mental arithmetic, vocabulary, verbal and nonverbal creativity, femininity, and achievement motivation) were largely the result of differences with respect to a spatial factor (author abstract).

Study incorrectly states that Sherman hypothesized that feminine, dependent women would have lower spatial ability than women with more masculine identifications. Sherman hypothesized that sex-role linked practice with spatial tasks is a causal factor in sex-related differences in spatial skill. In so far as masculine or feminine identification measured differences in spatial practice, it would be a test of the Sherman hypothesis. Masculine and feminine identifications, however, would not necessarily reflect that practice.

Johnson, S.: Effects of practice and training in spatial skills on sex-related differences in performance on embedded figures. Unpublished thesis, Fairfax, Virginia, George Mason University, 1976.

Scores on the Embedded Figures Test were compared at the beginning of courses and six weeks later for twelve male and twelve female undergraduates in a mathematics course, a language course, and a drafting course. Only the latter was expected to include sufficient spatial training to improve scores on the spatial test. No significant difference between the sexes was found overall. Regardless of sex, the liberal arts groups scored more poorly than both the drafting and mathematics groups on the spatial task. There was a significant sex-related difference on the spatial task in favor of males at the beginning of the drafting course, but no significant difference between the sexes after six weeks. Prior to the training of the drafting course, the women in the three different courses did not differ significantly. After six weeks, however, the women who had taken drafting performed significantly better than the others. Data indicate that (a) spatial performance in women can be easily improved, (b) course of study significantly affects and is related to spatial performance, and (c) females are frequently farther from the asymptote of their spatial ability than males.

Kato, N.: A fundamental study of rod frame test, *Japanese Psychological Research*, 7:61-68, 1965.

Witkin et al. have studied the rod frame test as the problem of the perception of upright. Present study investigated the basic characteristics of this test and its relations to the personality traits. Main findings are as follows: (1) Large error in RFT (field dependent) correlates with high inferiority, subjectiveness, lack of cooperativeness, social introversion and social maladjustment. (2) There are sex differences in extent of the error at adjusting the rod to the true vertical, e.g., women showed larger errors than men, so that women are more field dependent. (3) By practice the errors were eliminated gradually. (4) Individual and conditional differences in the mean errors are large, but the internal consistency was high (author abstract).

Lambert, P.: Mathematical ability and masculinity. *Arithmetic Teacher, 7*:19-21, 1960.

This study was designed to test the relationship between arithmetical ability and masculinity or femininity. The subjects were undergraduates at the University of California at Los Angeles. Group I consisted of eighty students enrolled in advanced courses in mathematics or physics, most of whom were majoring in these subjects. Group II consisted of 1,292 senior students entering practice teaching over a three-year period. All subjects were given two arithmetic tests: Section A of the arithmetic examination of the American Council on Education and a Basic Arithmetic Skills Survey test created by Dr. John Gowan. In addition all were given the Minnesota Multiphasic Personality Inventory (MMPI).

There was no significant difference between the arithmetic test scores of male and female mathematics majors. There was a significant difference between the arithmetic scores of female mathematics majors and female non-mathematics majors, and between male mathematics majors and male non-mathematics majors.

On the masculinity-femininity scale of the MMPI no significant differences were reported between the male mathematics majors and the male non-mathematics majors. The female mathematics majors, however, were shown to be significantly more feminine than the female non-mathematics majors. It was decided to check these results on a new sample of ten additional female mathematics majors. Again this group was rated as significantly more feminine than the group of female non-mathematics majors. There was no correlation found between arithmetic proficiency and masculinity of interest pattern for either sex (from Tobin et al., 1976).

Landy, F.; Rosenberg, B. G.; and Sutton-Smith, B.: The effect of limited father absence on cognitive development. *Child Development, 40*:941-944, 1969.

This study examines the effects of father shift work on girls' cognitive performances. The prediction, based on a previous study, was that girls whose fathers were on shift work for long periods between the ages of five and ten would show a depressed performance on tests of quantitative ability.

The subjects were 100 female students enrolled in a developmental psychology course, predominantly college sophomores with a median age of nineteen years. The subjects were categorized into five groups on two related dimensions of father absence: 1) the period in the subject's life when the father worked the night shift, and 2) the number of years that the father worked on the night shift. Night-shift work was defined as eight consecutive hours with the major portion falling between the hours of 8:00 PM and 8:00 AM, and all the night-shift jobs as well as the father-present jobs were of a manual nature in an effort to minimize socio-economic differences between groups. The subjects' scores on the quantitative part of the American College Entrance Examination were examined.

The only significant difference found was between the father-present group and the total father-absent group, although directionally scores on Q tend to decrease with the degree of father absence. A more important variable seems to be the period of father absence, and this study indicates that the years from one to nine compose a critical period for the development of quantitative skills in girls (from Tobin et al., 1976).

Lynn, D. B.: Determinants of intellectual growth in women. *School Review, 80*:241-260, 1972.

This theoretical discussion draws on pertinent research literature to postulate that the intellectual development of women is based on an interaction of biologically rooted potentials which predispose them toward certain roles, parent-child relationships within the typical family which predispose them toward certain cognitive styles, and cultural reinforcement of their traditionally prescribed roles.

Males surpass females on measures of skills considered essential to scientific, technical, professional, and administrative excellence. Males have also surpassed females in actual intellectual achievement. Evidence from research studies suggests that certain sex differences appear in earliest infancy and are biologically based. These differences function to keep women closer to home and childbearing activities, and most cultures reinforce these biological potentials. It is hypothesized that the process of learning appropriate identification habituates each sex to a different method of perceiving, thinking, and learning, which is subsequently applied generally. The male cognitive style primarily involves defining the goal, restructuring the situation, and abstracting principles. The female cognitive style primarily involves a personal relationship and lesson learning. Traditional feminine role prescriptions are culturally reinforced through the image of females presented in school readers, discriminatory vocational counseling, family disciplinary patterns, advertising images of women, and the patriarchal foundations of the society. Research and educational practices should be aimed at changing stereotypic attitudes and at improving female intellectual performance. Certain experimental procedures for researchers, teachers, and parents are described and suggested (from Astin et al., 1975).

Milton, G. A: Sex differences in problem solving as a function of role appropriateness of the problem content. *Psychological Reports, 5*:705-708, 1959.

This study was designed to test the hypothesis that when the characteristics of problems are altered so as to make them less appropriate to the masculine sex role, the sex differences in problem-solving will be reduced.

The subjects were twenty-four undergraduate men and twenty-four undergraduate women from the University of Colorado. They were all given a set of twenty problems, half with content appropriate to the masculine role and half with content appropriate to the feminine role.

The results showed that sex differences in problem solving were reduced when the content of the problems was more appropriate to the feminine role than to the masculine role (from Tobin et al., 1976).

Naditch, S. F.: Sex differences in field dependence: The role of social influence. Paper presented at the convention of the American Psychological Association, Washington, D. C., 1976.

It was argued that an unacknowledged factor accounting for at least part of the variability in findings of sex differences in field dependence is related to the demand characteristics of the experimental situations. Results of an experiment designed to assess the effects of alteration in the sex-typing of the task upon sex differences in performance were reported. Sixty-four subjects were assigned in equal numbers of males and females to the standard Rod-and-Frame condition and to a modified version substituting the figure of a female person for the rod. Instructions described the standard condition as a test of perceptual abilities related to spatial aspects of intelligence and the person condition as a test of empathy. There was a highly significant Sex X condition interaction, with males being more field independent than females in the standard rod condition and females becoming significantly more field independent in the person condition. This finding documents a situational source of variance in sex differences in field dependence, presumably related to the sex-role appropriateness of the experimental condition (author abstract).

Nash, S. C.: The relationship among sex-role stereotyping, sex-role preference, and the sex difference in spatial visualization. *Sex Roles, 1*:15-32, 1975.

At an early age, children attain concepts of sex-appropriate activities, behaviors, attitudes, and goals, i.e., sex-role stereotypes. These conceptual stereotypes seem to assign a less favorable role to females. Thus it seems plausible that their acceptance (by both sexes) might be at least partly responsible for the performance differences that begin to arise in adolescence and adulthood. In view of the importance of early adolescence as a transitional period during which sex-role requirements are augmented and intellectual sex differences emerge, 105 eleven-year-olds and 102 fourteen-year-olds were selected as subjects. Their spatial abilities, sex-role concepts, and sex-role preferences were assessed. Stereotyping sex roles (in general) was not associated with spatial performance; stereotyping sex roles that included information regarding subjects' views about intellectual competence was related to performance. The sex difference in spatial ability that emerged at age fourteen was among subjects with own-sex preferences only; there were no sex differences among subjects who preferred to be boys (author abstract).

Nelson, E. A. and Maccoby E. E.: The relationship between social development and differential abilities on the Scholastic Aptitude Test. *Merrill-Palmer Qurterly,* *4*:269-284, 1966.

This study was designed to investigate hypotheses centering around sex typing and the interfering effects of certain tension producing experiences upon cognitive processes. A biographical questionnaire concerning family and social relationships was given to 1,956 college freshmen. The responses to this questionnaire were analyzed in relation to differential verbal and mathematical abilities. For boys it was found that a high-verbal, low-mathematics pattern was associated with reports of father absence, punishment exclusively by the mother, fear of father, and reports of having been a "mamma's boy," or "daddy's boy." A high-mathematics, low-verbal pattern was found among boys who reported punishment exclusively by the father, and having talked over personal problems with the father. For girls a high-verbal, low-mathematics pattern was associated with reports of fearfulness of one's mother and "only sometimes" talking over personal problems with the father. A high-mathematics, low-verbal pattern was found for Ss of both sexes who reported having many friends and some close friends. Consideration of the results led to an interpretation relating dependency conflict and sex typing to the tension-interference hypothesis (author abstract, from Tobin et al., 1976).

Rosenkrantz, P. S.; Vogel, S. R.; Bee, H.; Broverman, I. K.; and Broverman, D. M.: Sex-role stereotypes and self-concepts in college students. *Journal of Consulting and Clinical Psychology, 32*:287-295, 1968.

A questionnaire administered to college students probed the extent to which sex-role stereotypes, with their associated social values, influence the self-concepts of men and women. The seventy-four male and eighty female students were asked to characterize the behaviors, attitudes, and personality traits of typical adult males, adult females, and themselves, by means of 122 bipolar items.

In contrast to expected results, self-concepts did not differ from stereotypic concepts of masculinity and femininity as a function of the social desirability of the stereotype. Results indicated strong agreement between sexes about differences between men and women, corresponding differences between the self-concepts of the sexes, and more frequent high valuation of stereotypically masculine characteristics by both sexes. Women seemed to hold negative values of their worth relative to men, indicating the influence of the factors that create this sex stereotyped self-concept. A cultural lag may account for the persistence of sex-role stereotypes despite contemporary changes in the prescribed sex-role behavior in this society. It is also noted that older or married subjects or subjects of other educational and social class levels might produce different patterns of responses (from Astin et al., 1975).

Sherman, J.: Problem of sex differences in space perception and aspects of intellectual functioning. *Psychological Review, 74*:290-299, 1967.

Key measures of analytical cognitive approach are substantially related to space perception, and therefore are sex biased. Consequently a conclusion of sex differences in analytical ability based on these data appears unwarranted. The construct of analytical cognitive approach, itself, appears questionable. Space perception also appears to be a relevant variable to control in studies of sex differences in geometric and mathematical problem solving. A causal explanation of the development of sex differences in spatial perception is presented based partly on differential practice. Other causal explanations of sex differences in analytical approach are discussed and an attempt is made to accommodate them within this framework (author abstract).

Sherman, J.: Field articulation, sex, spatial visualization, dependency, practice, laterality of the brain and birth order. *Perceptual and Motor Skills, 38*:1223-1235, 1974.

Among twenty-five female and twenty-five male college students, field-articulation measures—Rod and Frame Test (RFT), Embedded Figures Test, Space Relations Test of DAT—correlated highly with spatial visualization, but not consistently with each other or with measures of dependency. Practice significantly affected RFT performance for both sexes ($p<.01$), but no sex-related differences were found for measures of field-articulation or dependency. Males' mean for spatial visualization was higher ($p<.05$); males were more confident than females on RFT performance even though no more accurate ($p<.05$). Among Ss oldest of sibs, females were less field-articulated, males more. Males had higher RFT errors when the frame top was tilted to Ss left; females had higher RFT errors when the frame was tilted to the right ($p<.05$). This finding can be explained by the hypothesis that the left hemisphere of the brain is more frequently important for spatial function for females than for males. Previously unanalyzed data from a temporal lobectomy study also supported this hypothesis (author abstract).

Sherman, J. and Fennema, E.: The study of mathematics by high school girls and boys: Related variable. *American Educational Research Journal, 14*:159-168, 1977.

Reported is a study comparing females and males enrolled in high school mathematics classes on their intent to enroll in additional mathematics classes and affective variables related to this intent. Significantly more males than females, especially from the lower half of the achievement distribution, intended to continue to study mathematics. Controlling for cognitive differences 10th and 11th grade students differing in intent to take mathematics (n = 716) responded differently to nearly all of the Fennema-Sherman Mathematics Attitudes Scales. When girls and boys were "equated" for cognitive variables and intent to study mathematics, few sex-related differences in attitudes toward mathematics were found (author abstract).

Stein, A. H. and Smithells, J.: Age and sex differences in children's sex-role standards about achievement. *Development Psychology, 1*:252-259, 1969.

This study is the second in a series of investigations of children's sex-role standards for achievement in the areas of athletic, spatial and mechanical, arithmetic, reading, artistic, and social skills. Sex-role standards were defined as an individual's conception of the behaviors and attributes appropriate to each sex. Subjects were 120 middle-class boys and girls from the 2nd, 6th, and 12th grades of Ithaca, New York, public schools. They were asked in an interview to make forced choices and to rank order sex-role judgments on activities reflecting the above skills. The two measures allowed achievement areas to be rated separately for masculinity and femininity as well as on a masculine-feminine continuum.

Despite age and sex differences, the sample as a whole considered artistic, social, and reading skills to be most feminine, and athletic, spatial and mechanical, and arithmetic skills to be most masculine. As expected, older subjects generally had more definite and extreme sex-role standards. Girls tended to view more activities as feminine than did boys, especially in athletic and reading skills, but sex differences decreased with age. Twelfth graders showed an awareness of both adolescent and adult standards. Significant age-sex interactions in some skill areas suggest that the change in sex-role standards from 2nd to 12th grade is primarily concerned with learning what is inappropriate for one's own sex, rather than what is appropriate (from Astin et al., 1975).

Strauch, A. B.: The development of sex differences in spatial and verbal abilities. Paper presented at the convention of the American Psychology Association, Washington, D. C., 1976.

The issue of the development of sex differences has become of major interest to researchers. To account for the male superiority in spatial visualization three theoretical models postulating biological origins have been forwarded. With regard to female superiority in verbal skills, however, there is little such agreement. Developmental trends in the sex differences in these two abilities were examined to ascertain if assertions about the ages at which these differences occur would be replicated and thereby determine if the models would be supported. The results revealed that the male spatial superiority was consistent across ages six to sixteen, thereby failing to support one of the models which theorized its development at adolescence. In verbal ability, the female superiority was fairly strong at younger ages but practically disappeared by middle adolescence. The need for further research was outlined (author abstract).

THE WISCONSIN STUDY:
SPECIAL CONSIDERATIONS

DURING 1974 to 1976, data were carefully collected from a large sample of 6-12th grade students (about 3,000) in one midwestern city. A primary purpose of the investigation was to compare the sexes in their performance in mathematics, to evaluate the extent of the differences, if any, and to study factors which might be related to the differences.

The problems of unbiased testing for sex-related differences are many, as have been described. In the Wisconsin study, differential drop out of the two sexes from high school was not found to be a problem. Plenty of other problems remained. When the two sexes have basically the same curriculum, at least a massive, environmental source of variance is controlled. When the curricula differ, however, serious problems of bias can occur. If one takes a true random sample, or representative sample, of the entire population, the effects of differential training are not controlled. If one takes a sample of students with the same course of study, one cannot be sure that the two sexes have been equally selected into the course of study. In the Wisconsin study this problem was handled by (a) obtaining a more than usually detailed population description (see Fennema and Sherman, 1977), (b) keeping track of major relevant differences in courses, (c) controlling course of study for the major dependent variable, mathematics, and (d) controlling for general intelligence.

Students included in the main high school study had followed the same basic sequence of mathematics courses, e.g., in high school: 9th grade — algebra, 10th grade — geometry, 11th grade — algebra, trigonometry, or precalculus; 12th grade — advanced algebra or calculus. Count was also kept of the number of space-related courses, e.g., drafting; and math-related courses, e.g., physics, which the students had taken.

For grades six to eight, there was no problem about biased selection into courses since the two sexes were enrolled in the same curriculum. Because of a desire to look at age trends in students of ability similar to those in the high school sample, teachers were asked to eliminate the lower 15 percent of the 6th to 8th grade sample. While no known bias in comparing the sexes was introduced by this procedure, that possibility cannot be ruled out. A more objective way of proceeding would have been preferable. In grade nine, one slice of the data (at School 4) included a representative sample of all students, i.e., including general math students. (Reported in Sherman and Fennema, 1978.) The main body of the 9th grade data concerns only algebra students. Nearly 100 percent of 9th grade students were enrolled in mathematics; depending on the school, 5 to 9 percent more males than females were enrolled in general mathematics. In the 10th grade, 53 percent of both sexes were enrolled in geometry. Hence the two sexes should be very comparable from grades six to ten with any bias being in favor of males in the algebra only comparison in grade nine. Since more boys than girls took general math, boys in algebra might be more select than girls. This bias in favor of males would not apply to the extended representative sample at School 4 but would apply to the main data. In grade eleven, 5 percent more males were enrolled in algebra-trig or precalculus and in grade twelve, 9 percent more males were enrolled in advanced algebra or calculus. (See Fennema and Sherman, 1977 for more detail.)

The point could be raised that the girls in the 11th and 12th grade samples are *particularly* select. However, a check of the general intelligence, as measured by vocabulary, of the two groups did not show any significant differences between the sexes at any grade. (Though see exception, Sherman and Fennema, 1977.) Girls might be disinclined to take advanced mathematics not because they are any less able than other students, but because of other complex reasons. In this event the 11th and 12th grade samples of girls in mathematics would not necessarily be any more intellectually select than the boys. Such appears to be the case with this sample.

Because of the skepticism that has greeted negative findings of sex-related differences, some further notes of explanation may be helpful. The results cannot be attributed to any special mobilizing of motivation on the part of girls. No discussions about sex-related differences were held with either students or teachers until after testing was finished. Both male and female testers were used. As mentioned, a possible factor, however, may be the fact that for the last several years in grades six to eight the school system has required both boys and girls to take industrial art, which includes a section on drafting. It is possible that the sexes have a more similar curriculum than in some other cities.

BIBLIOGRAPHY

Aiken, L. R., Jr.: Non-intellective variables and mathematics achievement: Directions for research. *Journal of School Psychology, 8*:28-36, 1970.

Aiken, L. R. Jr.: Research on attitudes toward mathematics. *Arithmetic Teacher, 19*:229-234, 1972.

Aiken, L. R., Jr.: Two scales of attitude toward mathematics. *Journal for Research in Mathematics Education, 5*:67-71, 1974.

Aiken, L. R., Jr.: Some speculations and findings concerning sex differences in mathematical abilities and attitudes. In Fennema, E. (Ed.): *Mathematics Learning: What Research Says about Sex Differences.* Columbus, Ohio, ERIC Mathematics, Science and Environmental Education Clearinghouse, December, 1975.

Aiken, L. R., Jr.: Update on attitudes and other affective variables in learning mathematics. *Review of Educational Research, 46*:293-311, 1976.

Alexander, K. L. and Eckland, B. K.: Sex differences in the educational attainment process. *American Sociological Review, 39*:668-682, 1974.

Allen, M. J.: Sex differences in spatial problem solving styles. *Perceptual and Motor Skills, 39*:843-846, 1974.

Anastasi, A.: *Differential Psychology.* New York, Macmillan, 1949.

Anastasi, A.: *Differential Psychology: Individual and Group Differences in Behavior,* 3rd ed., New York, Macmillan, 1958.

Anastasi, A.: Four hypotheses with a dearth of data: Response to Lehrke's "A theory of X-linkage of major intellectual traits." *American Journal of Mental Deficiency, 76*:620-622, 1972.

Andrew, R. J. and Rogers, L. J.: Testosterone, behavior and persistence. *Nature, 237*:343-346, 1972.

Angoff, W. H. (Ed.): *The College Board Admissions Test Program.* New York, College Entrance Examination Board, 1971.

Archer, J.: Biological explanations of psychological sex differences. In Lloyd, B. and Archer, A. (Eds.): *Exploring Sex Differences.* London, Academic Press, 1976.

Astin, H. S.: Sex difference in mathematical and scientific precocity. In Stanley, J. C.; Keating, D. P.; and Fox, L. H. (Eds.): *Mathematical Talent: Discovery, Description, and Development.* Baltimore, Johns Hopkins, 1974.

Astin, H. S.; Parelman, A.; and Fisher, A.: *Sex Roles: A Research Bibliography.* Washington, D. C., National Institute of Mental Health, 1975.

239

Bakan, D.: The test of significance in psychological research. In Morrison, D. E. and Henkel, R. E. (Eds.): *The Significance Test Controversy: A Reader.* Chicago, Aldine, 1970.

Bakan, P.: Hypnotizability, laterality of eye-movements and functional brain asymmetry. *Perceptual and Motor Skills, 28*:927-932, 1969.

Bakan, P.: The eyes have it. *Psychology Today, 4*:64-67, 96, 1971.

Bakan, P. and Putnam, W.: Right-left discrimination and brain lateralization: Sex differences. *Archives of Neurology, 30*:334-335, 1974.

Baker, S. and Ehrhardt, A. A.: Prenatal androgen, intelligence and cognitive sex differences. In Friedman, R. C.; Richart, R. M.; and Vande Wiele, R. L. (Eds.): *Sex Differences in Behavior.* New York, Wiley, 1974.

Bardwick, J. M.: *Psychology of Women,* New York, Har-Row, 1971.

Barry, H.; Bacon, M. K.; and Child, I. L.: A cross-cultural survey of some sex differences in socialization. *Journal of Abnormal and Social Psychology, 55*:327-332, 1957.

Bayley, N.: Individual patterns of development. *Child Development, 27*:45-74, 1956.

Bennett, G. K.; Seashore, H. G.; and Wesman, A. G.: *A Manual for Differential Aptitude Test.* New York, Psych Corp, 1952.

Bennett, G. K.; Seashore, H. G.; and Wesman, A. G.: *Differential Aptitudes Tests Manual,* 3rd ed., New York, Psych Corp, 1959.

Bennett, G. K.; Seashore, H. G.; and Wesman, A. G.: *Differential Aptitude Tests Manual.* 4th ed., New York, Psych Corp, 1966.

Bennett, G. K.; Seashore, H. G.; and Wesman, A. G.: *Differential Aptitude Tests, Forms S and T* 4th ed, New York, Psych Corp, 1973.

Bentzen, F.: Sex ratios in learning and behavior disorders. *Journal of Orthopsychiatry, 23*:92-98, 1963.

Bernard, J.: Sex differences: An overview. Paper presented to the American Association for the Advancement of Science, Washington, D. C., 1972.

Berne, E.: *What Do You Say After You Say Hello?* New York, Grove, 1972.

Berry, J. W.: Temne and Eskimo perceptual skills. *International Journal of Psychology, 1*:207-229, 1966.

Blade, M. and Watson, W. S.: Increase in spatial visualization test scores during engineering study. *Psychological Monographs, 69* (397), 1955.

Bleier, R.: Myths of the biological inferiority of women: An exploration of the sociology of biological research. *University of Michigan Papers in Women's Studies, 2*:39-63, 1976.

Block, J. H.: Conceptions of sex role: Some cross-cultural and longitudinal perspectives. *American Psychologist, 28*:512-526, 1973.

Block, J. H.: Review of The Psychology of Sex Differences by Maccoby, E. E. and Jacklin, C. N. *Contemporary Psychology, 21*:517-522, 1976a.

Block, J. H.: *Review of The Psychology of Sex Differences* by Maccoby, E. E. and Jacklin, C. N. *Merrill-Palmer Quarterly, 22*:283-308, 1976b.

Block. J. H.: Another look at sex differentiation in the socialization behaviors of mothers and fathers. In Sherman, J. and Denmark, F., (Eds.):

Psychology of Women: Future Directions of Research. New York, Psych Dimensions, in press, 1978.

Bock, R. D.: A family study of spatial visualizing ability. *American Psychologist*, 22:571, 1967, (Abstract)

Bock, R. D.: Word and image: Sources of the verbal and spatial factors in mental test scores. *Psychometrika*, 38:437-457, 1973.

Bock, R. D. and Kolakowski, D.: Further evidence of sex-linked major-gene influence on human spatial visualizing ability. *American Journal of Human Genetics*, 25:1-14, 1973.

Bogen, J. E. and Bogen, G. M.: The other side of the brain III: The corpus callosum and creativity. *Bulletin of the Los Angeles Neurological Societies*, 34:191-221, 1969.

Bogen, J. E.; DeZure, R.; Tenhouten, W. D.; and Marsh, J. F.: The other side of the brain IV: The A/P ratio. *Bulletin of the Los Angeles Neurological Societies*, 37:49-61, 1972.

Bouchard, T. J. and McGee, M. G.: Sex differences in human spatial ability: Not an X-linked recessive gene effect. *Social Biology*, in press, 1977.

Briggs, G. G.; Nebes, R. D.; and Kinsbourne, M.: Intellectual differences in relation to personal and family handedness. *Quarterly Journal of Experimental Psychology*, in press, 1976.

Brinkmann, E. H.: Programmed instruction as a technique for improving spatial visualization. *Journal of Applied Psychology*, 50:179-184, 1966.

Brooks, G. W. and Mueller, E. F.: Serum urate concentrations among university professors. *Journal of the American Medical Association*, 195:415-418, 1966.

Broverman, D. M.: Generality and behavioral correlates of cognitive styles. *Journal of Consulting Psychology*, 28:487-500, 1964.

Broverman, D. M.: Personal communication, April 1977.

Broverman, D. M.; Broverman, I. K.; Vogel, W.; Palmer, R. D.; and Klaiber, E. L.: The automatization cognitive style and physical development. *Child Development*, 35:1343-1359, 1964.

Broverman, D. M. and Klaiber, E. L.: Negative relationships between abilities. *Psychometrika*, 34:5-20, 1969.

Broverman, D. M.; Klaiber, E. L.; Kobayashi, Y.; and Vogel, W.: Roles of activation and inhibition in sex differences in cognitive abilities. *Psychological Review*, 75:23-50, 1968.

Broverman, D. M.; Klaiber, E. L.; Kobayashi, Y.; and Vogel, W.: Reply to the "Comment" by Singer and Montgomery on "Roles of activation and inhibition in sex differences in cognitive abilities." *Psychological Review*, 76:328-331, 1969.

Broverman, I. K.; Vogel, S. R.; Broverman, D. M.; Clarkson, F. E.; and Rosenkrantz, P. S.: Sex-role stereotypes: A current appraisal. *Journal of Social Issues*, 2:59-78, 1972.

Bryden, M. P.: Tachistoscopic recognition, handedness, and cerebral dominance. *Neuropsychologia*, 3:1-8, 1965.

Buckley, F.: Preliminary report on intelligence quotient scores of patients with Turner's syndrome: A replication study. *British Journal of Psychiatry, 119*:513-514, 1971.

Buffery, A. W. H. and Gray, J. A.: Sex differences in the development of spatial and linguistic skills. In Ounsted, C. and Taylor, D. C. (Eds.): *Gender Differences: Their Ontogeny and Significance.* Baltimore, Williams & Wilkins, 1972.

Burt, C.: *The Factors of the Mind.* London, University of London Press, 1940.

Burt, C. and Moore, R. C.: The mental differences between the sexes. *Journal of Experimental Pedagogy, 1*:355-388, 1912.

Byrne, D.: The repression-sensitization scale: Rationale, reliability, and validity. *Journal of Personality, 29*:344-349, 1961.

Cancro, R. (Ed.): *Intelligence: Genetic and Environmental Influences.* New York, Grune, 1971.

Carey, G. L.: Sex differences in problem-solving performance as a function of attitude differences. *Journal of Abnormal and Social Psychology, 56*:256-260, 1958.

Carlsmith, L.: Effect of early father absence on scholastic aptitude. *Harvard Educational Review, 34*:3-21, 1964.

Carlson, E. R. and Carlson, R.: Male and female subjects in personality research. *Journal of Abnormal and Social Psychology, 61*:482-483, 1961.

Carlson, R.: Where is the person in personality research? *Psychological Bulletin, 75*:203-219, 1971.

Carr, B. M.: Ear effect variables and order of report in dichotic listening. *Cortex, 5*:63-68, 1969.

Carroll, J. B.: Fitting a model of school learning to aptitude and achievement data over grade levels. In Green, D. R. (Ed.): *The Aptitude-Achievement Distinction.* Monterey, California, CTB/McGraw-Hill, 1974.

Castle, C. A.: A statistical study of eminent women. *Columbia Contributions to Philosophy and Psychology, 22*(27), 1913. (Cited in Shields, 1975.)

Castore, C. H. and Stafford, R. E.: The effect of sex role perception on test taking performance. *Journal of Psychology, 74*:175-180, 1970.

Cattell, J. McK.: A statistical study of eminent men. *Popular Science Monthly, 62*:359-377, 1903. (Cited in Shields, 1975.)

Chance, J. E. and Goldstein, A. G.: Internal-external control of reinforcement and embedded-figures performance. *Perception and Psychophysics, 9*:33-34, 1971.

Childs, B.: Genetic origins of some sex differences among human beings. *Pediatrics, 35*:798-812, 1965.

Clarke, E. H.: *Sex in Education: Or, a Fair Chance for Girls.* Buffalo, New York, Heritage Press, 1873.

Coates, S.: Sex differences in field dependence-independence between the ages of 3 and 6. *Perceptual and Motor Skills, 39*:1307-1310, 1974a.

Coates, S.: Sex differences in field independence among preschool children. In Friedman, R. C.; Richart, R. M.; and Vande Wiele, R. K. (Eds.): Sex Differences in Behavior. New York, Wiley, 1974b.

Coates, S.; Lord, M.; and Jakabovics, E.: Field dependence-independence, social-non-social play and sex differences in preschool children. *Perceptual and Motor Skills, 40*:195-202, 1975.

Cohen, B. D.; Berent, S.; and Silverman, A. J.: Field-dependence and lateralization of function in the human brain. *Archives of General Psychiatry, 28*:165-167, 1973.

Cohen, B. D.; Noblin, C. D.; Silverman, A. J.; and Penick, S. B.: Functional asymmetry of the human brain. *Science, 162*:475-477, 1968.

Cohen, D.: Sex differences in the organization of spatial abilities in older men and women. Doctoral dissertation, Los Angeles, University of Southern California, 1975. *Dissertation Abstracts International,* in press. (University Microfilms, No. 75-15, 522.)

Coleman, J. S.: *The Adolescent Society.* New York, Free Press of Glencoe, 1963.

Condry, J. and Dyer, S.: Fear of success: Attribution of cause to the victim. *Journal of Social Issues, 32*:63-84, 1976.

Connor, J. M.; Schackman, M.; and Serbin, L. A.: Sex differences in response to practice on a visual spatial test and generalization to a related test. *Child Development,* in press, 1978.

Connor, J. M.; Serbin, L. A.; and Schackman, M.: Sex differences in children's response to training on a visual-spatial test. *Developmental Psychology, 13*:293-294, 1977.

Constantinople, A.: Masculinity-femininity: An exception to a famous dictum? *Psychological Bulletin, 80*:389-407, 1973.

Corah, N. L.: Differentiation in children and their parents. *Journal of Personality, 33*:300-308, 1965.

Crandall, V. C.: Achievement behavior in young children. In Hartup, W. H. and Smothergill, N. L. (Eds.): *The Young Child: Reviews of Research.* Washington, D. C., National Association for the Education of Young Children, 1967.

Culliton, B. J.: Patients' rights: Harvard is site of battle over X and Y chromosomes. *Science, 186*:715-717, 1974.

Culliton, B. J.: XYY: Harvard researcher under fire stops newborn screening. *Science, 188*:1284-1285, 1975.

Dalton, K.: Ante-natal progesterone and intelligence. *British Journal of Psychiatry, 114*:1377-1382, 1968.

Dawson, J.: Cultural and physiological influences upon spatial-perceptual processes in West Africa. *International Journal of Psychology, 2*:171-185, 1967.

Dawson, J.: Effects of sex hormones in cognitive style in rats and men. *Behavior Genetics, 2*:21-42, 1972.

Day, M. E.: An eye-movement indicator of type and level of anxiety: Some clinical observations. Journal of Clinical Psychology, 23:433-441, 1967.

Deaux, K.: The Behavior of Women and Men. Monterey, California, Brooks/Cole, 1976.

DeFries, J. C.; Ashton, G. C.; Johnson, R. C.; Kuse, A. R.; McClearn, G. E.; Mi, M. P.; Rashad, M. N.; Vandenberg, S. G.; and Wilson, J. R.: Parent-offspring resemblance for specific cognitive abilities in two ethnic groups. Nature, 261:131-133, 1976.

DeRussy, E. A. and Futch, E.: Field dependence-independence as related to college curricula. Perceptual and Motor Skills, 33:1235-1237, 1971.

Dimond, S. J. and Beaumont, J. G.: A right hemisphere basis for calculation in the human brain. Psychonomic Science, 26:137-138, 1972.

Dimond, S. J. and Beaumont, J. G. (Eds.): Hemisphere Function in the Human Brain. New York, Wiley, 1974.

Donlon, T. F.: Content factors in sex differences on test questions. Paper presented at the meeting of the New England Educational Research Organization, Boston, June 1971.

Donlon, T. F.; Ekstrom, R. B.; and Lockheed, M.: Comparing the sexes on achievement items of varying content. Paper presented at the annual meeting of the American Psychological Association, Washington, D. C., September 1976. (Cited in Fox, 1977.)

Dornbusch, S. M.: To try or not to try. The Stanford Magazine, 2:50-54, 1974.

Doughty, C. and McDonald, P. G.: Hormonal control of sexual differentiation of the hypothalamus in the neonatal female rat. Differentiation, 2:275-285, 1974.

Droege, R. C.: Sex differences in aptitude maturation during high school. Journal of Counseling Psychology, 14:407-411, 1967.

Duke, J. D.: Lateral eye-movement behavior. Journal of General Psychology, 78:189-195, 1968.

Dunn, J. P.; Brooks, G. W.; Mausner, J.; Rodnan, G. P.; and Cobb, S.: Social class gradient of serum uric acid levels in males. Journal of the American Medical Association, 185:431-436, 1963.

Dwyer, C. A.: Influence of children's sex role standards on reading and arithmetic achievement. Journal of Educational Psychology, 66:811-816, 1974.

Edwards, A. L.: Edwards Personal Preference Schedule, Manual. New York, Psych Corp, 1959.

Edwards, D. A. and Herndon, J.: Neonatal estrogen stimulation and aggressive behavior in female mice. Physiology Behavior, 5:993-995, 1970.

Ehrhardt, A. A. and Money, J.: Progestin-induced hermaphroditism: IQ and psychosexual identity in a study of ten girls. Journal of Sex Research, 3:83-100, 1967.

Ehrlichman, H. I.: Hemispheric functioning and individual differences in cognitive abilities. Doctoral dissertation, New York, New School for Social Research, 1971. Dissertation Abstracts Internationl, 33:2319B, 1972.

(University Microfilms No. 72-27, 869.)

Ekstrom, R. B.; Donlon, T. F.; and Lockheed, M. E.: The effect of sex biased content on achievement test performance. Paper presented at the annual meeting of the American Educational Research Association, San Francisco, California, April 1976. (Cited in Fox, 1977.)

Ellis, H.: *Man and Woman: A Study of Human Secondary Sexual Characteristics.* London, Walter Scott: New York, Scribner, 1894.

Ellis, H.: *Man and Woman: A Study of Secondary and Tertiary Sexual Characteristics* 8th rev. ed. London, Heinemann, 1934. (As quoted in Shields, 1975.)

Elton, C. F. and Rose, H. A.: Traditional sex attitudes and discrepant ability measures in college women. *Journal of Counseling Psychology, 14*:538-543, 1967.

Englander-Golden, P.; Willis, K. A.; and Dienstbier, R. A.: Intellectual performance as a function of repression and menstrual cycle. Paper presented at the convention of the American Psychology Association, Washington, D. C., 1976.

Erlenmeyer-Kimling, L. and Jarvik, L. F.: Genetics and intelligence: A review. *Science, 142*:1477-1479, 1963.

Ernest, J.: *Mathematics and Sex.* Santa Barbara, U of Cal Pr, 1976.

Etaugh, C. F.: Personality correlates of lateral eye movement and handedness. *Perceptual and Motor Skills, 34*:751-754, 1972.

Fairweather, H.: Sex differences in cognition. *Cognition, 4*:231-280, 1976.

Federman, D. D.: *Abnormal Sexual Development: A Genetic and Endocrine Approach to Differential Diagnosis.* Philadelphia, Saunders, 1968.

Fee, E.: Science and the woman problem: Historical perspectives. In Teitelbaum, M. S. (Ed.): *Sex Differences.* Garden City, New York, Anchor, 1976.

Fennema, E.: Mathematics learning and the sexes: A review. *Journal for Research in Mathematics Education, 5*:126-139, 1974.

Fennema, E.: Influences of selected cognitive, affective and educational variables on sex-related differences in mathematics learning and studying. In Fox, L. H.; Fennema, E.; and Sherman, J.: *Women and Mathematics: Research Perspectives for Change.* Washington, D. C., United States Government Printing Office, 1977.

Fennema, E. and Sherman, J.: Fennema-Sherman Mathematics Attitudes Scales. *Journal Supplement Abstract Service, Catalog of Selected Documents in Psychology, 6*:31, 1976. (Ms. No. 1225.)

Fennema, E. and Sherman, J.: Sex-related differences in mathematics achievement, spatial visualization and affective factors. *American Educational Research Journal, 14*:51-71, 1977.

Fennema, E. and Sherman, J.: Sex-related differences in mathematics achievement and related factors: A further study. *Journal of Research in Mathematics Education,* in press, 1978.

Ferguson, L. R. and Maccoby, E.: Interpersonal correlates of differential abilities. *Child Development*, 37:549-571, 1966.

Ferguson-Smith, M. A.: Karotype-phenotype correlations in gonadal dysgenesis and their bearing on the pathogenesis of malformations. *Journal Medical Genetics*, 2:142-155, 1965.

Fernberger, S. W.: Persistence of stereotypes concerning sex differences. *Journal of Abnormal and Social Psychology*, 43:97-101, 1948.

Flanagan, J. C.: Changes in school levels of achievement: Project Talent ten and fifteen year retests. *Educational Researcher*, 5:9-12, 1976.

Flanagan, J. C.; Dailey, J. T.; Shaycoft, M. F.; Gorham, W. A.; Orr, D. B.; Goldberg, I.; and Neyman, C. A., Jr.: *Counselor's Technical Manual for Interpreting Test Scores.* Palo Alto, California, Project Talent 1961. (Cited in Maccoby and Jacklin, 1974.)

Flanagan, J. C.; Davis, F. B.; Dailey, J. T.; Shaycoft, M. F.; Orr, D. B.; Goldberg, I.; and Neyman, C. A., Jr. *The American High School Student Today.* Pittsburgh, University of Pittsburgh, 1964.

Fox, L. H.: A mathematics program for fostering precocious achievement. In Stanley, J. C.; Keating, D. P.; and Fox, L. H. (Eds.): *Mathematical Talent: Discovery, Description and Development.* Baltimore, Johns Hopkins, 1974.

Fox, L. H.: Sex differences in mathematical precocity: Bridging the gap. In Keating, D. P. (Ed.): *Intellectual Talent: Research and Development.* Baltimore, Johns Hopkins, 1976.

Fox, L. H.: The effects of sex role socialization on mathematics participation and achievement. In Fox, L.; Fennema, E.; and Sherman, J.: *Women and Mathematics: Research Perspectives for Change.* Washington, D. C., United States Government Printing Office, 1977.

Freeman, J.: The legal basis of the sexual caste system. *Valparaiso University Law Review*, 5:203-236, 1971.

Freire-Maia, A.; Freire-Maia, D. V.; and Morton, N. E.: Sex effect on intelligence and mental retardation. *Behavior Genetics*, 4:269-272, 1974.

Friedman, H.: Magnitude of experimental effect and a table for its rapid estimation. *Psychological Bulletin*, 70:245-251, 1968.

Friedman, R. C.; Richart, R. M.; and Vande Wiele, R. L. (Eds.): *Sex Differences in Behavior.* New York, Wiley, 1974.

Frieze, I. H.; Fisher, J.; Hanusa, B.; McHugh, M.; and Valle, V. A.: Attributions of the causes of success and failure as internal and external barriers to achievement in women. In Sherman, J. and Denmark, F. (Eds.): *Psychology of Women: Future Directions of Research.* New York, Psych Dimensions, in press, 1978.

Fruchter, B.: Measurement of spatial abilities: History and background. *Educational and Psychological Measurement*, 14:387-395, 1954.

Garai, J. E. and Scheinfeld, A.: Sex differences in mental and behavioral traits. *Genetic Psychology Monographs*, 77:169-299, 1968.

Garron, D. C.: Sex-linked, recessive inheritance of spatial and numerical abilities, and Turner's syndrome. *Psychological Review*, 77:145-152,

1970.
Garron, D. C. and Vander Stoep, L. R.: Personality and intelligence in Turner's syndrome. *Archives of General Psychiatry, 21*:339-346, 1969.
Geddes, P. and Thomson, J. A.: *The Evolution of Sex.* New York, Scribner & Welford, 1890. (As quoted in Shields, 1975.)
Gibson, E. J.: Improvement in perceptual judgments as a function of controlled practice or training. *Psychological Bulletin, 50*:401-431, 1953.
Gill, N. T.; Herdtner, T. J.; and Lough, L.: Perceptual and socio-economic variables, instruction in body-orientation, and predicted academic success in young children. *Perceptual and Motor Skills, 26*:1175-1184, 1968.
Goldberg, P.: Are women prejudiced against women? *Transaction, 5*:28-30, 1968.
Goldberg, S.: *The Inevitability of Patriarchy.* New York, Morrow, 1973.
Goldberg, S. and Lewis, M.: Play behavior in the year-old infant: Early sex differences. *Child Development, 40*:21-31, 1969.
Goldstein, A. and Chance, J.: Effects of practice on sex-related differences in performance on embedded figures. *Psychonomic Science, 3*:361-362, 1965.
Gordon, R. E.; Lindeman, R. H.; and Gordon, K. K.: Some psychological and biochemical correlates of college achievement, *Journal of the American College Health Association, 15*:326-331, 1967.
Graham, D. T. and Stevenson, I.: Disease as response to life stress: I. The nature of the evidence. In Lief, H. I.; Lief, V. F.; and Lief, N. R. (Eds.): *The Psychological Basis of Medical Practice.* New York, Hoeber, 1963.
Gray, J. A. and Buffery, A. W. H.: Sex differences in emotional and cognitive behavior in mammals including man: Adaptive and neural bases. *Acta Psychologica, 35*:89-111, 1971.
Green, D. R. (Ed.): *The Aptitude-Achievement Distinction.* Monterey, California, CTB/McGraw-Hill, 1974.
Guilford, J. P.: *The Nature of Human Intelligence.* New York, McGraw, 1967.
Gump, J. P.: Reality and myth: Employment and sex role ideology in black women. In Sherman, J. and Denmark, F. (Eds.): *Psychology of Women: Future Directions of Research.* New York, Psych Dimensions, in press, 1978.
Guttman, R.: Genetic analysis of analytical spatial ability: Raven's Progressive Matrices. *Behavior Genetics, 4*:273-284, 1974.
Hall, G. S.: *Youth: Its Education, Regimen and Hygiene.* New York, Appleton, 1918.
Hamburg, B. A.: The psychobiology of sex differences: An evolutionary perspective. In Friedman, R. C.; Richart, R. M.; and Vande Wiele, R. L. (Eds.): *Sex Differences in Behavior.* New York, Wiley, 1974.
Hamburg, D. A. and Lunde, D. T.: Sex hormones in the development of sex

differences in human behavior. In Maccoby, E. E. (Ed.): *The Development of Sex Differences*, Stanford, California, Stanford U Pr, 1966.

Hannay, H. J. and Malone, D. R.: Visual field effects and short term memory for verbal material. *Neuropsychologia, 14*:203-209, 1976a.

Hannay, H. J. and Malone, D. R.: Visual field recognition memory for right-handed females as a function of familial handedness. *Cortex, 12*:41-48, 1976b.

Harris, L. J.: Interaction of experiential and neurological factors in the patterning of human abilities: The question of sex differences in 'right hemisphere' skills. Expanded version of a paper presented at Biennial Meetings of the Society for Research in Child Development, Denver, 1975.

Harris, L. J.: Sex differences in the growth and use of language. In Donelson, E. and Gullahorn, J. (Eds.) *Women: A Psychological Perspective*, New York, Wiley, 1977.

Harshman, R. A. and Remington, R.: Sex, language and the brain, part I: A review of the literature on adult sex differences in lateralization. Unpublished manuscript, Los Angeles, Phonetics Laboratory, University of California, 1976. See also *UCLA Working Papers in Phonetics, 31*:86-103, 1976.

Harshman, R. A.; Remington, R.; and Krashen, S. D.: Sex, language, and the brain, Part II: Evidence from dichotic listening for adult sex differences in verbal lateralization. Unpublished manuscript, Los Angeles, Phonetics Laboratory, University of California, 1976.

Hart, R. and Moore, G.: The development of spatial cognition: A review. In Downs, R. and Stea, D. (Eds.): *Image and Environment*. Chicago, Aldine, 1973.

Hartlage, L. C.: Sex-linked inheritance of spatial ability. *Perceptual and Motor Skills, 31*:610, 1970.

Haven, E. W.: Factors associated with the selection of advanced academic mathematics courses in high school. Doctoral dissertation, Philadelphia, University of Pennsylvania, 1971. *Dissertation Abstracts International, 32*:1747A. (University Microfilm No. 71-26027.)

Hays, W. L.: *Statistics for the Social Sciences*, 2nd ed. New York, H. R. & W. 1973.

Heilbrun, A. B., Jr.: Parent identification and filial sex role behavior: The importance of biological context. In Cole, J. K. and Dienstbier, R. (Eds.): *Nebraska Symposium on Motivation, 1973*. Lincoln, U of Nebr Pr, 1974, 125-195.

Helson, R.: Women mathematicians and the creative personality. *Journal of Consulting and Clinical Psychology, 36*:210-220, 1971.

Helson, R.: Creativity in women. In Sherman, J. and Denmark, F. (Eds.): *Psychology of Women: Future Directions of Research*. New York, Psych Dimensions, in press, 1978.

Herrnstein, R.: IQ. *Atlantic Monthly, 228*:43-64, 1971.

Hicks, M. M.; Donlon, T. F.; and Wallmark, M. M.: Sex differences in item responses on the Graduate Record Examination. Unpublished manuscript, Princeton, Educational Testing Service, 1976.

Hilton, T. L. and Berglünd, G. W.: Sex differences in mathematics achievement: A longitudinal study. *Journal of Education Research,* 67:231-237, 1974.

Hollingworth, L. S.: The frequency of amentia as related to sex. *Medical Record,* 84:753-756, 1913. (Cited in Shields, 1975.)

Hollingworth, L. S.: Variability as related to sex differences in achievement. *American Journal of Sociology,* 19:510-530, 1914. (Cited in Shields, 1975.)

Horner, M.: Achievement-related conflicts in women. *Journal of Social Issues,* 28:157-175, 1972.

Huarte, Jr.: *The Examination of Men's Wits* (Trans. from Spanish to Italian by M. Camilli; trans. from Italian to English by R. Carew.) Gainesville, Florida, Scholars' Facsimiles and Reprints, 1959. (As quoted in Shields, 1975.)

Humphreys, L. G.: The misleading distinction between aptitude and achievement tests. In Green, D. R. (Ed.): *The Aptitude-Achievement Distinction.* Monterey, California, CTB/McGraw-Hill, 1974.

Husén, T.: *International Study of Achievement in Mathematics.* New York, Wiley, 1967.

Hutt, C.: *Males & Females.* Baltimore, Penguin Education, 1972.

Hyde, J. S.; Geiringer, E. R.; and Yen, W. M.: On the empirical relation between spatial ability and sex differences in other aspects of cognitive performance. *Multivariate Behavioral Research,* 10:289-309, 1975.

Hyde, J. S. and Rosenberg, B. G.: *Half the Human Experience: The Psychology of Women.* Lexington, Massachusetts, Heath, 1976.

Irving, D. D.: The field-dependence hypothesis in cross-cultural perspective. *Dissertation Abstracts International,* 31(6-B):3691, 1970.

Jensen, A. R.: How much can we boast IQ and scholastic achievement? *Harvard Educational Review,* 39:81-82, 1969.

Johnson, D. D.: Sex differences in reading across cultures. *Reading Research Quarterly,* 9:67-86, 1973.

Johnson, M. M.: Sex role learning in the nuclear family. *Child Development.* 34:319-334, 1963.

Johnson, S.: Effects of practice and training in spatial skills on sex-related differences in performance on embedded figures. Unpublished thesis, Fairfax, Virginia, George Mason University, 1976.

Kagan, J.: Acquisition and significance of sex typing and sex role identity. In Hoffman, M. L. and Hoffman, L. W. (Eds.); *Review of Child Development Research.* New York, Russell Sage, 1964.

Kask, S. V.; Brooks, G. W.; and Cobb, S.: Serum urate concentrations in male high-school students: A predictor of college attendance. *Journal of the American Medical Association,* 198:713-716, 1966.

Kato, N.: A fundamental study of rod frame test. *Japanese Psychological Research,* 7:61-68, 1965.

Kimura, D.: Spatial localization in left and right visual fields. *Canadian Journal of Psychology,* 23:445-458, 1969.

Kimura, D.: The asymmetry of the human brain. *Scientific American,* 228:70-78, 1973.

Kinsbourne, M.: Mechanisms of hemispheric interaction in man. In Dimond, S. and Beaumont, J. G. (Eds.): *Hemisphere Function in the Human Brain.* London, Paul Elek, 1974a.

Kinsbourne, M.: Lateral interactions in the brain. In Dimond, S. and Beaumont, J. G. (Eds.): *Hemisphere Function in the Human Brain.* London, Paul Elek, 1974b.

Kinsbourne, M.: Direction of gaze and distribution of cerebral thought process. *Neuropsychologia,* 12:279-281, 1974c.

Kinsbourne, M. and Smith, W. L. (Eds.): *Hemispheric Disconnection and Cerebral Function.* Springfield, C C Thomas, 1974.

Klaiber, E. L.; Broverman, D. M.; and Kobayashi, Y.: The automatization cognitive style, androgens and monoamine oxidase. *Psychopharmacology,* 11:320-336, 1967.

Klaiber, E. L.; Broverman, D. M.; Vogel, W.; Abraham, G. E.; and Cone, F. L.: Effects of infused testosterone on mental performances and serum LH. *Journal of Clinical Endocrinology and Metabolism,* 32:341-349, 1971.

Kohlberg, L.: A cognitive-developmental analysis of children's sex-role concepts and attitudes. In Maccoby, E. E., (Ed.): *The Development of Sex Differences.* Stanford, California, Stanford, U Pr, 1966.

Kohlberg, L. and Zigler, E.: The impact of cognitive maturity on the development of sex-role attitudes in the years 4 to 8. *Genetic Psychology Monographs,* 75:89-165, 1967.

Kostick, M. M.: Study of transfer: Sex differences in the reasoning process. *Journal of Educational Psychology,* 45:449-458, 1954.

Krathwohl, D. R.; Bloom, B. S.; and Masia, B. B.: *Taxonomy of Educational Objectives: Handbook II: Affective Domain.* New York, McKay, 1964.

Kundsin, R. B. (Ed.): *Women and Success: The Anatomy of Achievement.* New York, Morrow, 1974.

Lake, D. A. and Bryden, M. P.: Handedness and sex differences in hemispheric asymmetry. *Brain and Language,* 3:266-282, 1976.

Lambert, P.: Mathematical ability and masculinity. *Arithmetic Teacher,* 7:18-21, 1960.

Lancaster, J. B.: Sex roles in primate societies. In Teitelbaum, M. S.: *Sex Differences: Social and Biological Perspectives.* New York, Anchor, 1976.

Landy, F.; Rosenberg, B. G.; and Sutton-Smith, B.: The effect of limited father absence on cognitive development. *Child Development,* 40:941-944, 1969.

Lansdell, H.: The effect of neurosurgery on a test of proverbs. *American Psychologist, 16:*448, 1961.

Lansdell, H.: A sex difference in effect on temporal-lobe neurosurgery on design preference. *Nature, 194:*852-854, 1962.

Lansdell, H.: The use of factor scores from the Wechsler-Bellevue Scale of Intelligence in assessing patients with temporal lobe removals. *Cortex, 4:*257-268, 1968.

Lehrke, R. G.: A theory of X-linkage of major intellectual traits. *American Journal of Mental Deficiency, 76:*611-619, 1972.

Lehrke, R. G.: *X-Linked Mental Retardation and Verbal Disability.* New York, Intercontinental Medical Book Corporation, 1974.

Levitan, M. and Montagu, A.: *Textbook of Human Genetics.* New York, Oxford U Pr, 1971.

Levy, J.: Information processing and higher psychological functions in the disconnected hemispheres of human comissurotomy patients. Doctoral Dissertation, Pasadena, California Institute of Technology, 1970. *Dissertation Abstracts International, 31:*1542B, 1970. (University Microfilms No. 70-14, 844.)

Levy, J.: Lateral specialization of the human brain: Behavioral manifestation and possible evolutionary basis. In Kiger, J. A. (Ed.) *The Biology of Behavior.* Corvalis, Oregon U Pr, 1972.

Levy, J.: Psychobiological implications of bilateral asymmetry. In Dimond, S. and Beaumont, J. G. (Eds.): *Hemisphere Function in the Human Brain.* London, Paul Elek, 1974.

Levy, J.: Cerebral lateralization and spatial ability. *Behavior Genetics, 6:*171-188, 1976.

Levy, J. and Nagylaki, T.: A model for the genetics of handedness. *Genetics, 72:*117-128, 1972.

Levy-Agresti, J. and Sperry, R. W.: Differential perceptual capacities in major and minor hemispheres. Paper presented at fall meetings, National Academy of Sciences, California Institute of Technology, Pasadena. *Proceedings of the National Academy of Science, 61:*1151, 1968.

Lewis, H.: *Psychic War in Men & Women.* New York, New York U Pr, 1976.

Lewis, M.: State as an infant-environment interaction: An analysis of mother-infant interaction as a function of sex. *Merrill-Palmer Quarterly, 18:*95-121, 1972.

Ljung, B.: The adolescent spurt in mental growth. *Stockholm Studies in Educational Psychology 8.* Stockholm, Almquist & Wiksell, 1965.

Lloyd, B.: Social responsibility and research on sex differences. In Lloyd, B. and Archer, J. (Eds.): *Exploring Sex Differences.* London, Academic Press, 1976.

Lloyd, B. and Archer, A. (Eds.): *Exploring Sex Differences.* London, Academic Press, 1976.

Lombroso, C. and Ferrero, W.: *Female Offender.* New York, Philos Lib, 1958.

Luchins, A. S.: Mechanization in problem-solving — the effect of

Einstellung. *Psychological Monographs, 54*(6), 1942.

Lynn, D. B.: *Parental and Sex Role Identification: A Theoretical Formulation.* Berkeley, California, McCutchan, 1969.

Lynn, D. B.: Determinants of intellectual growth in women. *School Review, 80*:241-260, 1972.

Lyon, M. F.: Gene action in the X-chromosome of the mouse *(Mus musculus L.) Nature, 190*:372, 1961.

MacArthur, R.: Sex differences in field dependence for the Eskimo: Replication of Berry's findings. *International Journal of Psychology, 2*:139-140, 1967.

McCall, J. R.: *Sex Differences in Intelligence: A Comparative Factor Study.* Washington, D. C. Catholic U Pr, 1955.

McCall, R. B.: Smiling and vocalization in infants as indices of perceptual cognitive processes. *Merrill-Palmer Quarterly, 18*:341-347, 1972.

McCarthy, D.: Language development of the preschool child. In Barker, R. G.; Kounin, J. S.; and Wright, R. F. (Eds.): *Child Behavior and Development.* New York, McGraw, 1943.

Maccoby, E. E.: Woman's intellect. In Farber, S. M. and Wilson, R. H. (Eds.): *The Potential of Women.* New York, McGraw, 1963.

Maccoby, E. E.: (Ed.): *The Development of Sex Differences.* Stanford, California, Stanford U Pr, 1966.

Maccoby, E. E. and Jacklin, C. N.: *The Psychology of Sex Differences.* Stanford, California, Stanford U Pr, 1974.

McDonald, P. G. and Doughty, C.: Androgen sterilization in the neonatal female rat and its inhibition by an estrogen antagonist. *Neuro-endocrinology, 13*:182-188, 1973/74.

McGlone, J.: *Sex differences in functional brain asymmetry.* (Research Bulletin # 378 Department of Psychology) London, Canada, University of Western Canada, July 1976.

McGlone, J. and Davidson, W.: The relation between cerebral speech processing of laterality and spatial ability with special reference to sex and hand preference. *Neuropsychologia, 11*:105-113, 1973.

McGlone, J. and Kertesz, A.: Sex differences in cerebral processing of visuospatial tasks. *Cortex, 9*:313-320, 1973.

McGuinness, D.: Sex differences in the organization of perception and cognition. In Lloyd, B. and Archer, A. (Eds.): *Exploring Sex Differences.* London, Academic Press, 1976.

McKerracher, D. W.: Psychological aspects of a sex chromatin abnormality. *The Canadian Psychologist, 12*:270-281, 1971.

Marañon, G.: *The Evolution of Sex and Intersexual Conditions.* London, George Allen & Unwin, 1932.

Marshall, J. C.: Some problems and paradoxes associated with recent accounts of hemispheric specialization. *Neuropsychologia, 11*:463-470, 1973.

Masica, D. N.; Money, J.; Ehrhardt, A. A.; and Lewis, V. G.: IQ, fetal sex hormones and cognitive patterns: Studies in the testicular feminizing syndrome of androgen insensitivity. *Johns Hopkins Medical Journal*, *124*:34-43, 1969.

Matarazzo, J. D.: *Wechsler's Measurement and Appraisal of Adult Intelligence*, 5th ed. Baltimore, Williams & Wilkins, 1972.

Mazurkiewiez, A. J.: Social-cultural influences and reading. *Journal of Developmental Reading*, *3*:254-263, 1960.

Mead, M.: In Tanner, J. M. and Inhelder, B. (Eds.): *Discussion on Child Development*. New York, Intl Univs Pr, 1958.

Mebane, D. and Johnson, D. L.: A comparison of the performance of Mexican boys and girls on Witkin's cognitive tasks. *Interamerican Journal of Psychology*, *4*:227-239, 1970.

Mednick, M. T. S.; Tangri, S. S.; and Hoffman, L. W. (Eds.): *Women and Achievement: Social and Motivational Analysis*. Washington, D. C., Hemisphere Pub, 1975.

Meissner, L.: Personal communication, 1975.

Merenda, P. F.; Clarke, W. V.; and Kessler, S.: AVA and KPDS as measures of passive dependency. *Journal of Clinical Psychology*, *3*:338-341, 1960.

Merenda, P. F.; Clarke, W. V.; Musiker, H. R.; and Kessler, S.: AVA and KPDS as construct validity coordinates. *Journal of Psychological Studies*, *12*:35-42, 1961.

Messent, P. R.: Female hormones and behavior. In Lloyd, B. B, and Archer, J. (Eds.): *Exploring Sex Differences*, London, Academic Press, 1976.

Messer, S. B. and Lewis, M.: Social class and sex differences in the attachment and play behavior of the year-old infant. *Merrill-Palmer Quarterly*, *18*:295-306, 1972.

Meyer, R. A.: A study of the relationship of mathematical problem solving performance and intellectual abilities of fourth-grade boys and girls. (Working Paper No. 60) Madison, Wisconsin Research and Development Center for Cognitive Learning, 1976.

Meyer, V. and Jones, H. G.: Patterns of cognitive test performance as functions of lateral localization of cerebral abnormalities in the temporal lobe. *Journal of Mental Science, 103*:758-772, 1957.

Michael, W. G.; Guilford, J. P.; Fruchter, B.; and Zimmerman, W. S.: The description of spatial-visualization abilities. *Educational and Psychological Measurement, 17*:185-199, 1957.

Mikkelsen, W. M.; Dodge, H. J.; and Valkenburg, H.: The distribution of serum uric acid values in a population unselected as to gout or hyperuricemia. *American Journal of Medicine, 39*:242-251, 1965.

Mill, J. S.: *The Subjection of Women*. London, Dent, 1955.

Miller, E.: Handedness and the pattern of human ability. *British Journal of Psychology, 62*:111-112, 1971.

Millett, K.: *Sexual Politics*, New York, Doubleday, 1970.

Milner, B.: Interhemispheric differences in the localization of psychological processes in man. *British Medical Journal, 27*:272-277, 1971.

Milstein, V.; Small, I. F.; Malloy, F. W.; and Small, J. G.: Influence of sex and handedness on hemispheric functioning. *Diseases of the Nervous System*, in press, 1977.

Milton, G. A.: The effects of sex-role identification upon problem-solving skill. *Journal of Abnormal and Social Psychology*, 55:208-212, 1957.

Milton, G. A.: Sex differences in problem solving as a function of role appropriateness of problem content. *Psychological Reports*, 5:705-708, 1959.

Mobius, P. J.: The physiological mental weakness of woman (Trans. by A. McCorn.) *Alienist and Neurologist*, 22:624-642, 1901. (As quoted in Shields, 1975)

Molfese, F. L.; Freeman, R. B.; and Palermo, D. S.: The ontogeny of brain lateralization for speech and nonspeech stimuli. *Brain Language*, 2:356-368, 1975.

Monday, L. A.; Hout, D. P.; and Lutz, S. W.: *College Student Profiles: American College Testing Program*. Iowa City, ACT Publications, 1966-67.

Money, J.: Two cytogenetic syndromes: Psychologic comparisons 1. Intelligence and specific-factor quotients. *Journal of Psychiatric Research*, 2:223-231, 1964.

Money, J. and Granoff, D.: IQ and the somatic stigmata of Turner's syndrome. *American Journal of Mental Deficiency*, 70:69-77, 1965.

Money, J. and Ehrhardt, A. A.: *Man & Woman: Boy & Girl*. Baltimore, Johns Hopkins, 1972.

More, H.: *Strictures on the Modern System of Female Education. With a View of the Principles and Conduct Prevalent among Women of Rank and Fortune*. Philadelphia, Dobson, 1800. (Cited in Shields, 1975.)

Morrison, D. E. and Henkel, R. E. (Eds.): *The Significance Test Controversy: A Reader*. Chicago, Aldine, 1970.

Moss, H. A.: Sex, age and state as determinants of mother-infant interaction. *Merrill-Palmer Quarterly*, 13:19-35, 1967.

Mueller, E. F.; Kasl, S. V.; Brook, G. U.; and Cobb, S.: Psychosocial correlates of serum urate levels. *Psychological Bulletin*, 73:238-257, 1970.

Mullis, I. V. S.: *Educational Achievement and Sex Discrimination*. Denver, National Assessment of Educational Progress, 1975.

Munroe, R. L. and Munroe, R. H.: Effect of environmental experience on spatial ability in an East African society. *Journal of Social Psychology*, 83:15-22, 1971.

Murray, J. E.: An analysis of geometric ability. *Journal of Educational Psychology*, 40:113-124, 1949.

Myrdal, G.: How scientific are the social scientists? *Journal of Social Issues*, 28:151-170, 1972.

Naditch, S. F.: Sex differences in field dependence: The role of social influence. Paper presented at the convention of the American Psychological Association, Washington, D. C., 1976.

Nakamura, C. Y.: Conformity and problem solving. *Journal of Abnormal and Social Psychology, 56*:315-320, 1958.

Nance, W. E. and Engel, E.: One X and four hypotheses: Response to Lehrke's "A theory of X-linkage of major intellectual traits." *American Journal of Mental Deficiency, 76*:623-625, 1972.

Nash, S. C.: The relationship among sex-role stereotyping, sex-role preference, and the sex difference in spatial visualization. *Sex Roles, 1*:15-32, 1975.

Naslund, R. A.; Thorpe, L. P.; and Lefever, D. W.: *Mathematics Concepts Test.* Chicago, Sci Res, 1971.

Nebes, R. D.: Hemispheric specialization in commissurotomized man. *Psychological Bulletin, 81*:1-14, 1974.

Nelson, E. A. and Maccoby, E. E.: The relationship between social development and differential abilities on the Scholastic Aptitude Test. *Merrill-Palmer Quaterly, 4*:269-284, 1966.

Nelson, K.: Structure and strategy in learning to talk. *Monographs of the Society for Research in Child Development, 38*(2, Serial No. 149), 1973.

Nerlove, S. B.; Munroe, R. H.; and Munroe, R. L.: Effects of environmental experience on spatial ability: A replication. *Journal of Social Psychology, 84*:3-10, 1971.

Newcombe, F. and Radcliffe, G.: Handedness, speech lateralization and spatial ability. *Neuropsychologia, 11*:399-407, 1973.

O'Connor, J.: *Structural Visualization.* Boston, Human Eng Lab, 1943.

Oetzel, R.: Classified summary of research in sex differences. In Maccoby, E. (Ed.): *The Development of Sex Differences.* Stanford, California, Stanford U Pr, 1966.

O'Faolain, J. and Martines, L. (Eds.): *Not in God's Image.* New York, Har-Row, 1973.

Orowan, E.: Origins of man. *Nature, 175*:683-684, 1955.

Osen, L.: *Women in Mathematics.* Cambridge, MIT Pr, 1974.

Ounsted, C. and Taylor, D. C.: The Y chromosome message: A point of view. In Ounsted, C. and Taylor, D. C. (Eds.): *Gender Differences: Their Ontogeny and Significance.* Baltimore, Williams & Wilkins, 1972.

Park, J.; Johnson, R. C.; DeFries, J. C.; Ashton, G. C.; McClearn, G. E.; Mi, M. P.; Rashand, M. N.; Vandenberg, S. G.; and Wilson, J. R.: Parent-offspring resemblance for specific cognitive abilities in Korea. *Behavior Genetics,* in press, 1977.

Parlee, M. B.: Comments on "Roles of activation and inhibition in sex differences in cognitive abilities" by D. M. Broverman, E. L. Klaiber, Y. Kobyashi, and W. Vogel. *Psychological Review, 79*:180-184, 1972.

Parlee, M. B.: Sex differences in perceptual field dependence: A look at some data embedded in theory. Unpublished manuscript, New York, Barnard, 1974.

Payne, A. P. and Swanson, H. H.: The effect of sex hormones on the aggressive behavior of the female golden hamster *(Mesocricetus auratus Waterhouse). Animal Behavior, 20*:782-787, 1972.

Pearson, K.: Variation in man and woman. In *The Chances of Death,* Vol. I London, Edward Arnold, 1897. (Cited by Shields, 1975.)

Pedersen, D. M.; Shinedling, M. M.; and Johnson, D. L.: Effects of sex of examiner and subject on children's quantitative test performance. *Journal of Personality & Social Psychology, 10:*251-254, 1968.

Petersen, A. C.: Physical androgyny and cognitive functioning in adolescence. *Developmental Psychology, 12:*524-533, 1976.

Petersen, A. C.: Personal communication, 1977.

Pheterson, G. I.; Kiesler, S. B.; and Goldberg, P. A.: Evaluation of the performance of women as a function of their sex, achievement and personal history. *Journal of Personality and Social Psychology, 19:*114-118, 1971.

Phillips, J. R.: Syntax and vocabulary of mothers' speech to young children. Age and sex comparisons. *Child Development, 44:*182-185, 1973.

Plank, E. M. and Plank, R.: Emotional components in arithmetical learning as seen through autobiographies. *Psychoanalytic Studies of the Child, 9:*274-296, 1954.

Pleck, J.: Males' traditional attitudes toward women: Conceptual issues in research. In Sherman, J. and Denmark, F. (Eds.): *Psychology of Women: Future Directions of Research.* New York, Psych Dimensions, in press, 1978.

Polani, P. E.: Errors of sex determinance and sex chromosome anomalies. In Ounsted, C. and Taylor, D. C. (Eds.): *Gender Differences: Their Ontogeny and Significance.* Baltimore, Williams & Wilkins, 1972.

Reid, I. S.: Science, politics, and race. *Signs, 1:*397-422, 1975.

Reinisch, J. M.: Fetal hormones, the brain, and human sex differences: A heuristic, integrative review of the recent literature. *Archives of Sexual Behavior, 3:*51-90, 1974.

Rogers, L.: Male hormones and behavior. In Lloyd, B. B. and Archer, J. (Eds.): *Exploring Sex Differences.* London, Academic Press, 1976.

Rosen, B. and Jerdee, T. H.: Influence of sex role stereotypes on personnel decisions. *Journal of Applied Psychology, 59:*511-512, 1974.

Rosenkrantz, P. S.; Vogel, S. R.; Bee, H.; Broverman, I. K.; and Broverman, D. M.: Sex role stereotypes and self-concepts in college students. *Journal of Consulting and Clinical Psychology, 32:*287-295, 1968.

Rudel, R. G.; Denckla, M. B.; and Spalten, E.: The functional asymmetry of Braille letter learning in normal, sighted children. *Neurology, 24:*733-738, 1974.

Ryan, K. H.; Naftolin, F.; Reddy, V.; Flores, F.; and Petro, Z.: Estrogen formation in the brain. *American Journal Obstetrics and Gynecology, 114:*454-560, 1972.

Sarbin, T. R.: Role: Psychological aspects. In *International Encyclopedia of the Social Sciences,* Vol. 13. New York, Macmillan, 1968.

Scannell, D. P.: *Test of Academic Progress, Manual, Form S.* Boston, H M, 1972.

Schaie, K. W. and Strother, C. R.: Cognitive and personality variables in college graduates of advanced age. In Talland, G. A. (Ed.): *Human Aging and Behavior*. New York, Academic Press, 1968.

Schildkamp-Kündiger, E.: *Studien zur Lehrforschung: Frauenrolle und Mathematikleistung*. Düsseldorf, Schwann, 1974.

Schonberger, A. K.: The interrelationship of sex, visual spatial abilities and mathematical problem solving. Unpublished doctoral dissertation, University of Wisconsin, 1976.

Schwabacher, S.: Male vs. female representation in psychological research: An examination of the *Journal of Personality and Social Psychology*, 1970, 1971, *Journal Supplement Abstract Service*, 2:20-21, 1972.

Schwartz, D. W. and Karp, S. A.: Field dependence in a geriatric population. *Perceptual and Motor Skills*, 24:495-504, 1967.

Scottish Council for Research in Education: *The Intelligence of Children*. London, University of London Press, 1933.

Scottish Council for Research in Education: *The Trend of Scottish Intelligence*. London, University of London Press, 1949.

Sears, R. R.; Rau, L.; and Alpert, R.: *Identification and Child Rearing*. Stanford, California, Stanford U Pr, 1965.

Sells, L. W.: High school mathematics as the critical filter on the job market. Unpublished manuscript, Berkeley, University of California, 1973.

Shaffer, J.: A specific cognitive deficit observed in gonadal aplasia (Turner's syndrome). *Journal of Clinical Psychology*, 18:403-406, 1962.

Sherman, J.: Problem of sex differences in space perception and aspects of intellectual functioning. *Psychological Review*, 74:290-299, 1967.

Sherman, J.: *On the Psychology of Women: A Survey of Empirical Studies*. Springfield, C C Thomas, 1971.

Sherman, J.: Field articulation, sex, spatial visualization, dependency, practice, laterality of the brain and birth order. *Perceptual and Motor Skills*, 38:1223-1235, 1974.

Sherman, J.: Review of The Psychology of Sex Differences by Maccoby, E. E. and Jacklin, C. N. *Sex Roles*, 1:297-301, 1975.

Sherman, J.: Psychological "facts" about women: Will the real Ms. please stand up? In Roberts, J. I. (Ed.): *Beyond Intellectual Sexism: A New Woman, A New Reality*. New York, McKay, 1976a.

Sherman, J.: Social values, femininity, and the development of female competence. *Journal of Social Issues*, 32:181-196, 1976b.

Sherman, J.: Cognitive performance as a function of sex and handedness: An evaluation of the Levy hypothesis. *Psychology of Women Quarterly*. in press, 1978.

Sherman, J. and Fennema, E.: The study of mathematics by high school girls and boys: Related variables. *American Educational Research Journal*, 14:51-71, 1977.

Sherman, J. and Fennema, E.: Distribution of spatial visualization and mathematical problem solving scores: A test of Stafford's X-linked hypotheses. *Psychology of Women Quarterly*, in press, 1978.

Shields, S. A.: Functionalism, Darwinism, and the psychology of women. *American Psychologist*, 30:739-754, 1975.

SIECUS (Sex Information and Education Council of the United States): *Sexuality and Man*. New York, Scribner, 1970.

Simon, R. J.; Clark, S. M.; and Galway, K.: The woman Ph.D.: A recent profile. *Social Problems*, 15:211-236, 1967.

Singer, G. and Montgomery, R. G.: Comment on "Role of activation and inhibition in sex differences in cognitive abilities." *Psychological Review*, 76:325-327, 1969.

Smith, I. M.; *Spatial Ability*. San Diego, California, Knapp, 1964.

Smith, K. U.: Personal Communication, October 1976.

Smith, M. O.; Chu, J.; and Edmonston, W. E., Jr.: Cerebral lateralization of haptic perception: Interaction of responses to braille and music reveals a functional basis. *Science*, 197:689-690, 1977.

Smith-Rosenberg, C. and Rosenberg, C.: The female animal: Medical and biological views of woman and her role in nineteenth century America. *The Journal of American History*, 60:332-336, 1973.

Sommer, B.: Menstrual cycle changes and intellectual performance. *Psychosomatic Medicine*, 34:263-269, 1972.

Spence, J. T. and Helmreich, R.: *The Psychological Dimensions of Masculinity and Femininity*. Austin, U of Tex Pr, in press, 1978.

Spencer, H.: Psychology of the sexes. *Popular Science Monthly*, 4:31-32, 1873. (As quoted in Fee, 1976.)

Sperry, R. W.: Left-brain, right-brain. *Scientific American*, 233:30-33, 1975.

Stafford, R. E.: Sex differences in spatial visualization as evidence of sex-linked inheritance. *Perceptual and Motor Skills*, 13:428, 1961.

Stafford, R. E.: An investigation of similarities in parent-child test scores for evidence of hereditary components. Doctoral dissertation, Princeton, Princeton University, 1963. *Dissertation Abstracts International*, 11:4785-4786, 1964. (University Microfilms No. 64-2713.)

Stafford, R. E. *Mental Arithmetic Problems (Form AA)*, re. ed. Vocational and Educational Guidance Associates, 1965a.

Stafford, R. E.: Spatial visualization and quantitative reasoning: One gene or two? Paper presented at the meeting of the Eastern Psychological Association, Atlantic City, New Jersey, April 1965b.

Stafford, R. E.: Bimodal distribution of "true scores" by twins on the Differential Aptitude Tests. *Perceptual and Motor Skills*, 23:470, 1966.

Stafford, R. E.: Hereditary and environmental components of quantitative reasoning. *Review of Educational Research*, 42:183-201, 1972.

Stanley, J. C.; Keating, D. P.; and Fox, L. H. (Eds.): *Mathematical Talent Discovery, Description, and Development*. Baltimore, Johns Hopkins, 1974.

Stassinopoulos, A.: *The Female Woman*. London, Davis-Poynter, 1973.

Stein, A. A. and Bailey, M. M.: The socialization of achievement orientation in females. *Psychological Bulletin, 80*:345-366, 1973.

Stein, A. H. and Smithells, J.: Age and sex differences in children's sex-role standards about achievement. *Developmental Psychology, 1*:252-259, 1969.

Stetten, D., Jr. and Hearon, J. Z.: Intellectual level measured by Army Classification Battery and serum uric acid concentration. *Science, 129*:1737, 1969.

Stewart, V.: Social influences on sex differences in behavior. In Teitelbaum, M. S. (Ed.): *Sex Differences: Social and Biological Perspectives.* Garden City, New York, Anchor Pr. Doubleday, 1976.

Strauch, A. B.: The development of sex differences in spatial and verbal abilities. Paper presented at the convention of the American Psychology Association, Washington, D. C., 1976.

Strassberg-Rosenberg, B. and Donlon, T.: Content influences on sex differences in performance on aptitude tests. Unpublished manuscript, Princeton, Educational Testing Service, 1975.

Tanner, J. M.: *Education and Physical Growth.* London, University of London Press, 1961.

Tanner, J. M.: *Growth at Adolescence,* 4th ed. Springfield, C C Thomas, 1962.

Tavris, C. and Offir, C.: *The Longest War: Sex Differences in Perspective.* New York, Har Brace J, 1977.

Taylor, D. C.: The influence of sexual differentiation on growth, development and disease. In Davis, J. A. and Dobbing, J. (Eds.): *Scientific Foundations of Paediatrics.* London, Heinemann, 1974.

Teitelbaum, M. S.: Introduction. In Teitelbaum, M. S. (Ed.); *Sex Differences.* Garden City, New York, Anchor, 1976.

Terman, L. M. et al.: *Genetic studies of genius,* Vol. 1. Stanford, California, Stanford U Pr, 1925.

Thomas, W. L.: The mind of woman. *American Magazine, 67*:150, 1908. (Cited in Fee, 1976.)

Thompson, H. B.: *The Mental Traits of Sex.* Chicago, U of Chicago Pr, 1903.

Thorndike, E. L.: Sex in education. *The Bookman, 23*:211-214, 1906. (Cited in Shields, 1975.)

Thurstone, L. L.: *A Factoral Study of Perception.* Chicago, U of Chicago Pr, 1944.

Tiger, L.: *Men in Groups.* New York, Random, 1969.

Tiger, L.: The possible biological origins of sexual discrimination. *Impact of Science on Society, 20*:29-45, 1970.

Tittle, C. K.; McCarthy, K.; and Steckler, J. F.: *Woman and Educational Testing.* Princeton, Educational Testing Service, 1974.

Tobias, S.: Math anxiety. *Ms, 5*:56-59, 1976.

Tobin, D.; Brody, L; and Fox, L. H.: The effects of sex role socialization on mathematics participation and achievement: Annotations. Washington, D. C., National Institute of Education, 1976.

Tresemer, D.: Measuring "sex differences." *Sociological Inquiry, 45*:29-32, 1975.

Tyler, L. E.: *The Psychology of Human Differences.* New York, Appleton-Century-Crofts, 1965.

Unger, R. K. and Denmark, F. L. (Eds.): *Woman: Dependent or Independent Variable?* New York, Psych Dimensions, 1975.

Vandenberg, S. G.: Sources of variance in performance of spatial tests. In Eliot, J. and Salkind, N. J. (Eds.): *Children's Spatial Development.* Springfield, C C Thomas, 1975.

Vandenberg, S. G.: Personal communication, July 1977.

Van den Berghe, P. L.: *Age and Sex in Human Societies: Biosocial Perspectives.* Belmont, California, Wadsworth, 1973.

Very, P. S.: Differential factor structures in mathematical ability. *Genetic Psychology Monographs, 75*:169-207, 1967.

Waber, D. P.: Sex differences in cognition: A function of maturation rates? *Science, 192*:572-574, 1976.

Waber, D. P.: Sex differences in mental abilities, hemispheric lateralization, and rate of physical growth at adolescence. *Developmental Psychology, 13*:29-38, 1977.

Wada, J. A.; Clarke, R; and Hamm, A.: Cerebral hemispheric asymmetry in humans. *Archives of Neurology, 32*:239-246, 1975.

Warrington, E. K. and Pratt, R. T. C.: Language laterality in left-handers assessed by unilateral E.C.T. *Neuropsychologia, 11*:423-428, 1973.

Wearne, D. C.: Development of a test of mathematical problem solving which yields comprehension, application and problem solving scores. Unpublished doctoral dissertation, Madison, University of Wisconsin, 1976.

Wechsler, D.: *The Measurement of Adult Intelligence,* 3rd ed. Baltimore, Williams & Wilkins, 1944.

Wechsler, D.: *Manual for the Wechsler Adult Intelligence Scale.* New York, Psych Corp, 1955.

Wechsler, D.: *Measurement and Appraisal of Adult Intelligence.* Baltimore, Williams & Wilkins, 1958.

Weininger, O.: *Sex and Character* (Trans.) London, Heinemann, 1906.

Weisenburg, T. and McBride, K. E.: *Aphasia: A Clinical and Psychological Study.* New York, The Commonwealth Fund, 1935.

Weiss, P.: Some aspects of femininity. Unpublished doctoral dissertation, Boulder, University of Colorado, 1961.

Weisz, J. and Gibb, ⸱C.: Conversion of testosterone and androstanedione to estrogens in vitro by the brain of female rats. *Endocrinology, 94*:616-620, 1973.

Weitan, W. and Etaugh, C. F.: Lateral eye movements as related to verbal and perceptual-motor skills and values. *Perceptual and Motor Skills, 36*:423-428, 1973.

Weitan, W. and Etaugh, C. F.: Lateral eye-movement as a function of cognitive mode, question sequence, and sex of subject. *Perceptual and Motor Skills, 38*:439-444, 1974.

Weitz, S.: *Sex Roles: Biological, Psychological and Social Foundations.* New York, Oxford U Pr, 1977.

Werdelin, I.: *Geometrical Ability and the Space Factors in Boys and Girls.* Lund, Sweden, University of Lund, 1961.

Wesley, F. and Wesley, C.: *Sex-Role Psychology.* New York, Human Sci Pr, 1977.

Whalen, R. E.; Battie, C.; and Luttge, W. G.: Anti-estrogen inhibition of androgen induced sexual receptivity in rats. *Behavioral Biology, 1*:311-320, 1972.

White, L.: *Educating our Daughters.* New York, Harper, 1950.

White, R. W.: Motivation reconsidered: The concept of competence motivation. *Psychological Review, 66*:297-333, 1959.

Williams, T.: Family resemblance in abilities: The Wechsler Scales. *Behavior Genetics, 5*:405-409, 1975.

Wilson, J. W.: *Patterns of Mathematics Achievement in Grade 11: Z Population.* (National Longitudinal Study of Mathematical Abilities, No. 17 (Stanford, California, Stanford U Pr, 1972.

Witelson, S. F.: Sex and the single hemisphere: Specializaton of the right hemisphere for spatial processing. *Science, 193*:425-427, 1976.

Witkin, H. A.: *The Effect of Training and of Structural Aids on Performance in Three Tests of Space Orientation.* (Report No. 90) Washington, D. C., Division of Research, Civil Aeronautics Assoc., 1948.

Witkin, H. A.: Sex differences in perception. *Transactions of the New York Academy of Science, 12*:22-26, 1949.

Witkin, H. A.: A cognitive style approach to cross-cultural research. *Internatinal Journal of Psychology, 2*:233-250, 1967.

Witkin, H. A.; Dyk, R. B.; Faterson, H. F.; Goodenough, D. R.; and Karp, S. A.: *Psychological Differentiation.* New York, Wiley, 1962.

Witkin, H. A.; Goodenough, D. R.; and Karp S. A.: Stability of cognitive style from childhood to young adulthood. *Journal of Personality and Social Psychology, 7*:291-300, 1967.

Witkin, H. A.; Lewis, H. B.; Herzman, M.; Machover, K.; Meissner, P. B.; and Wapner, S.: *Personality Through Perception.* New York, Harper, 1954.

Witkin, H. A.; Oltman, P. K.; Raskin, E.; and Karp, S. A.: *A Manual for the Embedded Figures Tests,* Palo Alto, California, Consulting Psychologists Press, 1971.

Wittig, M. A.: Sex differences in intellectual functioning: How much of a difference do genes make? *Sex Roles, 2*:63-74, 1976.

Wolf, V. C.: Age and sex differences as measured by a new non-verbal visual perceptual test. *Psychonomic Science, 25*:85-87, 1971.

Wyckoff, H.: The stroke economy in women's scripts. *Transactional Analysis Journal, 1*:16-20, 1971.

Yalom, I. D.; Green, R.; and Fisk, N.: Prenatal exposure to female hormones.

Archives of General Psychiatry, 28:554-561, 1973.

Yen, W. M.: Sex-linked major-gene influences on selected types of spatial performance. *Behavior Genetics, 5*:281-298, 1975a.

Yen, W. M.: Independence of hand preference and sex-linked genetic effects on spatial performance. *Perceptual and Motor Skills, 41*:311-318, 1975b.

Zimmerman, E. and Parlee, M. B.: Behavioral changes associated with the menstrual cycles: An experimental investigation. *Journal of Applied Social Psychology, 3*:335-344, 1973.

INDEX

263